Labour and the Left
in the 1930s

Labour and the Left in the 1930s

BEN PIMLOTT

LECTURER IN POLITICS
UNIVERSITY OF NEWCASTLE UPON TYNE

CAMBRIDGE UNIVERSITY PRESS

CAMBRIDGE
LONDON · NEW YORK · MELBOURNE

Published by the Syndics of the Cambridge University Press
The Pitt Building, Trumpington Street, Cambridge CB2 1RP
Bentley, House, 200 Euston Road, London NW1 2DB
32 East 57th Street, New York, NY 10022, USA
296 Beaconsfield Parade, Middle Park, Melbourne 3206, Australia

First published 1977

Printed in Malta by
Interprint (Malta) Ltd

Library of Congress Cataloguing in Publication Data

Pimlott, Ben, 1945–

Labour and the Left in the 1930s.

Bibliography: p.
Includes index.

1. Labour Party (Great Britain)—History.
2. Socialism in Great Britain—History.
3. Great Britain—Politics and government—1910–1936.
4. Great Britain—Politics and government—1936–1945.   I. Title.

JN1129. L33   1930   329.9′41   76–27906

ISBN 0 521 21448 3

Contents

Contents

To the memory of my parents
John and Ellen Pimlott

Acknowledgements

My first debt is to the British Academy, and to the benefactors of the Academy's Thank Offering to Britain Fund, for the generous award of a one-year Fellowship which made research for this book possible. I am also grateful to the Newcastle University Research Committee for a grant towards travelling expenses during the early stages of the project.

I would like to express my thanks to Newcastle University for giving me leave of absence; to my colleagues, for their good humoured acceptance of the inconvenience which this inevitably caused; to the staff of the British Academy who were unfailingly helpful during my year as Fellow; and to the staff of the Labour Party Library at Transport House, for their assistance and cheerful tolerance over many months.

For permission to quote from private papers, I would like to thank University College, Oxford (Attlee papers), Dame Margaret Cole (Cole papers), the British Library of Economics and Political Science (Dalton and Passfield papers) and Mrs Pauline Dower CBE (Trevelyan papers).

Of the many individuals who helped me while I was preparing this book, I am particularly grateful to the Rt Hon. Lord Beswick, Mr Arthur Blenkinsop MP, Miss Joan Bourne, Lord Brockway, the Rt Hon. Lord Citrine GBE, the Rt Hon. Lord Duncan-Sandys CH, Sir Trevor Evans CBE, the late Lord Garnsworthy OBE, Lady Garnsworthy, Mr Reginald Groves, Professor G. W. Jones, Dame Leah Manning, Mr G. Grant Mackenzie, Mr John Parker CBE, MP, and the Rt Hon. G. R. Strauss MP.

I would like to thank my friends Angela Rathbone, Janet Watts, Janet Lewis, Ken Young and Rod and Gilly James for their encouragement and their help in other important ways; Peter Pulzer, who suggested that I should write this book and later gave invaluable advice; and Iain McLean, Rod Hague, Alice Prochaska, Albert Weale and Hugh Berrington who read the manuscript and made many helpful suggestions.

I also wish to thank members of the Newcastle East, Arundel, and Cleveland and Whitby Constituency Labour Parties for a practical schooling in local and electoral politics which has helped me to understand parties and how they work.

Acknowledgements

I owe a very special debt to Mrs Rule, who typed the whole manuscript with amazing speed and accuracy and sustained me with her kindness and enthusiasm.

Finally I want to thank Jean Seaton, who read everything in draft, often disagreed, usually argued, and always made valuable comments which profoundly affected the final version of this book. She bears no responsibility for what I have written, but I am deeply aware of how much I owe to her intelligence, her generosity and her interest.

Ben Pimlott

Newcastle upon Tyne
March 1977.

Glossary of initials

AEU	Amalgamated Engineering Union
ASLEF	Associated Society of Locomotive Engineers and Firemen
BUF	British Union of Fascists
CP, CPGB	Communist Party, Communist Party of Great Britain
DLP	Divisional Labour Party
ECCI	Executive Committee of the Communist International
HCLA	Home Counties Labour Association
IFTU	International Federation of Trade Unions
ILP	Independent Labour Party
LBC	Left Book Club
LCC	London County Council
LRC	Labour Representation Committee
L & SI	Labour and Socialist International
MFGB	Miners' Federation of Great Britain
NCL	National Council of Labour
NEC	National Executive Committee
NFRB	New Fabian Research Bureau
NJC	National Joint Council
NUDAW	National Union of Distributive and Allied Workers
NUGMW	National Union of General and Municipal Workers
NUPE	National Union of Public Employees
NUR	National Union of Railwaymen
NUT	National Union of Teachers
NUWM	National Unemployed Workers' Movement
PEP	Political and Economic Planning
PLP	Parliamentary Labour Party
POUM	Partido Obrero de Unificación Marxista
PPS	Parliamentary Private Secretary
RPC	Revolutionary Policy Committee
SDF	Social Democratic Federation
SL	Socialist League
SSIP	Society for Socialist Inquiry and Propaganda

SSP	Scottish Socialist Party
TGWU	Transport and General Workers' Union
TUC	Trades Union Congress
WEA	Workers' Educational Association

1
Introduction

1

Introduction

Two great national anxieties, mass unemployment and the threat of war, dominated British politics in the 1930s and preoccupied British politicians, who failed to provide an answer for either of them. It was the 'Red Decade' – the decade of Auden, Spender and Cornford, of *Love on the Dole* and *The Road to Wigan Pier*. It was the decade of the Jarrow March, the International Brigade and the Left Book Club, of Fabian schools, mass rallies and demonstrations. Yet it was a decade in which the impact of the entire British Left on practical problems and immediate events was virtually nil. No major national policy or decision, from the formation of Ramsay MacDonald's first National Government in August 1931 to the declaration of war eight years later, was made or prevented by anything any politician on the Left said, wrote or did.

Perhaps this was inevitable. The National Governments responsible for taking decisions were unusually insulated from normal political pressures – the 1931 and 1935 Parliaments were controlled by the largest Conservative majorities of modern times. It might, therefore, be argued that the Left should be acquitted of any responsibility for the political failures which preceded the Second World War; that after the 1935 election, when Labour took a larger share of the popular vote than ever before but won a mere 154 seats, the Left had no chance of shifting the Government or influencing its behaviour before the circumstances of war changed the rules of the Parliamentary game; and that socialists had no option short of revolution but to take a spectator role, propagating their views and planning for the future, but blamelessly incapable of affecting the present.

This is one view. Another is that Labour's impotence was the fault, not of the electors, but of a weak, right-wing, union dominated, 'Parliamentarist' leadership which, like the MacDonald clique before it, betrayed the working class with its caution and pusillanimity. Labour was actively hostile to left-wing attempts to organise the unemployed; it refused to give unequivocal backing to the Republican cause in the Spanish Civil War; and its campaigns against fascism at home and abroad, and against Chamberlain's foreign policy, were weak and half-hearted. The result (so it is argued) was

1

that Labour lost a great opportunity to mobilise the working class movement and force a change in domestic and foreign policy through political
and industrial action. The British Left had the strength and ability to alter
the course of history – what it lacked was the will. It failed because its leaders
pursued a policy of 'MacDonaldism without MacDonald':

> when it came to *doing* anything, here and now, about the evil they
> denounced, they showed the same inhibitions they had always shown
> before. Throughout the decade [the 1930s] they never swerved from the
> belief that opposition meant opposition in Parliament and that Labour
> could achieve little, and must not attempt much, until it had been re-
> turned as a majority Government.[1]

Neither of these two views is satisfactory. Labour might have exercised a
major influence in the 1930s, but the mass movement did not provide the
means for it to do so. The Labour leadership certainly showed little initiative in channelling the anger and frustrations of the depressed areas, and
allowed itself to be outflanked by the Communist Party as champion of the
unemployed. It may also be blamed for failing to provide an inspirational
lead in the country against fascism. But unless marches and demonstrations
had been aimed at the forceful overthrow of the Government – something
which nobody of any standing in the Labour Party was prepared to advocate
– there is no reason to suppose that an intensification of such action would
have had a dramatic impact on policy.

A repetition of the General Strike for political ends, advocated by some
left-wingers, was a pipe-dream. Trade union membership had fallen steadily as unemployment increased, and only began to pick up after 1934; the
only two large-scale strikes of the thirties resulted in victory for the employers.[2] The trade union movement was concerned with industrial defence
in the 1930s; it had no resources for political attack. Purely political action
in the country – hunger marches, mass meetings, propaganda campaigns –
could, and did, have an effect on the general climate of opinion. But such
activities were no sanction against a Government which regarded it as a virtue to resist such pressures, and was determined to keep its own counsel.

To say this, however, is not to accept the first argument – that Labour
could do nothing but wait and watch. The position of the Right in Parliament
was far less secure than its paper strength suggested. The right-wing
'National' majorities which dominated the House of Commons were not
undifferentiated or monolithic. Indeed, from the Government whips' point
of view, a smaller Parliamentary following would have been more manageable. There were many Conservatives of ability and imagination, excluded
from Government and with no prospect of preferment, who felt as frustrated as the Opposition, and became as keen for a fundamental change of
policy, and if necessary, for a change of control.

2

Introduction

In domestic policy a group of young Tory planners centred around Harold Macmillan and Robert Boothby pressed for a Keynesian approach to unemployment and the management of the economy. In foreign policy, especially after 1936, factional groups increasingly concerned about the need for rearmament and for collective security against the Dictators developed around Churchill, Amery and then Eden. On the Opposition benches, the small body of Liberals contained men strongly hostile to Government policy in both foreign and domestic spheres who were looking for allies. These groups showed a willingness to cooperate with Labour – in Parliament, and at the polls.

Given the overall balance of forces in the Commons in the 1930s, an anti-Government majority was scarcely conceivable. But a split in the Tory ranks was a real possibility. Long before 1940, opportunities existed for substantial cooperation in Parliament across party lines – with the chance of a grand anti-Government alliance of Labour, Liberals and rebellious Tories. What effect this might have had cannot now be judged. But a big loss of support for the Government would arguably have been the only kind of pressure capable of changing policy and forcing resignations. The most serious criticism, then, that can be levelled at the Labour Party is that it failed to exploit such opportunities. Labour's Parliamentary leaders held themselves aloof from Liberal and Tory critics of the Government, and did little to encourage Tory rebels when they sought assistance from across the floor. Not until 1940, with the country on the brink of a military catastrophe, was a successful combination achieved.

The idea of a progressive alliance was not new or revolutionary. For half a century third and fourth parties – Irish Nationalist, Labour and Liberal – had been an important factor in Parliamentary and electoral calculations. Cooperation across the floor of the House of Commons had been a recurring feature of British political life. Successive Liberal and Labour Governments had held office only because of 'progressive' support from other parties. Major crises – over Ireland, war, the economy – had been marked by lasting schisms and major realignments. On occasion these had taken place suddenly and dramatically. At other times the process had been more gradual. Thus the 1920s had been a period of steady recruitment to Labour from other parties – mainly from the Liberals, but from Conservatives as well.[3]

The obstacles to any anti-Government combination after 1931 were great, none the less. The biggest problem was a legacy of bitterness left by the Labour Party split in 1931. The formation of the National Government by Ramsay MacDonald, regarded in the Labour Movement as an act of treachery, had created a powerful taboo. There developed a strong feeling against fraternisation with 'capitalist' politicians and a deep suspicion of anybody in the Party who favoured deals with them.

Before 1935 the Labour Opposition in Parliament was in any case too

3

small, too left-wing and too lacking in talent to hold many attractions as a potential ally. Even after the 1935 election, when Labour's Parliamentary strength increased, resistance to any kind of arrangement with socialists remained strong among the most dissatisfied of Tories, whose dislike of Labour was quite as emphatic as their hostility towards the Government. The feeling was mutual. Churchill, who had sent troops against the miners and who staunchly defended the British Raj, was the kind of Tory most hated and distrusted on the Left – as an out-and-out reactionary, an imperialist and a warmonger.

An alliance only became a serious proposition when the impact of events abroad had begun to create common ground among Government critics over Chamberlain's handling of foreign policy. Attempts by Harold Macmillan and Lord Allen[4] in the middle of the decade to bring together people 'of all parties or none',[5] on the basis of a scheme for planning and national development, were regarded coldly on the Left. Before 1938 even foreign policy and defence contained little to unite and a great deal to separate anti-Government forces. The pacifist strain in the Labour Party ran deep. Until 1937 the Parliamentary Labour Party regularly opposed the annual defence estimates, and even in 1939 it voted against conscription. The Party moved only gradually to the belief that fascist aggression must be met by the threat of armed resistance. And it was with the greatest reluctance that Labour shed the opinion, long dominant on the non-pacifist Left, that a capitalist government, even an anti-fascist one, must never be trusted with arms.

Yet the change did come. The rhetoric of Labour leaders, and official Labour propaganda, continued to show many traces of earlier attitudes. Labour continued to regard all capitalists as potential aggressors, to see war as an inherent feature of an imperialist system in which Britain was an arch-offender, and to be deeply suspicious of rearmament programmes. Nevertheless, by the beginning of 1938 the Party was pressing for a system of collective security through the League of Nations, and accepting that such a policy must be backed by a military deterrent. Since a League policy meant, in practice, an alliance of the three great powers within the League – France, Britain and the Soviet Union – this brought Labour closely in line with dissident Tories such as Churchill and Amery.[6]

As the international situation worsened, some kind of anti-Government combination began to have attractions for politicians of all parties. The idea was often discussed. The most widely canvassed proposal was for an alliance of all Government opponents, which might be backed by electoral pacts to enable Tory rebels to survive the withdrawal of the whip and a possible general election. In private, the scheme had support among the Tory dissidents, Liberals, and some of Labour's most influential leaders: as Dalton put it, 'To split the Tory Party would be real big politics.'[7] In public, however, the most united, vocal and passionate support for a 'Popular

4

Front' came from the left-wing of the Labour Party and from the Communists. It was this that killed it.

Until the end of 1937, the Labour Left had vehemently opposed a Popular Front. Left-wingers had preferred a 'United Front', which meant an alliance of Labour, Independent Labour Party (ILP) and Communists, and the exclusion of all non-socialists. The Left's 'Unity Campaign' in support of a united front preoccupied Labour throughout 1937 with an internal quarrel which arose from a powerful bid by the Communists to gain affiliation to the Labour Party. When this failed, and the extreme left began instead to advocate a wider alliance, the new line was regarded by many as another device to increase the influence of those sympathetic to Communist aims. The result was the most bitter battle of the decade between Left and Right for the loyalty of Labour's rank and file, the identification of support for a Popular Front with disruptionism and disloyalty, and the expulsion of the most prominent left-wing advocates of a Popular Front from the Labour Party. At the moment when an alliance was most practical and promising, a factional struggle obscured the issue and hardened attitudes in the Labour Movement against it.

The influence of the Labour Left in the 1930s on British politics has been profound, and long lasting. Labour's 'class of 1945' – many of whom had been schooled in the campaigns of the thirties[8] – carried the ideals and concerns of the far left into post-war Parliaments. The controversies which split Labour in the fifties over German rearmament, unilateralism and Clause 4 were rooted in pre-war debates. 'Means Test' remains a rallying cry in the Labour Movement; so does 'Spain'. The Tribune Group, stronger in the 1970s than ever before, owes its name to the newspaper established in 1937 by Sir Stafford Cripps as part of the left-wing Unity Campaign. Since then, there has been a continuity in the political attitudes and causes of Labour's left-wing which no other British parliamentary group has matched. That the British Labour Party is now the most socialist of European social democratic parties owes much to the resilience of this tradition.

Nevertheless, the pre-war Labour Left, to its credit, claimed that its main concern was not the long-term, but the here and now. The 1930s was a decade in which problems were immediate and time was short. The Labour Left's advocacy of the Popular Front sprang from a feeling, shared by the whole Labour Movement, that a change of policy was urgent and could not wait. Yet in the immediate situation left-wing activity defeated its own ends.

It is a major theme of this book that in the 1930s the Labour Left was consistently wrong on tactics. Some left-wing ideas appear in retrospect blinkered or utopian; others were far-sighted and highly practical. We are concerned, however, not with judging policies, but with political action:

with attempts to put favoured policies into practice. If political effectiveness is the measure, the Labour Left in the 1930s scores very poorly indeed. A predilection for the noisy confrontation, the public battle with standards held high, made the far left an exciting place in British politics in the 1930s; but it gained little ground. Led by the brilliant and egotistical figure of Sir Stafford Cripps, taking its cue from an elitist, inward-looking, intellectual coterie, the Labour Left engaged in factional fight after factional fight whose main effects were to alienate Labour opinion, and taint its own proposals. Throughout the decade, left-wing leaders showed a disastrous insensitivity to the realities of political power and influence *within the Labour Movement*.

Part One
Labour and the Crisis

2

Watershed

Labour's second period of office shattered the illusion of the 'inevitability of gradualness', and ended an inglorious era of Party history in which electoral success had outpaced ability and effectiveness. The 1929 general election nearly doubled Labour's parliamentary representation, bringing the Party close to an overall majority for the first time. Yet with scarcely any exceptions, MacDonald's senior ministers – men in their fifties and sixties, few of whom had as much as a year of governmental experience behind them – lacked the imagination and confidence which the economic crisis required. Long before the collapse of August 1931, a demoralisation and sense of purposelessness had permeated all levels of the Party.

It is hard to exaggerate the importance of this episode of failure for the future development of the Labour Party. Even now, the memory and the legend remain as a sombre warning and powerful constraint. At the time, the lessons seemed all pervading, and dominated the events and debates described later in this book. The defections of Mosley, of the 'National' leaders and finally of the ILP, created in the end a more cohesive and more manageable party. But the most significant effect was the sharpening and redefinition of some old political traditions.

As the slump worsened, the view that the crisis of capitalism had arrived gained strength. This was accompanied by a belief that Labour's impotence derived both from sabotage by financial and class interests, and from a lack of socialist determination which could only be cured by a moral as well as political regeneration. On the other hand, the government's lack of direction was also encouraging a new sense of the inadequacy of aspiration and political faith as agents of social change, and a feeling that radical policies could only be carried out against a background of research and detailed policy making. These two, by no means contradictory, diagnoses – the first concentrating on attitudes and intentions, the second on the availability and content of plans – initially developed side by side. Later they diverged, providing the major rival ideological themes of the Left in the 1930s. But for both, the point of departure was the mistakes and weaknesses of Labour in office after 1929.

Labour and the Crisis

BACKGROUND: THE SECOND LABOUR GOVERNMENT

Almost as soon as MacDonald had returned to Downing Street in May 1929, it became clear that one issue would dominate the new administration. Unemployment had been a serious problem throughout the 1920s – the total of insured unemployed had never fallen below a million. Within a few months of Labour taking office for the second time, the collapse of world markets had pushed the unemployment figure to a higher level than at any time since 1922. By December 1930, it had reached a record $2\frac{1}{2}$ million.

The burden was unevenly distributed. Areas of expanding industry – especially the South and Home Counties – suffered relatively little. The national percentage of insured workers unemployed was nearly twice as great in 1930 as in 1923; in London the change was from 9.0 per cent to 9.8 per cent. On the other hand, where the old, declining industries – coal, iron and steel, engineering, ship-building, textiles – were concentrated, a bad situation became suddenly, dramatically worse, and worklessness and the dole became a way of life. In Wales, one worker in three was on the dole in 1930. In the North-East, unemployment rose from 12.6 per cent in July 1929 to 24.5 per cent in 1930; in the North-West from 12.7 per cent to 29.3 per cent; in Scotland from 11.2 per cent to 23.5 per cent in the same period.[1] Thus there were two nations: for millions living and working in the first, the destitution and miseries of the second remained distant and incomprehensible.

Labour's 1929 election manifesto, which had contained few specific proposals, included a pledge to deal 'immediately and practically' with the problem of unemployment, and schemes of 'National Development' were outlined. However it became plain that little of this programme would be implemented.[2] The Chancellor of the Exchequer, Philip Snowden, upon whom the Prime Minister depended unquestioningly on economic matters, soon showed that he would adhere rigidly to Treasury policies of minimising Government spending and preserving existing parities, and that he would not contemplate any departure from the Free Trade principle. He treated the expansionist proposals of the left-wing ILP as impudent and irrelevant; and he refused to consider suggestions put forward by the Government's own Economic Advisory Council (on which Maynard Keynes and Ernest Bevin, General Secretary of the Transport and General Workers' Union, served), or by a committee of ministers set up by the Prime Minister to handle the unemployment problem, consisting of Sir Oswald Mosley, George Lansbury and Tom Johnston.

Early in 1930 Mosley, exasperated by the Government's inactivity, and influenced both by the 'Hobsonian' economics of the ILP and by Keynes, presented the Cabinet with the so-called 'Mosley Memorandum' which set out a radical plan for dealing with unemployment by expanding credit,

10

increasing purchasing power through a development of social services and
the raising of pensions, and by planning in industry and the introduction
of either import controls or a tariff to protect the home market. Snowden
first ignored the document, then secured its rejection. Mosley resigned from
the Government, and began a vigorous campaign against Snowden's policy
and in favour of his own. Though he narrowly failed to carry the Labour
Party Conference in October, extensive sympathy in the Movement for
Mosley's position was reflected in his election to a coveted place on the
Party's National Executive.

This challenge to the Government's economic orthodoxy soon foundered. Mosley's wisdom on policy was combined with a restless ambition
and a lack of political judgement which destroyed him. In December 1930,
with the support of 17 other MPs (including John Strachey and Aneurin
Bevan), he published the 'Mosley Manifesto' – a restatement of the
'Memorandum' aims. When this achieved no success, he left the Labour
Party and founded a 'New Party' in the mistaken belief that he could build
up a rival political body. This was the first of three splits in the Labour
Party which occurred within the space of eighteen months – and which
demonstrated the firmness of Labour's hold on its mass working-class
support.

After Mosley's defection, attacks on the Government were intensified
by the ILP, which advocated measures similar to Mosley's. Relations between leading ministers, always difficult, became increasingly tense.
MacDonald exhausted himself with overwork, isolated himself from
Cabinet colleagues whom he despised, and withdrew for social comforts to
the company of rich, aristocratic friends outside the Labour Movement. By
July 1931 unemployment had reached 2¾ million – imposing a heavy burden
in unemployment benefit on the Exchequer.

Impervious to radical and left-wing criticisms, Snowden determined on
a policy of economic retrenchment. In February 1931 he had set up a Committee under Sir George May, Chairman of the Prudential Assurance Company, to advise on reductions in Government expediture; membership of
the Committee had been balanced to ensure that recommendations would
be drastic. The Committee's report in July was not a disappointment. It
announced that Britain was on the brink of bankruptcy, and proposed £97m
cuts in national expenditure – of which two thirds should come from cutting
unemployment benefit, raising contributions and imposing a means test.

The May Report had been intended as a stick with which to beat soft-
hearted Labour MPs. It had a quite different, devastating, effect. Foreign
holders of sterling became convinced of Britain's insolvency and started to
sell. To save the gold standard, which for Snowden was an article of faith,
the Bank of England borrowed heavily from France and the United States.
An initial £50m loan proved insufficient. The Bank tried to borrow an addi-

tional £80m. It was met with a demand from the New York Federal Reserve Bank that the Government should first show its intention of making economies in-line with the May Report – including a heavy cut in unemployment benefit.

There was no minister with the financial expertise to stand up to Snowden's cold economic logic, and under heavy pressure from bankers, Tories, Liberals and its own Economy Committee, the Cabinet gave way on almost every point. However, a proposal to make a 10 per cent cut in the rate of unemployment benefit proved too much for many ministers to take. Twelve ministers accepted it as necessary; but a minority of nine refused to agree to what seemed the negation of everything the Labour Party stood for.

Thus the Cabinet reached deadlock, and late on 23 August MacDonald went to the Palace ostensibly to offer the resignation of the Government, and advise the King to hold a conference with the leaders of the other two parties. When the Prime Minister reported to his colleagues later that he had told the King that 'it was impossible for them to continue in office as a united Cabinet',[3] many assumed that this meant that a Baldwin administration would be formed. Next day, however, MacDonald presented ministers with a *fait accompli*. Assuring the Cabinet that once the emergency was over 'the political Parties would resume their respective positions', and that there would be no 'Coupon' election, the Prime Minister announced that the King was to invite 'certain individuals, as individuals, to take upon their shoulders the burden of the Government',[4] and indicated that he, MacDonald, was to be one of these individuals.

Three ministers, Snowden, J. H. Thomas and Lord Sankey, were invited to join the new Cabinet and agreed to do so. Lord Amulree joined the Government later. All other Cabinet Ministers lost their jobs and were replaced by Conservatives and Liberals.

THE SPLIT

Outside the Labour Movement, the Prime Minister's action was greeted as statesmanlike and selfless. Among his former supporters it came to be regarded as a wicked betrayal which split the Party and duped the public. In itself, the formation of the National Government – for which there were honourable precedents[5] – does not account for this. As far as the ex-Cabinet ministers were concerned, the main grievance was the lack of any proper consultation. A myth developed later that Labour ministers were completely taken aback by MacDonald's announcement on the 24th. There is evidence that this was not the case – that the decision was half-expected.[6] However, at no stage had the Prime Minister taken the full Cabinet into his confidence.

Yet it is clear that MacDonald did not want a permanent breach in the

Party. Nor did many ex-ministers. Arthur Henderson's view – which carried most weight in the Party – was pragmatic, and entirely in accord with the Prime Minister's own. MacDonald was the indispensable leader; he must not be lost to the Movement. 'We mustn't drive J. R. M. and the others out,' he told a 'Council of War' at Transport House on the afternoon of the 24th, 'this is only an interlude in the life of the Party, like the war'.[7] Others among the Party's leaders continued to speak of MacDonald's 'sincerity and courage' and held back from recrimination.[8] What decided the issue was the tactless behaviour of the 'National' Labour ministers (and of Mac-Donald especially) over the next few days – infuriating opponents, silencing sympathisers, and alienating many who felt more bewilderment than outrage.

Three crucial meetings determined that the split would be permanent. The first was held in Downing Street on the 24th shortly after the final Cabinet had ended. MacDonald explained himself to junior ministers, and did it badly. 'Christ crucified speaks from the cross' Hugh Dalton wrote in disgust.[9] Attlee later wrote of the Prime Minister's performance: 'Having already distributed the offices in the new Government, he would have been embarrassed if any Labour Ministers had wished to join'.[10] But this was wrong. Immediately after the meeting MacDonald began a frantic campaign of attempted patronage, and it rapidly became clear that he was prepared to make an offer to anybody who might be prepared to follow him.[11] Few accepted.[12]

The other two decisive meetings were called by the ruling bodies of the Labour Movement. MacDonald damned himself at both by not attending. On 26 August, a Joint Meeting of the TUC General Council, the Executive of the PLP, and the Labour Party National Executive accepted an NEC resolution that the PLP should go into opposition – yet it still held back from any explicit mention of the Prime Minister.[13] Two days later, however, the absence of the 'National' Labour leaders from a full meeting of the Parliamentary Party ensured the unity of the PLP against them. In the whole Party only one MP was prepared to vote for the Prime Minister – his own son, Malcolm.[14]

Having rejected MacDonald, the PLP then elected Arthur Henderson to succeed him. Henderson appeared, at this moment of crisis and uncertainty, as a symbol of what the Party felt that it stood for. As General Secretary since 1911, he had had a greater hand in turning Labour into a major party than any other leader, and as Foreign Secretary since 1929 he had been one of the Labour Government's few ministerial successes. His incorruptibility, his immunity from the 'aristocratic embrace' which had so undermined other leaders, and above all his dedication to the concept of 'the Movement', greater than its component parts, gave him an unrivalled authority. Nevertheless, Henderson's own instinct to avoid accepting the leadership was sound. As Party Leader, he ruined his health, shortened his life, and added nothing to his reputation.

The change in the Party leadership brought no shift in policy. When Parliament reassembled on 8 September, Opposition leaders were at pains to declare their financial orthodoxy. 'I entirely repudiate the suggestion', declared William Graham, former President of the Board of Trade, 'that there was ever the slightest hesitation among those sitting on this side of the House – those charged with responsibility – about balancing the Budget'.[15] Most other Labour speakers also crossed themselves reverently before the altar of 'sound' finance.

Even Jimmy Maxton, from the revolutionary left, accepted the Treasury view that an unchecked flight from gold would be catastrophic; the difference was that he wanted a catastrophe. 'The economies are not going to do more than postpone the real crisis for a very few weeks,' he predicted, 'and then you are going to have a real, genuine, economic collapse – not merely a flight from the pound, but a breakdown of your economic system.'[16]

This was not, however, the only left-wing position. Frank Wise, also of the ILP (but soon to break with Maxton, and found a new left-wing body, the Socialist League) was a rare but significant exception in that he questioned gold standard dogma. Describing 'all this talk about preserving the gold standard for the benefit of the cost of living' as a delusion, he argued that the main beneficiaries were the rentiers and the City.[17] Mosley, similarly, asked if 'any hon. member (would) suggest that we are in danger of inflation in a period in which prices are sharply falling.'[18]

Such views were shortly to be vindicated. By 20 September the Cabinet was left with no choice but to accept the Bank of England's advice to suspend the obligation to sell gold at a fixed price. When the Government had 'done what it was formed in order not to do',[19] none of the expected disasters happened. The pound did not lose half its value, nor did unemployment rise to ten million, as Snowden had predicted to a disbelieving Walter Citrine, General Secretary of the TUC.[20] The price level did not rise; unemployment remained static, and then began to fall slowly. It is likely that this devaluation, forced upon a Cabinet hitherto convinced that it would bring a cataclysmic collapse, helped to stimulate a recovery of trade and employment.

It did not, however, bring any immediate revolution in Labour attitudes, as Party Conference, which opened at Scarborough two weeks later – 'dull, drab, disillusioned but not disunited'[21] – revealed. 'I cannot claim to have any knowledge of the movements of the exchange,' Aneurin Bevan confessed in Parliament on 21 September, 'or indeed, any clear understanding of the Gold Standard. The only thing that consoles me in that regard is that my ignorance is shared by almost every other member of the House of Commons.'[22] Scarborough showed that lack of economic understanding was not restricted to the Palace of Westminister. Speeches were heavily spiced with references to the 1928 policy document, *Labour and the Nation*, as if nothing at all had changed, and the NEC's policy resolutions created 'a feeling of having heard all that before on quite a number of occasions and of having heard it better put'.[23]

On the first day of Conference, the Labour Party approved the expulsion of the 'National' rebels. A few hours later MacDonald told the Cabinet that he had decided to ask for an immediate dissolution. Promises to Labour ministers on 24 August were tossed aside. Preparations began for an election in which 'National' Labour and Liberal candidates were to be protected by inter-party arrangements in the constituencies similar in all essentials to the 'Coupon' of 1918.

THE HOLOCAUST

The 1931 election was a savage affair. It was also a confused one. As in 1918 the main battles were within parties rather than between them. Labour was not alone in its preoccupation with family quarrels: the Liberals were divided three ways between followers of Sir John Simon, uncritical in support of the Government, followers of Sir Herbert Samuel who supported the Government but took a firm stand on free trade, and a tiny group led by Lloyd George which would have nothing to do with the Government at all.

The centre of the stage was taken by the battle between former members of the Labour Cabinet. Labour's position was peculiarly difficult because the Party had nothing new to offer; it could only defend a dismal record in Government, blaming for failures those who had led it. The Labour Manifesto, *Labour's Call to Action: The Nation's Opportunity*, accepted 'a balanced Budget as the first condition of sound national finance' and attacked 'men who are now acting in direct contradiction to their own previous convictions', yet did not attempt to explain how it was that these same men had been principally responsible for the programme on which Labour had fought the last election and was now fighting this one. And it included among excuses the 'intolerable restrictions' of its minority position – a compelling argument for not voting Labour since the most incorrigible optimist could scarcely imagine that an overall majority was possible in 1931.

Labour had no premonition of disaster. Some Labour candidates reported the best canvass for years.[24] 'No one would have guessed either from meetings or the canvass that we were not the winning party',[25] wrote Harold Laski, who accompanied Henderson during the campaign. On the morning of the poll, the *Manchester Guardian* reported a guess by 'an expert electioneer properly so called': Conservatives 316, Labour 215, Liberals (including Lloyd George Liberals) 35, Simonites 30, National Labour 10, Independents 9. As it turned out, Labour was not merely defeated; it was all but wiped out.

The 1931 election was the greatest landslide of British democratic history, producing the most unbalanced Parliament since the Great Reform Act. Labour had been reduced from 288 seats in 1929 to 52. Only nine other members would not support the new Government – Lloyd George's family group of 4 independent Liberals, and 5 Independents. The new House would contain 554 Government supporters, including 473 Conservatives, 13 National Labour, 35 Liberal National (Simonites) and 33 Liberals (Samuelites).

Only one member of the old Labour Cabinet who was not now in the National Government survived the holocaust – George Lansbury. Of ex-ministers outside the Cabinet, only Clement Attlee, former Post-Master General, and Sir Stafford Cripps, briefly Solicitor-General, hung on with hairsbreadth majorities. Otherwise, five former under-secretaries, George Hall, Morgan Jones, Jack Lawson, Willy Lunn and Allen Parkinson were all that remained of the old Labour Government in the Opposition.

Why did it happen? Morrison gave a Hackney audience a list of factors a week later:

> the mendacious campaign of the Tory press, particularly the utterly baseless story which was encouraged by Mr MacDonald and Mr Snowden that the Labour Government had endangered the savings of Post Office depositors; pressure and intimidation by the employers; reckless promises by Tory candidates of an end to unemployment under tariffs; the preferential use of broadcasting by Government spokesmen during and before the election; the widespread combinations of Toryism and Liberalism against Labour, despite Mr Lloyd George's courageous appeals for sanity; and the inadequacy of Labour canvassing in many constituencies.'[26]

Yet the most plausible explanation is that Labour had manifestly failed to deal with unemployment. 'The Pits Are Closed', ran a Labour election poster in 1929, 'But the Ballot Box is Open!' In two years the total of registered unemployed had more than doubled – from 1 164 000 in June 1929 to 2 880 000 in September 1931.

Nevertheless Labour's massive loss of seats was mainly a product of the simple majority electoral system, in the context of the National 'Coupon'. The fall in Labour's proportion of the total vote was relatively small – from 37.1 per cent in 1929 to 30.6 per cent in 1931.[27] 1929, however, had been Labour's best election year ever; and a comparison with 1924, when Labour contested about the same number of seats as in 1931 and polled 33.0 per cent of the total poll, shows that the 1931 vote, though a severe setback, did not indicate a disintegration of support.

A calculation by the Proportional Representation Society just after the election puts Labour's defeat into a clearer perspective. According to this estimate, based on votes cast in contested seats, under PR Labour would have won only 225 seats in 1929, instead of 288, and 168 in 1931, instead of 52.[28] The electoral system worked strongly in favour of Labour in 1929, and drastically against it in 1931. This was because of pacts among Government supporters in 1931, which would have caused a big drop in the number of Labour seats even if Labour's vote and percentage of the poll had remained steady. Political alignments, more than fickle voters, were the main cause of the enormity of Labour's defeat.[29]

POWER IN THE LABOUR PARTY

Nevertheless, the impact of the election result on the Party was immense. Even before the election, in the PLP there had been an important shift of balance. Those ex-ministers who had supported MacDonald and Snowden in Cabinet on the question of cuts in unemployment benefit, but who had stayed with Labour, retired to a tactful or embarrassed silence, both in Parliament and at Conference.[30] This shift was powerfully reinforced by the polls in November, ending the era of Labour's pioneers. Of those who had built up the Party only Henderson, Clynes and Lansbury remained in positions of prominence.[31] Labour's second generation now emerged and took control of the Party for the next twenty years. The union organisers and socialist propagandists for whom office had come as a disorientating surprise gave way to men who had fixed their eyes early on the Treasury bench, and who by their forties had solid experience of Government behind them.

The events of 1931 had another important effect. During the twenties there had been an increasing tendency for the Parliamentary leaders to gain control of the Party and of policy; now this was reversed. A major reason for the growing power of the PLP after 1918 had been that the National Executive, constitutionally sovereign between Conferences, had contained an increasing proportion of Parliamentary leaders among its members. In Labour's period of opposition after 1924, on average nearly half of the NEC was made up of MPs. After 1929 this rose to two thirds, with an average of 10 members of the Government on the 24 man Executive.[32] Since the non-parliamentary members of the NEC were usually trade unionists of the second rank the Parliamentary leadership had little difficulty in carrying the Executive with it on most issues. This changed after 1931. The electoral carnage was greatest among leaders, and the close link which had tied the Party in Parliament to the Party outside it was broken. The only member of the NEC who held his seat was George Lansbury, also one of only two survivors from the post-crisis Parliamentary Executive.[33] The average Parliamentary membership of the NEC fell from over 16 in 1929–31 to 3 between 1931 and 1935 – lower absolutely than for any Parliament since 1900, and proportionately lowest ever.[34]

The result was a lack of unity and direction. Within the Commons, the PLP maintained its autonomy, its leaders sometimes expressing views widely at variance with those of the Executive; but outside it, the National Executive and strengthened National Joint Council issued policy statements which coolly overruled the PLP. For at least four years there were in effect two separate political bodies within the Movement – one at Transport House, directed by the National Executive, moderate and cautious, the other in Parliament, taking its cue from its own Executive, and leaning to the left, especially on foreign policy issues. Divisions within the Party during the 1931 Parliament and after it were, in part, a reflection of a conflict between these two bodies for the right to speak for the political wing of the Movement.

In this conflict the NEC generally came out on top – largely because of the weakness and mediocrity of the PLP. With Labour MPs in only the most homogenous of working-class constituencies there was a lack of skills in the Parliamentary Party other than those of the union branch and the miners' lodge. Of 46 endorsed Labour MPs (the total of 52 included 6 who had fought as unendorsed candidates) exactly half were sponsored by the Miners' Federation, and 9 by other trade unions.[35] There were 137 lawyers in the new House; only 3 were Labour. Of 111 businessmen, 3 were Labour. Of 42 journalists, retired civil servants, doctors, teachers and accountants Labour provided 2 doctors and 4 teachers.[36] The vagaries of the electoral system had produced a Parliamentary Party which was highly sectional and unrepresentative of the Movement as a whole, and also little equipped either to function as an effective Opposition, or to beat off an intrusive National Executive.

Indeed, more than at any other time after 1918, the NEC dominated the Party, and the PLP often appeared as a junior partner, engaged in a gallant but unreal battle of secondary importance to the serious business of the Party carried on at Transport House. The Executive determined official policy, making extensive use of its new Policy Committee and specialist sub-committees; it also reproved and disciplined party members who stepped out of line with all the tight-lipped prudery of a Victorian governess. It was on the attitudes and actions of the Executive that the main controversies in the Party during the decade ultimately turned.

Some coordination was provided by the revamped National Joint Council. Since 1921 the Council had operated as a consultative body of small importance on which the General Council of the TUC, the Parliamentary Executive and the National Executive had been equally represented. Now, at the initiative of the General Council, it was given new powers. Trade union leaders moved quickly in the atmosphere of shock and confusion which followed the election. Irritated by the disdain shown in the past by

Parliamentary leaders, vindicated in their stand against the Labour Cabinet in August, they demanded more say in the affairs of the Party.

'The National Joint Council had scarcely ever functioned', Walter Citrine, General Secretary of the TUC, told a joint meeting of the General Council and the NEC on 10 November. 'One felt that in the life-time of the Government, so far as the Parliamentary side of the Council was concerned, the Ministers were preoccupied by their own duties, which made it impossible for the Council to carry out the work it was designed to do. The General Council ... did not seek in any shape or form to say what the Party was to do, but they did ask that the primary purpose of the creation of the Party should not be forgotten. It was created by the Trade Union Movement to do those things in Parliament which the Trade Union Movement found ineffectively performed by the two-party system.'[37]

In December the National Joint Council was reconstituted in a fundamental way. Henceforth it was to be made up of seven members of the General Council with three each from the NEC and the Parliamentary Executive, thus giving the trade union movement a majority, and with a rotating chairmanship. It was to meet monthly and hold emergency meetings when necessary. Its new duties included, in particular, the duty to 'consider all questions affecting the Labour Movement as a whole, and make provisions for taking immediate and united action on all questions of national emergency', and to 'endeavour to secure a common policy and joint action, whether by legislation or otherwise, on all questions affecting the workers as producers, consumers and citizens.'[38]

The new Council (from 1934 called the National Council of Labour) became a powerful body. It organised national campaigns and made frequent declarations, mainly concerned with foreign policy. But its position did not justify the claim that the Labour Party in the 1930s was 'The General Council's Party', as one historian has suggested.[39] The main function of the National Joint Council was to give weight to Party pronouncements by demonstrating that the Movement spoke with a united voice. It was never out of step with the majority view on the NEC. When war came in 1939, the National Council was designated 'the authority of the Movement'. Yet it was the National Executive which determined and negotiated Labour's entry into the Coalition Government.[40] Indeed, quite early in the 1931 Parliament Lansbury, as Party Leader, made clear that he did not regard his role as in any sense a subservient one. Bevin had tried to use the authority of the National Joint Council to prevent Lansbury's attendance at a left-wing meeting at the Albert Hall. 'I do not think,' replied Lansbury, 'that I am called upon to ask permission from anybody to do this – and certainly have no intention of doing so.'[41]

The crisis and the bitterness engendered by it also brought another change. In the nine years since Labour had become the main Opposition Party the heritage of cooperation with non-Labour politicians had been maintained. A steady influx of former Liberals (and a trickle of former Conservatives) had served to reinforce MacDonald's view of Parliament as a 'Council of State' composed of men of goodwill with as much to bind as to separate them. The 1931 crisis set Labour on a course of purist exclusiveness. There was a powerful reaction not only against the aristocratic embrace but against the political embrace as well. A strong feeling developed that Labour could only regain its integrity and effectiveness by standing aloof from the enticements of capitalist parties and rejecting any temptation to compromise.

This feeling was strongest on the left-wing of the Party, which could claim to have assessed MacDonald correctly while the rest of the Party was allowing itself to be betrayed by him. Over the next few years, the Left was able to argue persuasively that any contact with those intrinsically hostile to the interests of the working-class was dangerous and unacceptable. Ironically, this argument succeeded only too well. When, after 1937, the Labour Left switched from the advocacy of an exclusive working-class unity to that of a broad Popular Front alliance, it found itself fighting the effects of its own propaganda.

3
Leadership

A major effect of the 1931 election was to move the most prominent of those in the PLP who survived it suddenly to the forefront, and, among those who were defeated to give younger, brighter men unexpected influence. The party hierarchy was turned upside down. It was not just that most of the older leaders who had not deserted to the other side had lost their seats. Within the space of a few months, almost all had ceased to be central figures in the Labour Party.

Sir Charles Trevelyan retired to manage his huge estates in Northumberland; Tom Johnston returned to Scotland; Margaret Bondfield went back to the NUGMW as a full-time official; Willie Adamson was taken back as a miners' official. William Graham – formerly President of the Board of Trade and widely regarded as one of the most promising of the younger ministers – fell victim to the combined shocks of domestic tragedy, electoral reverse and the break with Snowden, with whom he had been especially close. Just after Christmas 1931 he caught a chill, and died a fortnight later. 'I can't think why Philip did it!', he was heard to repeat in his last delirium.[1] A. V. Alexander, considered by Henderson as Labour's brightest hope for the future,[2] returned to full-time work in the Co-operative Movement, and became embroiled in a protracted battle between the Co-operative Party and the NEC; for the next few years his first loyalty was to the Co-operatives.[3]

For those who lost their seats, '[t]here was a danger,' wrote Dalton, who, though defeated, undoubtedly benefited from the decimation of the PLP, 'of losing one's place, perhaps decisively, in the ever-shifting Parliamentary queue'.[4] Certainly, those who now took their places near the head of the queue included men who would never have been seen as front rank leaders but for the paucity of talent in the PLP. Yet the weakness of the Party in Parliament and the disappearance of the old leadership meant that dominating positions fell to men who were placed at key power points in the extra-parliamentary party, especially on the NEC. Thus, while Lansbury, Attlee and Cripps gained a special strength until 1935 from their position as Parliamentary spokesmen, Greenwood (who returned to Parliament in

1932) could base his influence on Transport House, while Dalton maintained a strong position on the NEC, and Morrison had the London Labour Party behind him.

After the 1931 election the chairmanship of the PLP went to Lansbury as the only member of the old Labour Cabinet who had neither been expelled from the Party nor lost his seat. That he was scarcely the ideal choice was, however, acknowledged with the re-election, unopposed, of Henderson as Party Leader – even though Henderson was out of Parliament. This division of the functions of Leadership and PLP Chairmanship did not work well, and Henderson soon became more of an encumbrance than an asset. In January he was elected President of the Disarmament Conference, and he spent most of his remaining energies, when not overcome by illness, pursuing the chimera of international control of armaments at Geneva. 'Shrunken in frame and drawn in features,' Beatrice Webb noted in August 1932, 'inert and depressed, he is manifestly incapable of any general leadership of the Labour Party'.[5] He resigned the Leadership in October 1932, but frequent absences had meant that for the previous year the position had been little more than nominal. Lansbury succeeded him as full Party Leader, keeping the post until 1935.

GEORGE LANSBURY

Lansbury's politics, rooted in bitter experience of unemployment and hardship as an emigrant in Australia in the 1880s, and belonging to the oldest traditions of Christian Socialism and street corner demogoguery, were in some ways suited to the beleaguered Opposition of 1931.[6] One reaction to the crisis and defeat was an eagerness to return to fundamental principles: Lansbury reflected this mood.

With such a massive imbalance between the two sides in Parliament, there was a real danger that the Opposition powers of scrutiny would fall into disuse; Lansbury had to see that Government Bills and Votes of Credit were subjected to as vigorous a criticism as in a normal Parliament.[7] He also had to keep up the morale of outnumbered and outgunned backbenchers, organise the very small number of articulate Labour MPs to speak on every conceivable topic, and provide an inspirational lead for the demoralised rank-and-file outside. It was a measure of his success that when he found his position untenable in 1935 because of his pacifist objection to Labour's support for sanctions in the Italy–Abyssinia dispute, a large majority of the PLP asked him to reconsider his resignation.

Lansbury's reputation as a left-winger was based on his pacifism, his support for minority causes and his refusal to compromise on matters of principle, not on any inclinations towards marxism. He had little sympathy for the rebellious ILP. When Maxton gave trouble, Lansbury was as firm as Henderson that ILP members must subscribe to Labour Party Standing

Orders or get out. On domestic policy he was essentially orthodox, believing that *Labour and the Nation* and the 1931 Election Manifesto contained 'the real guts of the position'.[8] Before foreign policy became a major issue his only serious disagreement with official policy was one in which the Party was to the left of him: Lansbury favoured a personal means test (as opposed to the Government policy of a household means test), while the official Party view was against the means test altogether.[9]

Yet Lansbury's emotionalism and lack of incisiveness[10] infuriated trade unionists like Bevin and Citrine, while an irreverence of authority, and a stubborn resistence to influence when his convictions were challenged, irritated 'respectable' leaders outside Parliament and helped to create a gulf between the PLP and Transport House; from 1934 relations deteriorated badly over his refusal to countenance the possibility of armed resistance to the Dictators.

CLEMENT ATTLEE

More fateful than Lansbury's election as PLP chairman was the election of the deputy chairman. The choice of Attlee for this office went almost unnoticed and was considered of little importance at the time. Yet its direct consequence was that Attlee, hitherto regarded by nobody as a possibility for the Leadership, took over from Lansbury in 1935 and remained leader for twenty years, longer than anybody else in the Party before or since.

Roy Jenkins has described the election of Attlee in 1931 as 'almost automatic...Its inevitability although of very recent growth, was almost complete'.[11] It is not clear that this was so. Apart from Lansbury, Attlee had more solid ministerial experience than any other MP – though he had only served above the rank of under-secretary for a little over a year. Yet it is surprising that no miner was put forward for the deputy post. One MP who was well suited for it was D. R. Grenfell, MP for Gower since 1922, and later Minister for Mines in the Wartime Coalition. A man of considerable talents, with a self-taught fluency in French, he had been elected to the Parliamentary Executive (for which Attlee did not stand) in September, and retained a high position on it for the rest of the decade. In 1918, a PLP similarly dominated by miners had chosen as chairman Willie Adamson, a miner of meagre abilities and little standing, despite the far greater claims of Clynes and J. H. Thomas.

Attlee's own cryptic comment on the most fateful event of his Parliamentary career is interesting. 'On going to the first Party Meeting after the Election, I had a message from Arthur Henderson that George Lansbury would be proposed as Leader and myself as Deputy. These nominations went through without opposition.'[12] Henderson may have been concerned that the vague and emotional Lansbury shoud be balanced by the practical and efficient Attlee. At any rate, it is an open question whether without the intervention of Henderson the outcome would have been the same.[13]

Attlee's early life was singular mainly for its lack of distinction of a conventional kind. Born in 1883 the son of a City solicitor, he was educated at Haileybury and University College, Oxford; his progress at both institutions was unremarkable. A short career after Oxford as a barrister was a depressing failure. 'I had always been painfully shy', he wrote later,[14] and perhaps this was why he rapidly found that he was unsuited to work at the Bar. Instead he took up social work in the East End, where, affected by the poverty and miseries of the slums, his Anglican Toryism gave way to the doctrines of Ruskin, Morris and Webb. At the age of 25 he joined the ILP and became active in establishing the party in Stepney. 'The experience that he gained during this time was later of inestimable value to Attlee', his biographer has written. 'He treated the East End as his home, and not as a laboratory in which he could carry out social experiments. By so doing he dug himself into one of the great working-class areas of the country and grew roots of a firmness that few middle-class socialists have been able to achieve.'[15]

A series of temporary jobs led, through a brief association with Sidney Webb, to a post teaching social administration at the London School of Economics. 'I was not appointed on the score of academic qualification,' Attlee later wrote modestly, 'but because I was considered to have a good practical knowledge of social conditions.'[16] In 1914 Attlee rejected the pacifism prevalent in the ILP and joined up. He rose to the rank of major, saw action at Gallipoli, in Mesopotamia and in France, was wounded and suffered recurring bouts of illness. Recovered by 1919, he returned to Stepney, fought and lost an LCC contest, was co-opted mayor of Stepney, and in 1922 became MP for Limehouse.

Attlee's Parliamentary career started with a stroke of good luck. MacDonald, newly elected to the Leadership, picked him as his PPS. In 1924, however, he was given a meagre reward – one of the least promising posts in the first Labour Government – under-secretary at the War Office. Five years later he was passed over completely – partly because he was still serving on the Indian Statutory Commission, to which he was appointed in 1927. If Mosley had not resigned in May 1930 Attlee might never have served in the Second Labour Government; for the abrupt end to Mosley's career provided a crucial stepping-stone for Attlee who moved from the backbenches to the Chancellorship of the Duchy of Lancaster. In March 1931 he was transferred to the Post Office, and for five months, the only period in his whole career, he had responsibility for a Government department. At the election he held Limehouse with the slim majority of 551.[17]

Attlee's most fortunate characteristic was one which, in normal times, might have been a besetting handicap. He was not a prima donna. He appeared modest and unassuming to the point of self-effacement. 'In

24

stature slight and unimpressive,' recalled Francis Williams, 'he carried with him little of the aura of vitality and drama that one is inclined to look for when one is young in those who occupy a central place on the political stage. He was not easy to talk to. He listened but he did not give much and seemed more often to reflect a middle view than have one of his own.'[18]

Colleagues and journalists were patronising when they were not contemptuous. Attlee was often described as mediocre, unimaginative, lacking in personality. In 1935 Alexander still considered him 'negligible',[19] Susan Lawrence regarded him as 'inconspicuous',[20] and Dalton dismissed him as 'a nonentity'.[21] Few took him seriously until after 1939, and his imminent return to obscurity was confidently predicted throughout the decade. Yet taunts which would have upset a more glamorous and self-important man left Attlee curiously unruffled. He was content to get on with the job. He did not seek the lime-light. He was used to, and happy with, a life of apparently unproductive committees which more brilliant men found irredeemably tiresome. Lacking glittering talents, his qualities were of a kind which do not often lead to high office, but are invaluable if, by chance, it is obtained. He had an orderly mind, a shrewd understanding of men, and a great, but not neurotic, appetite for work; he was never a schemer; his integrity was known to be absolute. 'I was never an intellectual', he corrected an interviewer after his retirement; 'they would not have allowed me as such'.[22] This was crucial. He had not come into the Party through the back door as a renegade Liberal, or as a bright young man marked out for hasty preferment. He had risen from the rank-and-file like any other party worker, and so had a worm's-eye understanding of the Movement which others of his class, like Cripps or Dalton, always lacked.

The period from 1931 to 1935 was the making of Attlee. Lansbury invited Cripps and Attlee to share his office behind the Speaker's chair, and the three together organised the work of the Opposition, necessarily taking the heaviest burden of speaking upon themselves. Attlee had been an infrequent speaker before 1931. Now he was required to speak in almost every major debate; in the 1931–2 session, he made no fewer than 125 speeches in the Commons and took up 352 columns of Hansard.[23] In the process he gained a fuller knowledge of every aspect of policy, and a greater standing in the Party, than would ever have been possible in other circumstances, establishing himself as a credible candidate for the Leadership – something which would have been unimaginable in 1931.

ARTHUR GREENWOOD

By contrast, Arthur Greenwood, Minister of Health in the 1929 Government, and with a wider political and administrative experience than any other of the second generation of Labour Party leaders, would have been an obvious candidate against Lansbury if he had survived the 1931 holocaust. His stature was such that when he returned in April 1931, he found it necessary to deny rumours that he had contested a by-election in order to take over as chairman.[24]

Greenwood was a political rarity among the younger leaders in that he was both working-class in origin and an intellectual. Born in 1880 in Leeds, he made his way through elementary and secondary schools in the city, and started his career as an elementary school teacher. Largely self-taught, he moved on to become an economics lecturer, and build up a national reputation through his writings, in particular, on the welfare of schoolchildren. These, and connections with the Fabians, led to his selection for Lloyd George's Wartime 'Garden Suburb'. After a period as an Assistant Secretary at the Ministry of Reconstruction, where he worked closely with Addison and Arthur Henderson, he became Secretary of the new Joint TUC–Labour Party Research and Information Department. He entered Parliament as MP for Nelson and Colne in 1922, and in 1924 was given a junior post at the Ministry of Health. When the Labour Party set up its own Research Department in 1927 he became Head, and with only short breaks remained so until 1943. As Minister of Health in the Second Labour Government, he steered through Parliament the Widows', Orphans' and Old Age Contributory Pensions Act of 1929, and the Housing Act of 1930.

Greenwood was respected as a shrewd and balanced leader with a remorseless appetite for detail. He had worked with the trade unions in the twenties, and maintained closer relations with union leaders than almost any of his political rivals. Open-hearted, genial, and with great personal warmth, he aroused more affection than any other Labour leader. Yet he remained more of a back-room intellectual than a politician. In some ways he was too nice. He lacked forcefulness. A heavy and near-compulsive drinker, a point on which his enemies readily capitalised, he was too tolerant and kindly in his treatment of others to be a really effective administrator; by the mid-thirties, his direction of the Research Department had become weak, and his subordinates tended to be their own masters.[25]

Yet he remained one of Labour's most influential leaders until his appointment to Churchill's War Cabinet in 1940. His election as Deputy Leader in 1935 meant that he stood in during Attlee's illness in the summer of 1939, convincing many in the Party that he would make the better Leader.

HUGH DALTON

The most influential Labour politician in the 1930s who was not himself a contender for the Party Leadership was Hugh Dalton. Dalton was an academic economist; yet his greatest impact in the 1930s was in the field of foreign policy. He and Ernest Bevin were first among national leaders to seek to impress on the Movement the need for collective action and rearmament as counter-measures to fascist aggression, and the gradual conversion of the Party to this view was to a great extent their achievement.

John Strachey, when asked by dear old ladies why he became a Communist, had a stock answer. 'From chagrin, madam,' he would reply, 'from chagrin at not getting into the Eton Cricket Eleven.'[26] Perhaps Dalton joined the Labour Party because he was never elected to the Etonian elite society Pop.[27] Dalton's background was certainly bizarre for a Labour politician. His father had been Canon of St George's Chapel, Windsor, and for fourteen years tutor to the sons of the Prince of Wales, later Edward VII, remaining to his death in 1931 an intimate friend of George V. The young Hugh spent his early years in the atmosphere of the Court. After Eton, he went to King's College, Cambridge, where his three primary interests were 'Personal Relationships, Politics and Poetry',[28] and one of his closest friends was Rupert Brooke. At Cambridge he became a Fabian, exchanging Joseph Chamberlain for Hardie and Webb, and developing an early dislike for Ramsay MacDonald. Under the Webbs' influence he went on to take a doctorate at the London School of Economics, and was then briefly a barrister before serving in France during the War. Afterwards he returned to the School as a lecturer, and established a reputation as an economist with the publication of *The Principles of Public Finance* in 1922.

After four unsuccessful contests he became an MP in 1924. Once in the House his progress was meteoric. Within a year he was on the PLP Executive, and in 1926 took third place, beating Thomas, Henderson and Webb. In the same year he was elected to the Constituency Parties' section of the NEC, and though he lost his seat the following year, he was thereafter re-elected annually until 1952. 'I am inclined to agree with Henderson that if the Labour Government arrives during the next ten years Dalton will certainly attain Cabinet rank' wrote Beatrice Webb, who did not like him, in 1927.[29] But Dalton did not get into the Cabinet; he was given the Parliamentary Secretaryship at the Foreign Office, and in the course of the Second Labour Government his respect for Henderson grew into hero worship, while his scorn for MacDonald hardened into a bitter contempt.

In 1931 he narrowly lost his seat at Bishop Auckland. 'In the intense and self-regarding life of Westminster,' he wrote later, 'the absent are soon forgotten or left out of account.'[30] Yet Dalton was scarcely ignored; from a firm base on the NEC he was a directing force in the Labour Party in this period, and his absence from Parliament freed him to concentrate on reshaping Labour's economic and financial policies. A product of his efforts was *Practical Socialism for Britain*, published in March 1935, 'the first swallow of the post-1935 summer'[31] of socialist reformism, which dismissed 'all theatrical nightmares of violent head-on collisions',[32] and presented a detailed programme for the next Labour Government.

Dalton's main flaw was a boyish enjoyment of plots and behind-the-scenes deals. 'Rather a born intriguer', was Attlee's verdict.[33] Outgoing, worldly and gregarious, with a notoriously booming voice, politics remained for him on one level a compulsive, competitive undergraduate game. Revelling in personal success, with a huge confidence in his own abilities, he was distrusted both for his manoeuvrings and for his fierce careerism. '[I]n his curiously deferential and ingratiating method of address with persons who are likely to be useful to him, there is just a hint of insincerity', noted Mrs Webb; 'in his colourless face there is a trace of cunning'.[34]

On another level, he was a man of real socialist conviction and compassion, with a generous concern for the younger generation of socialist intellectuals which he did much to encourage and bring on; and his rare combination of intellectual power, economic sophistication and sound political judgement gained wide respect. 'With no sort of finesse or skill to hide an ambition thoroughly justified by a good and well-trained mind, first-rate experience and great drive,' wrote his friend, Mary Agnes Hamilton, 'he has forthright convictions of a robust kind ... No one could charge Hugh with having a thin skin; it is not a quality he admires or comprehends. He is the complete extrovert; he loves the rough and tumble, the shouting and the fight.'[35] All these qualities are revealed in his private diary, on which his memoirs were based – the shrewdest and sharpest reminiscences of any Labour politician of any era.

HERBERT MORRISON

Dalton and Morrison guided the National Executive during the 1930s. Of the two, Morrison was more powerful. His influence had a very solid basis. He had built up the London Labour Party to the point at which in 1934 it captured the LCC for the first time ever, an enormous boost to battered Labour morale. Thereafter, as Leader of the LCC majority, he was the exception among Labour's national leaders in that he was in a position of major executive power, and was able to prove his effectiveness in the day-to-day running of the metropolis.

For most of his life Morrison had been, in a literal sense, a professional politician. Born in Brixton in 1888, the son of a Tory policeman and a former housemaid, he left school at 14 to work as a Pimlico grocer's errand boy. An early interest in history and economics led him, via the ILP and the SDF, to Fabianism. Despite blindness in one eye, which would have exempted him on medical grounds, Morrison declared himself a conscientious objector in 1914. In 1915 came the opportunity which soon established him as a major political force – he became part-time secretary of the London Labour Party at £1 per week, and within a few years had established himself as a figure of national importance in the Movement. After a term as mayor of Hackney he became MP for South Hackney in 1923. In Parliament, he gained a reputation as a vigorous debater of pragmatic views, a keen admirer of MacDonald, and a hammer of the ILP.

In 1929 MacDonald made him Minister of Transport. It was a successful appointment and one of great long-term significance. As Minister Morrison was responsible for drafting plans for a unified, publicly-owned London Transport. In the process he became firmly committed to the public corporation principle for nationalised industries, and the exclusion of direct labour representation on public boards. After the Government's fall, Morrison used all his influence on the NEC to ensure that this view became integral to Labour Party policy. His views on nationalisation reflected his attitude to party organisation – efficiency must take precedence over abstract theory. 'We shall have to beware of the men who think that machinery and meetings do things of themselves,' he wrote in 1933, 'and we must remember at all times that industries cannot be run by committees, meetings and prolonged argument, but they must be managed and run by men of all grades with individual responsibilities which cannot await the convincing of a meeting and the conduct of lengthy arguments and negotiations.'[36]

Such a position was anathema to the TGWU, and Morrison prevailed only after some bitter clashes with Bevin and other leaders of the Transport workers. Bevin never forgave him, and the antagonism between the two continued into the post-war Labour Cabinet. This conflict with the most powerful figure in the trade union movement seriously undermined his claim to the leadership in the 1930s.

Yet he was regarded by many in all parties as Labour's most able leader. 'He wants results', wrote one of his admirers. 'He prods his lieutenants all the time for "output" . . . Faced with something wrong, his immediate concern is to find the quickest way of getting it put right. Where another would postpone action to indulge in a moving exhortation to the people on the theme of injustice, Morrison would be at once immersed in a practical examination of the circumstances and the definition of remedies.'[37] When the possibility of broadening the 'National' Government was raised during the thirties, Morrison's name was often mentioned as a possible recruit. This was partly because of his abilities; but also because of his frequently voiced intolerance of utopian approaches to socialism, which endeared him to politicians of the centre. 'Socialism in our time is romantic rot', he allegedly told an East End audience in 1932.[38] Deeply ambitious, he never came to terms with his defeat by Attlee in the Leadership contest of 1935, and continued to feel that the Leadership should, by rights, be his.

SIR STAFFORD CRIPPS

Herbert Morrison played a major part in launching Sir Stafford Cripps on one of the most dazzling and contradictory political careers of the twentieth century. During the post-war Labour Government Cripps acquired a reputation as the austere defender of financial virtue, a man of stern intellect and constant temperament, whose calls for national discipline reflected his own moral certitudes. This final period, however, followed a stormy and erratic political adolescence.

Early in the 1931 Parliament Cripps came to be regarded, in the Press and widely in the Party, as leader and chief spokesman of the Labour Left. This reflected, in part, the essential Parliamentarism of Labour's left-wing – Cripps' pre-eminence was founded on his possession of a scarce Labour seat. It was partly by default – the disaffiliation of the ILP in June 1932 had greatly undermined the Labour Left, which was singularly lacking in leaders with a popular appeal. But it was also because of Cripps' quite exceptional personality and intellect. The consequence – that Labour's left-wing was dominated in these critical years by a man of such brilliance, recklessness and political insensitivity – was of the greatest importance to British politics.

Cripps entered politics at the late age of 41, embarking on what was, in a sense, his third career. Cripps' background was one of inherited privilege and talent, and of outstanding personal success. His father was Alfred Cripps, a distinguished lawyer and Tory MP who as Lord Parmoor became, in his old age, a Labour Cabinet Minister; his mother was a member of the Potter family, a sister of Beatrice Webb. With such close links with the political world, an early interest in politics might have seemed inevitable. Apparently he showed none. At Winchester he specialised in science, and showed such promise that he was encouraged to throw up a scholarship at New College to work as a research assistant to Sir William Ramsay at University College, London.

Science however, did not satisfy him, and he decided instead to follow his father at the Bar. He became a barrister in 1913. The War turned him back into a scientist. After a brief spell driving Red Cross lorries in France, he was sent to work as a chemist and administrator at a munitions factory. In 1919, after the first attack of an intestinal illness that was to dog him throughout his life, he returned to the Bar, where he took a specialist interest in scientific and patent law. His progress was freakish, and in 1926 after a total of only eight years' practice, he became the youngest KC, began to earn a vast income, and gained a reputation as 'probably the most formidable cross-examiner of technical experts in the history of the Courts'.[39]

Morrison first made the suggestion that he should become a Labour politician in 1928, after Cripps had made an impressive appearance for the

LCC at the Railway Rates Tribunal. Cripps refused. 'I don't want to enter politics. I am more interested in the Church.'[40] Morrison renewed his efforts in 1929. This time he succeeded, and shortly after the General Election Cripps joined the Labour Party. His adoption as candidate for West Woolwich, narrowly held by the Conservatives, was quickly engineered; had he fought it, his political career would probably never have begun – for West Woolwich was a hopeless constituency for Labour in the conditions of the 1930s, and after 1931, with a large number of established leaders clamouring for seats, there were few to spare for newcomers. But Cripps did not have to wait until the General Election. In October 1930 the Solicitor-General, Sir James Melville, resigned because of ill-health. MacDonald chose Cripps to succeed him – a decision which may have owed something to the presence in the Cabinet of Cripps' father, Parmoor, and uncle, Passfield.

Cripps had to be found a seat. A by-election was pending at Bristol East. The Party managers decided that Cripps should fight it. Before he could do so, it was necessary to overcome some local opposition. The favourite for the candidature was Leah Manning, a prominent NUT official. Henderson ordered her peremptorily to stand down. She refused. So Henderson sent down Dalton, an old personal friend of Mrs Manning, to persuade her; Dalton's charm worked. 'I can remember only a few times when I have given way to tears,' she recalled; 'this was one of them.'[41] She withdrew, leaving an atmosphere of bitterness. There was fierce resistance 'to the Executive's method of dumping onto them a rich man, an aristocrat and a knight',[42] The National Agent was sent to exert maximum pressure: 'I urge the Local Party,' he told them, 'nay, I implore you, to accept him'.[43] After hours of deliberation, and by the narrowest of majorities, they agreed to do so. It was a grudging decision. 'East Bristol was a Left Party. And Cripps was a nominee of Transport House. They did not like it.'[44]

Cripps was elected in January 1931. Nine months later those who had secured this highly undemocratic selection –Morrison, Henderson, Dalton– were out of Parliament, and were soon to find that in giving Cripps one of the safest seats in the country Transport House had taken on very much more than it had bargained for.

Before the crisis, Cripps behaved impeccably as a tame Government lawyer, paying dutiful lip service to official policies, but showing little interest in them. It was therefore not surprising that when the Government fell he, like the other Law Officers, should have been invited to stay on. The others accepted and moved as a bloc into the National Government, retaining their posts. For a time it seemed that Cripps might join them.

When the crisis broke he was in Baden-Baden receiving treatment for his intestinal ailment. He received a telegram from MacDonald on 26 August:

HOPE YOU PROGRESSING STOP WOULD YOU LIKE TO GO ON–RAMSAY

MACDONALD.[45] Cripps cabled back ambiguously saying that he was returning at once, a message apparently read by the Prime Minister as an acceptance.[46] Back in England, he was Sir William Jowitt (the Attorney-General), on the evening of 27 August, and Lord Sankey (the Lord Chancellor), the next morning. He told Sankey he intended to resign. 'Then that ends our friendship', replied the Lord Chancellor.[47] Only after this meeting did he write to MacDonald explaining that he could not stay. Cripps' letter indicates how close he came to joining the National Government.

> It is with very great personal regret that I find myself unable to accept your kind offer.
> May I be allowed – without being considered impertinent – to say that I admire immensely the courage and conviction which have led you and other Labour Ministers associated with you to take the action you have taken. My own personal hope is that the rift in the Party may be quickly healed, and I shall do all I can to attain that end.[48]

In the General Election, Cripps was extraordinarily lucky. In 1929 there had been a straight fight in Bristol East between Liberal and Labour, with no Conservative standing. If this had been repeated in 1931 Cripps would probably have lost; as it happened, the electoral arrangement on the Government side meant that Cripps faced a Conservative opponent but no Liberal, and presumably gained the votes of some former Liberal supporters. Consequently Cripps held the seat by 429 votes, barely 1 per cent of the total poll, and found himself, little more than two years after joining the Party, one of Labour's three most prominent spokesmen in Parliament.

Meanwhile Cripps had begun a rapid move to the Left. The crisis, and the critical decision it had forced him to make, had affected him deeply. His speech at Scarborough on 6 October showed the impact on him of recent events.

> The recent crisis, which I think many people in the future will look back upon as the beginning of a new era in the politics of this country, has, I think, brought home to all of us that the time has come when we can no longer try with one hand to patch up the old building of Capitalism and with the other hand to build the new building of Socialism. . .
> It is not now a question of 'the inevitability of gradualness'. The one thing that is not inevitable now is gradualness. We are going forward with a complete system for immediate operation, and while I appreciate, as I am sure you all appreciate, the necessity for doing our utmost to support and sustain the unemployed . . . I am sure you also realise that it would be a vast mistake of policy on our part to put undue emphasis on that feature of our policy.[49]

This was the essence of Cripps' socialism for the next few years. There could be no compromise. Capitalism had proved its unworthiness and must be replaced. While it remained, public works programmes and relief for the unemployed were at best temporary ambulance work, at worst dangerous palliatives. They certainly provided no solution.

Beyond this, Cripps' political preoccupations switched and changed with disconcerting rapidity. With no political philosophy of his own to build on, he flitted from one attractive panacea to another. For a time he took up the quackish monetary schemes of Major Douglas; then, influenced by William Mellor, he gave support to a quasi-revolutionary marxism; later, this time under the influence of Harry Pollitt, he became increasingly uncritical in his support for the campaigns of the Communists.

Conflicts with the Party machine started early. Cripps' cool contempt for the views of Transport House exacerbated resentment of his new prominence in Parliament, which seemed a threat to established leaders frustrated in their exile. The close understanding between Lansbury, Attlee and Cripps, their left-wing sympathies and dislike of outside interference, aroused strong hostility on the NEC. 'The whole problem of personal relationships is increasingly difficult', wrote Dalton late in 1932. 'The Parliamentary Party is a poor little affair, isolated from the National Executive, whose only MP is George Lansbury. Attlee is Deputy Leader of the Parliamentary Party. He and Cripps, who are in close touch with Cole, sit in Lansbury's room at the House all day and all night, and continually influence the old man. With none of these are Henderson's relations close or cordial.'[50] In October 1932 Beatrice Webb reported 'serious friction between the Parliamentary Party led by G. L., guided by Stafford and forming a very united brotherhood in its own part, and the N. E.' and she regarded the Executive's pointed failure to ask Cripps to speak at the Party Conference as 'signifying that he is out of favour with the Labour Party Executive as too advanced in his views'.[51] As yet, however, Cripps exercised some restraint. Only after he had taken over the Chairmanship of the Socialist League, successor left-wing body to the ILP, in 1933, did he abandon caution and identify himself as an uncompromising rebel.

Cripps had many virtues. The sincerity of his convictions was universally respected; he was deeply religious, and maintained a rigorous asceticism in his habits and life-style; despite frequent bouts of illness, from which he was never entirely free, his energy and enthusiasm were prodigious; he was an outstanding speaker with a remarkable ability to communicate his idealism to others, especially to the young; though some found him strangely impersonal, he was always kind and concerned, and he was a devoted family man.

Largely through his legal practice, which he kept up throughout the thirties, he was extremely rich, a fact which some found offensive, and the Tory press was happy to exploit. 'The apostle of Socialism in Our Time enforced with machine guns lives in an old farmhouse converted into a large country mansion of 30 or 40 rooms', observed the *Daily Express* in 1934; 'in front of it, screening it from the common gaze, a row of weeping willows; a trout stream, a golf course, tennis courts, gardens of flowers, gardens of luxury fruit of the table, ornamental water, even yew hedges – all tended by three gardeners. Such is Goodfellows – the home of the Red Squire.'[52] Yet he was exceptionally generous. 'Of the "fabulous and fantastic" sums which Cripps earned at the Bar only a small part was used for personal expenditure', wrote one who knew the family well. 'Every year he and Lady Cripps sat down and worked out a budget – so much for the children's education, so much for housekeeping at Goodfellows, so much for the small London apartment, and so much for foreign travel. The difference between this budget and his income was given away ... He gives anonymously to causes which he believes are fighting for the good of all.'[53] Many of these causes were ones from which he could derive no political benefit – for example, European refugees from the Nazis, and the Republican side in the Spanish Civil War. On occasion, his principles led him to sacrifices which to those who did not share his principles seemed incomprehensible. Thus, after the 1931 General Election, he returned to the Treasury the bulk of the fees that would have accrued to him as Solicitor-General, 'in view of the economy need'.[54]

He had, on the other hand, a number of traits which were less endearing – in particular a messianic arrogance which made him impervious to the advice of any but a handful of close associates. He expected to lead; he was never prepared to follow. He seemed to relish notoriety and to take a mischievous delight in outraging his more conventional colleagues. He was peculiarly insensitive to the difficulties of those who, lacking his financial and professional security, were reluctant to jeopardise Party positions in the pursuit of what he considered to be right. He antagonised less talented leaders with a contempt which he did little to conceal. 'I can't come back this afternoon', he once told Dalton after a weary session of the NEC. 'It cost me £120 to be here this morning and I might just as well have sent my typist.'[55] He had absolutely no sense of the concepts of solidarity and loyalty to majority decisions upon which the Movement and the Party had been built.

Although some of his financial contributions were disinterested, others were not. A proliferation of left-wing bodies sympathetic to Cripps' political views owed much to his generous support. Certainly the Socialist League could not have functioned as a national political body, and the paper *Tribune*, founded in 1937, would have quickly collapsed, without massive contributions from Cripps. He may not have consciously sought to exploit this situation. Yet he was prepared to cut off funds and exert his full influence when it suited him, something which others in the Movement reasonably resented.

The most frequent charge levelled against him, however, by friends as well as by opponents, was that he lacked judgement. His aunt, Beatrice Webb, noted this at an early stage.

> In manners and morals, in tastes and preferences, Stafford would make an ideal leader for the Labour Party: he would be equally at home with the TU official, the Co-operative administrator and the Socialist intellectual. He has sufficient personality – physical and mental – for leadership: tall, good-looking, with a good voice and pleasant gestures. But he is oddly immature in intellect and unbalanced in judgement: a strange lack of discrimination and low standard of reasoning, in picking up ideas... He does not *know* his own limitations: he is ignorant and reckless in his statements and proposals.[56]

Part of the reason was that Cripps had no experience whatsoever of the political world in which he was suddenly and unexpectedly required to take a leading role. 'In private discussions he was invincible', recalled Morrison, who retained an affectionate pride in Cripps, despite frequent clashes. 'There was many an occasion when in our personal talks I took the opposite view to his. We would argue until he got me to a point where my case could no longer be argued, yet I knew in my bones that he was wrong and I was right – which subsequent events usually proved to be so.'[57] Other leaders were less tolerant of the curious combination in Cripps of dialectical brilliance and political innocence, and reacted strongly to actions and utterances which seemed to reveal the destructiveness of a precocious child.

4
Fabians and Keynesians

An immediate effect of electoral defeat was to induce the Labour Party to re-think its policy. In December the NEC set up an eight-man Policy Committee, composed of the Executive's three representatives on the National Joint Council, four other members of the Executive, and Lansbury, as leader of the PLP. '[F]or the next twenty years,' wrote Dalton, 'Morrison and I were the two whose membership was most continuous and who did most work.'[1] The Policy Committee flourished, spawned numerous sub-committees which made extensive co-options, and issued a series of documents which formed the basis for the policies adopted by the Executive and Conference. The Committee worked closely with the Party Research Department under Arthur Greenwood, and was fed with ideas and information by sympathetic experts and unofficial research groups. Of the latter, two of the most influential were the New Fabian Research Bureau (NFRB) and the XYZ Club.

The New Fabian Research Bureau had been founded in March 1931 by G. D. H. Cole 'to inject a more lively spirit into politics, not by trying, like the ILP, to write a new programme for the Party, but by calling attention to what had been promised and suggesting ways and means of carrying it out.'[2] Initially it operated as a siamese twin to another Cole body, the Society for Socialist Inquiry and Propaganda (SSIP), before the latter merged itself into the left-wing Socialist League.[3] NFRB membership was open, but always extremely small. By the autumn of 1932 there were only 133 members; four years later the Bureau was congratulating itself on an increase to 400; a target of 1000 had not been reached by the time the NFRB united with the Fabian Society in 1939.[4] Yet the NFRB included most of Labour's leading intellectuals[5] and its output was prolific. By the end of 1938 the Bureau had produced 42 research pamphlets, 7 books and a large number of private memoranda; and it was providing an expert advice service to the Labour Party and other progressive bodies.

There was no comparable body. Unlike SSIP, the New Fabians had no defined policy of their own – and indeed every wing of the Party was represented in its membership. Its direct contribution was in building up confidence in the viability of Labour's plans, offering detailed blueprints where, in the MacDonald era, there had been vague generalities. Thus NFRB produced a series of studies of particular industries – including pains-taking schemes for the nationalisation of electricity, gas, coal and anthra-cite, iron and steel, textiles, chemicals, shipping, aircraft manufacture, armaments, flour milling and milk distribution – and in so doing it con-centrated the minds of Labour's younger intellectuals on the practical problems which many of them would personally face after 1945.

The XYZ Club was started early in 1932. Founded at the initiative of Nicholas Davenport and H. V. Berry,[6] a director of the Union Discount Company who felt that 'the Labour Party was woefully short on expert knowledge of the City's financial institutions',[7] it provided an intelligence service on City activities and helped shape thinking on financial policy in the Labour Party. It included MPs, economists, financial journalists and 'a number of City people mostly young but sometimes of surprising rank and seniority'.[8] Hugh Gaitskell became secretary, Dalton, Pethick-Lawrence, Douglas Jay, Evan Durbin, Francis Williams, Cecil Spriggs (Financial Editor of the *Manchester Guardian*) and Hugh Quigley (Chief Economist of the Central Electricity Authority) were among its members.

The XYZ Club met above a pub in the City, and for a time worked as a secret society to spare its City members embarrassment. 'I circulated papers which they sent me,' wrote Dalton, 'but divulged no names'.[9] It drew up detailed proposals for the nationalisation of the Bank of England which were adopted, in essence, by the 1945 Labour Government. In Francis Williams' opinion, the Club could claim 'to have exercised in a quiet sort of way more influence on future government policy than any other group of the time and to have done so in the most private way without attracting publicity to itself ... It stands, perhaps, as an example of a democratic Socialist "cell" which far exceeded in its success anything that the numerous much vaunted Communist cells of the time managed to achieve.'[10]

Through the influence of economists who worked for NFRB and the XYZ Club, Labour came gradually to accept the new economics of Keynes and his disciples. *The General Theory of Employment, Interest and Money* did not appear until 1936. But by the end of 1932 most of the ingredients that went into it were available and the subject of eager discussion in academic circles. A collection of essays by nine Oxford economists including Cole, Gaitskell, Colin Clark and Roy Harrod, edited by Cole and called *What Everybody Wants to Know About Money* came out in 1933. This dealt with the need for deficit financing, the powers of banks to create credit, the employment multiplier, and the idea that when resources are idle an increase in pur-chasing power rather than an increase in prices will bring them into play

37

again.[11] Over the next couple of years, these ideas appeared more and more frequently in Labour Party policy documents and pamphlets.

LABOUR AND KEYNES

However, there was no Damascus Road, and Keynesian ideas scarcely became the linchpin of official Labour policy. Keynes offered – as Hobson, the ILP and Mosley had offered in varying ways since the late twenties – a practical, radical alternative to the orthodoxies of the Treasury and the financial Establishment which Labour might have taken up as the main plank in a crusade against Government policies on unemployment. It never did so, and Labour's major policy document of the decade, *For Socialism and Peace*, adopted in 1934, though more socialist in tone than *Labour and the Nation* and including more precise and extensive proposals for nationalisation, scarcely revealed a revolution in Labour's economic thinking.

For Socialism and Peace reiterated Labour's long-standing intention to nationalise coal, transport, power and the land, adding water supply, iron and steel, with a hint that other industries might be included as well. It promised to nationalise the Bank of England and the joint stock banks – though this in itself was scarcely a significant change, for bringing the Bank of England under closer public control had long been one of the Party's notional aims,[12] and nationalisation of the joint stock banks (regarded by Keynes as absurd, and by the main architects of Labour's financial policy as irrelevant) was included only because Conference had so decided in 1932 against the wishes of the Executive. What was more important than a list of aspirations was the raising of public ownership to a high priority – an emphasis reinforced by specific commitments in *Labour's Immediate Programme*, a short-term plan issued in 1937. In accordance with the wishes of the TUC, a 40-hour week replaced the 48-hour week goal of *Labour and the Nation*.

In terms of the new economics, the most radical proposal was for a National Investment Board for National Planning. But there was no explicit mention of deficit financing. A hint of the multiplier came only as an afterthought. 'It should not be forgotten that new expenditure on development not only creates employment, directly and indirectly, in respect of the particular schemes of work put in hand, but creates further employment in an ever-widening circle, through the payment of wages to those who are now employed, and who, through their increased purchasing power, are enabled to buy additional goods and services.'[13]

All the same, *For Socialism and Peace* represented a partial conversion. Dalton, in his exposition of Labour policy published in March 1935, *Practical Socialism for Britain*, went far in dressing up Keynes in socialist clothes. The process was completed by Douglas Jay's *The Socialist Case*, published in 1937, which 'superimposed Keynes on Webb',[14] and sounded a note which had gained increasing support from one wing of the party and increasing hostility from the other. Jay made out the case for those who were primarily concerned about economic management for prosperity rather than about the creation of a society based on new social and economic relationships. He took Morrison's emphasis on efficiency one stage further. Stressing the need for a redistribution of income, he was little interested in public ownership as an end in itself, relegating nationalisation to a low position in his own order of priorities, and indicating that for many industries nationalisation was, in his view, irrelevant. But for many people in the Labour Party public ownership was an ethical requirement only tangentially related to efficiency. 'Mr Jay entitles his book "The Socialist Case",' wrote G. D. H. Cole, reviewing it, 'but there is very little in it of what most people habitually think of as Socialism.'[15] This was true. It was also a major reason why Keynesianism, for all its apparent attractions, was such a hard doctrine for the Labour Party to swallow.

Up to a point, the new economics fitted in well with traditional socialist theory. Many Labour intellectuals were attracted to Keynes because he seemed to provide practical justifications for what socialists had long believed in their hearts – the more so because Keynes was indifferent to the moral claims of socialism. Labour favoured equality; Keynes presented the argument that inequality was inefficient. Labour had long favoured the central direction of the economy in order to distribute its fruits equitably; Keynes preferred a free market but felt that in the conditions of the 1930s state intervention was necessary to stimulate the economy and utilise idle resources. Labour wanted schemes of public works for humanitarian reasons, but was guiltily aware of the difficulty of combining such a policy with balancing budgets; Keynes removed the guilt by declaring that deficits were not only acceptable but necessary in a time of economic depression.[16]

For those who were mainly concerned with unemployment and inequalities, Keynes offered a vindication which opened up exciting new possibilities. But for those who looked to a new order, and for whom unemployment was merely symptomatic of the decline of an irredeemably rotten system, he appeared as a false and dangerous prophet. Though Keynes advocated many of the things Labour wanted to do, he did so from a fundamentally different premise. He offered no comfort to those who held that mass unemployment, a product of the contradictions of capitalism, could only be removed by a transition to socialism. His remedies were intended to modify and revitalise capitalism not to replace it. His firmly held view that capitalism *could* be made to work was far from palatable to those for whom the events of 1931 had been a welcome confirmation that it could not.

39

When unemployment was at its worst and Keynesian measures were most relevant the response to them in the Labour Party was lukewarm, and many on the extreme left were positively hostile. In 1932 John Strachey attacked Keynes furiously in *The Coming Struggle For Power*, the most influential application of marxism to British conditions in the 1930s. Later, when the economic situation improved, and it became clear that a cataclysmic breakdown was not imminent, reformist approaches were more widely acceptable. By 1938 even Strachey had come round to the view that 'the efforts of Mr Roosevelt, though many of them, to my mind, have been misdirected, and the recent theoretical work of Mr Keynes, have shown us that powerful weapons are at the disposal of a resolute progressive Government which is confronted with a slump, whether deliberately provoked or not.'[17]

For a time Keynes had hopes of working with the Labour Party. After the 1931 election, according to his biographer, he at first 'thought that he might galvanise the Labour Party into constructive opposition on the basis of a programme for expansion'.[18] He wrote some important articles for the *New Statesman and Nation*, and asked Francis Williams of the *Daily Herald* to help him to persuade the Labour Party to adopt his views. 'Since I regarded him as a genius with solutions that could save the world, I was both delighted and flattered by the invitation', recalled Williams. 'But not to much avail. Whenever Keynes actually met Labour or trade union leaders he managed to insult them.'[19] Keynes was not prepared to make concessions, and his snobbish distaste and intellectual contempt for most of the leaders of the Labour Movement (Ernest Bevin was a rare exception) meant that there was little useful contact.

Consequently he switched his attention back to the Liberals, with whom he had worked closely in the twenties, and who he found socially and politically more compatible. It was Lloyd George and a group of left-wing Tories who were the most passionate advocates of his ideas in the 1930s, and who were most enthusiastic in their demands for a British 'New Deal'. This did not help Keynes's standing in the Labour Party. Dark suggestions that the Tory and Liberal planners were fascists in disguise, advocates of 'the corporate state', found a ready audience on the Labour Left – and in particular in the Socialist League, left-wing successor to the ILP.

5
Labour and the Left:
the Socialist League

To the Labour Left, what happened in November 1931 was a well deserved and expiating chastisement. 'I honestly believe the movement is going to be purer and stronger for the very heavy defeat we have sustained', wrote Lansbury early in 1932.[1] 'We have been beaten,' observed Cole, 'no doubt, thoroughly, devastatingly, overwhelmingly beaten ... But all the same the predominant feeling in my mind, and in the minds of most of those whom I meet, is not depression, but rather elation and escape.'[2]

This view was particularly popular among upper class intellectuals, themselves immune from the allures of the aristocratic embrace. 'Ethel [Snowden] and Jimmy [Thomas] have caricatured social climbing,' wrote Beatrice Webb, 'and in so doing have put their particular type of ugly fawning out of bounds: they will find no imitators. MacDonald's act of treachery has, in fact, served as a drastic emetic'.[3] R. H. Tawney joined the Webbs in calling for a new socialist covenant. Those in the Labour Party who cultivated their financial betters and 'succumb to convivial sociabilities like Red Indians to fire-water' would be better off as footmen.[4]

The moral of 1931 seemed to be that Labour must have nothing to do with politicians who did not share a socialist determination to transform the system. 'Onions can be eaten leaf by leaf, but you cannot skin a live tiger paw by paw; vivisection is its trade, and it does the skinning first', wrote Tawney.

> The plutocracy consists of agreeable, astute, forcible, self-confident, and, when hard pressed, unscrupulous people... The way to deal with them is not to pretend, as some Labour leaders do, that, because many of them are pleasant creatures, they can be talked into the belief that they want what the Labour movement wants, and differ only as to methods.[5]

One expression of this mood was a new interest in the Communist Party, which many intellectuals joined in preference to the Labour Party in the 1930s. Another was in the new Socialist League – 'intellectuals and nothing else, all leaders and no followers'[6] – which became guardian of the Party's left wing conscience until defiance of NEC edicts provoked its own dis-affiliation in 1937.

The numerically tiny League contained an array of talent. G. D. H. Cole, E. F. Wise, William Mellor, Sir Charles Trevelyan, J. T. Murphy, H. N. Brailsford, D. N. Pritt, Harold Laski, Ellen Wilkinson, Aneurin Bevan and G. R. Strauss were all in it, or closely associated. Above all, the League came to be identified with its most glittering personality, Sir Stafford Cripps.

On economic policy, the League might have had a great deal to offer. Deriving much of its analysis from the 'under-consumptionist' J. A. Hobson, and from H. N. Brailsford and E. F. Wise, the League stressed planning and the expansion of credit to increase demand as the bases for any solution to mass unemployment. In these respects, its economic proposals shared common ground with those of Tory and Liberal planners, and of some of Labour's Keynesian economists on the right of the Party. Unlike the Keynesians, however, who concentrated on remedies for specific problems, the League was not prepared to consider solutions in the context of the existing political order. Hence it was deeply suspicious of all advocates of a British 'New Deal', whom it attacked as proponents of a 'Corporate State', and bitterly opposed any political dealings by the Labour Party with them.

At the outset, League leaders expressed a determination to avoid the mistakes of the rebellious ILP, and concentrate instead on socialist research. This resolve was soon forgotten. A momentum quickly developed which isolated the League from the mainstream of Labour politicians. Research was dropped. Taking its cue increasingly from the Communist Party, the League adopted the tactics of direct confrontation, and began to operate as a semi-independent political party. In the process it antagonised the official leadership without gaining significant support from the rank and file, destroyed its influence, and finally brought about its own proscription.

ORIGINS OF THE SOCIALIST LEAGUE

The Socialist League was founded in 1932 when a large minority group in the ILP refused to follow the ILP leadership and majority in its decision to break away from Labour and become an entirely separate political party.

Before 1918, the ILP had been the individual members' section of the Labour Party. The ILP had been the main way into the Labour Party for non-trade unionists, and the main centre for left-wing political activity. This traditional function was undermined by Henderson's reforms in 1918. These set up constituency Labour parties with provision for direct individual membership through affiliated ward and local parties.[7] From the early twenties the ILP and the expanding constituency parties were in direct competition for members. The ILP, no longer in effect the official body for Labour political activists, became increasingly factional, attracting those who were dissatisfied with the policies of the Labour Party. In 1925 the 'Clydesider' Jimmy Maxton captured the ILP Chairmanship for the extreme left, and set the ILP on a road which was to lead to its destruction as a significant political force.

Under Maxton's leadership, the ILP produced some of the most constructive policies to emerge from the Labour Party in the twenties, in particular those contained in *The Living Wage*,[8] adopted in 1926, whose proposals on economic and employment policy anticipated Keynes. Yet the ILP's revolutionary language and guerrilla tactics directed against the Labour Party's leaders in Parliament alienated moderate opinion in the PLP. Many MPs who had received their early political training in the ILP left it in disgust; others who had been elected under ILP auspices sought alternative backers.

During the 1929 Parliament relations between the ILP and the Government developed into open warfare. The ILP objected to the rigidity of party discipline, and declared that it was unreasonable to ask MPs to vote for Bills which had not been approved by the PLP or Party Conference. The Labour Party leadership was determined to bring ILP MPs to heel. Henderson stressed that there could not be 'a party within a party'.[9] Protracted negotiations over PLP Standing Orders were unresolved when the Government fell. MacDonald's departure made little difference to the quarrel; if anything it made the NEC and PLP leadership more insistent upon a rigid adherence to Party decisions. When the General Election came, ILP candidates who refused to sign a pledge to accept Party discipline were not given endorsement by the NEC. Of those who stood without Transport House backing many were opposed by official candidates and only five were elected.

The ILP had one foot out of the Labour Party, and in the new Parliament the ILP MPs were recognised as a separate Parliamentary group by the Speaker.[10] Inside the Commons, the ILP's tactics now included schoolboy pranks. In February an ILP demand that the new group should be allocated a separate House of Commons room was rejected; the group's MPs thereupon raided one of the Labour Party's rooms, removing the books, papers and other belongings of the incumbent, and installed themselves with a secretary. Lansbury complained to the Speaker, and the ILP was forced to retreat.[11]

The ILP militants had decided that they had so little in common with the PLP leadership in political terms that it was pointless to continue the alliance. At a special Conference in Bradford in July 1932 the ILP decided, by 241 votes to 142, to disaffiliate from the Labour Party.

Maxton and his associates, like Mosley in 1931, had misread the auguries. They believed, mistakenly, that there was a real possibility of crushing the Labour Party in open competition for working-class support in the country.

In the wake of Labour's humiliating defeat and with unemployment at its highest level ever, the feeling was strong on the extreme left that the final crisis of capitalism was at hand and that an unfettered socialist leadership should make itself available to the masses.

However, a large minority in the ILP, led by E. F. Wise and including a number of prominent intellectuals, refused to cut themselves off from the Labour Movement by accepting the Bradford decision. These 'affiliationists' who favoured continued affiliation to the Labour Party, 'as the only organisation which, whatever its imperfections, has any chance of achieving socialism in our time',[12] were nevertheless determined that the Labour Left should continue to have an organisational form. After the Bradford decision, they set up a National ILP Affiliation Committee and, as a result of negotiations between this body and Cole's intellectual ginger group, the Society for Socialist Inquiry and Propaganda (SSIP), the Socialist League was formed.

The SSIP, known as 'Zip', was started by G. D. H. Cole and his wife in June 1931 and contained several former Guild Socialist associates – in particular William Mellor and Frank Horrabin. 'Douglas and I recruited personally its first list,' wrote Margaret Cole, 'drawing upon comrades from all stages of our political lives, members of the "Movement" not irretrievably pledged to Communism, WEA students and tutors, Trade Union Secretaries and Trade Unionists with a Left tinge, and younger recruits from the Oxford and other university Labour Clubs.'[13] Their intention had been to be a society of 'Loyal Grousers', constructively critical of the Government from a socialist standpoint, putting forward carefully worked out policies but avoiding the dangers and disruptions that would be created by a political faction. It was decided not to seek affiliation to the Labour Party, or sponsor candidates.[14] The Society set up branches,[15] undertook to promote and carry out research, propaganda and discussion, issue pamphlets, reports and books, and organise conferences, meetings, lectures and schools. To this extent it was strongly in the Fabian tradition, and it worked in close conjunction with Cole's other group, the New Fabian Research Bureau, founded shortly after SSIP.

The most promising feature of SSIP was that Cole had managed to persuade Bevin to be Chairman. This was an improbable association, but one which seemed potentially an enormous asset to the intellectual Left. It had been Cole's dream to bring trade unionists and intellectuals together in SSIP in an attempt to bridge the gap between them. In fact SSIP retained the flavour of Hampstead and Bloomsbury, and apart from Bevin the only prominent trade unionist to be closely involved was Arthur Pugh. Bevin's association greatly improved the standing of the new group. SSIP's first pamphlet *The Crisis* was written jointly by Bevin and Cole in 1931, and seemed to herald a new alliance between Bevin and the intellectuals.

Bevin's attitude to intellectuals was double-edged. On the one hand he regarded left-wing intellectuals as 'people who stabbed you in the back';[16] on the other, he had no doubt that there was a place for intellectuals and middle-class people in the Movement. He saw them as an essential source of ideas, from whom practical experienced men involved in the day-to-day business of political and trade union affairs could make a hard-headed selection. 'We have kept clear of dogma,' Bevin wrote before the 1931 crisis, 'and this is an attempt to study and project in order to fill the needs for the next decade, like the Fabians and early socialists did for us.'[17] On one point, however, he was absolutely firm. 'We are not out to establish a new Party', he told an SSIP meeting in June 1931. If SSIP became an attempt to create any counter-organisation to the Labour Party, he would have no association with it.[18]

When the disaffiliation of the ILP from the Labour Party became imminent, the SSIP Executive proposed to appeal to loyal ILPers to join SSIP. Cole favoured this; and the affiliationists' leaders seemed interested. Then both had second thoughts. 'I thought at first that SSIP might suffice,' Wise wrote to Trevelyan at the beginning of September, 'but I soon discovered that this was not the case. In any case, the ILPers who will refuse to go out of the Party must number ten thousand or so in organised branches all over the country, whereas SSIP, though it has some very eminent members, still does not number more than a few hundreds.'[19] With the formation of Wise's affiliationist committee, SSIP took fright. The ex-ILPers no longer appeared as a source of vigorous new recruits, but became potential rivals. Cole now faced two alternatives. either to compete for members and attention with a new loyalist ILP, or to join forces with the affiliationists in the formation of a new body. Spurred on by Mellor and Horrabin, Cole reluctantly agreed to the latter course, to his subsequent bitter regret.

The most serious concern of SSIP was that any new body in which it became merged should not develop factional tendencies, like those of the ILP. Sir Stafford Cripps, later Chairman of the Socialist League, leading it in its battles with the NEC, was, ironically, especially worried about this danger.

When SSIP and affiliationist leaders had reached agreement, Cole wrote in identical terms to Attlee, Pugh, Pritt and Cripps, none of whom had participated in the negotiations, telling them what had happened. He added an extra paragraph to his letter to Cripps, which provides striking evidence of Cripps' anxieties at this time:

> So far I am sending you an exact replica of a letter which I am sending to several other people, but I know you have been specially concerned about the possibility of Wise and his friends wanting to make the Socialist League the nucleus for a political party with the possible danger of a row with the Labour Party at a later stage.[20]

45

In the negotiations, which took place in mid-September, the key issue was the distribution of posts in the new body, in particular the Chairmanship. Cole wanted to keep Bevin; the ILP insisted on having Wise. The meeting deadlocked and nearly broke down. Then SSIP gave way. 'I regarded it as indispensable to carry Bevin into the new body,' Cole wrote later, 'as the outstanding Trade Union figure capable of rallying Trade Union opinion behind it. I accordingly voted against the fusion of SSIP with the Wise group; but I was outvoted and agreed to go with the majority – a yielding of which I was soon to repent. Had I not been seriously ill at the time, I do not think I should have agreed.'[21]

Bevin was furious. 'I shall always watch, as long as I am in the Movement, the antics of careerists who seem to think we have created the Movement as a sort of ladder for individuals.' Cole tried to persuade Bevin to join the League's Executive, but he refused; he felt that the new body would 'always have a bias against Trade Unionists'. Furthermore, 'I do not believe the Socialist League will change very much from the old ILP attitude, whoever is in the Executive.'[22]

In not seeing to it that the new body had sound trade union connections the founders of the League blundered badly. Links with the PLP were strong. Attlee and Cripps were both directly involved; so were four other MPs: David Kirkwood, Alfred Salter, F. S. Cocks and Neil Maclean. Bevan, though refusing to take part in the foundation of the League, was sympathetic. With barely fifty Labour MPs altogether, this was significant support, and for a time, in the absence of the leading spokesmen of the Right, the Socialist League was able to exercise an important influence on the Party in Parliament. Outside Parliament, however, the League was poorly placed. Cole had tried to forge a link between trade unionists and intellectuals in SSIP, and fought hard to include trade union figures on the provisional Executive of the League. But when the new League elected a thirteen-man National Council in October, the only trade unionist to gain a place was Arthur Pugh, who soon dropped out. Harold Clay, assistant general secretary of the TGWU, became a regional member of the National Council, and served on it until 1935. Otherwise the League had no significant connection with the trade union leadership at any stage. SSIP had been led by upper class intellectuals from major public schools and Oxford; the ILP Affiliation Committee had consisted of middle-class socialists from Cambridge and the provinces.[23] When the two groups merged, they did so to the exclusion of the few working-class leaders who had previously been associated with either side. The 23 people who served as national members of the Socialist League's National Council between 1932 and 1937 included two Etonians, two Wykehamists, and a Harrovian. At least nine had been at Oxbridge, and four at London University.[24] The formal education of only two ended at elementary school level.[25]

46

Changing Leadership of the Socialist League

	SSIP Exec. 1932	NILPAC Exec. 1932	Oct. 1932	National Council of the Socialist League 1932–7 (National Membership)			
				Whitsun 1933	Whitsun 1934	Whitsun 1935	Whitsun 1936
Frank Wise		X	Ch	X/died			
Sir S. Cripps	X		X	Ch	Ch	Ch	X
William Mellor	X		X	X	X	X	Ch
Frank Horrabin	X	X	X	X	X	X	X
H. N. Brailsford		X	X	X	X		X
G. R. Mitchison	X		Jt Tr.		X		X
Sir C. Trevelyan			X	X	X		
F. Wynne Davies		X	Jt Tr.	Treas.	Treas.		
G. D. H. Cole	X		X	X/res.			
David Kirkwood		X	X				
F. Pethick-Lawrence			X				
Arthur Pugh	X		X/res.				
Dr Alfred Salter			X				
Constance Borrett		X		X	X	X	X
Donald Barber		X		X	X		
Jean Thompson		X		X			
Lionel Elvin					X	X	X
I. Davies					X	X	
R. George						X	X/res.
D. N. Pritt	X					X	
L. A. Finn						Treas.	Treas./res.
Ruth Dodds						X	X
Barbara Betts							X

Ch = Chairman; Treas. = Treasurer; Jt Tr. = Joint Treasurer; res. = resigned before next National Council election; NILPAC = National ILP Affiliation Committee.

This was hardly a social mixture ideally suited to the task of enticing the Movement from its inherent suspicion of left-wing intellectuals. Kingsley Martin recalled a conversation which aptly sums up the incongruity of many of the League's positions. When Sir Charles Trevelyan, a baronet, land-owner and Lord Lieutenant for Northumberland (and also a member of the Socialist League's Council) suggested that British workers should use the strike weapon to check Government foreign policy, Bevin retorted: 'You want a strike? OK, I am to call out 600 000 dockers; will you call out the Lord Lieutenants?'[26]

The Socialist League was inaugurated at a stormy and inauspicious meeting in Leicester on 2 October 1932, the eve of the Labour Party Conference. An ex-ILP majority rejected the attempts of an SSIP group[27] to amend the draft constitution so as to increase safeguards against the recrudescence of the old ILP. The *Manchester Guardian* noted that 'among the rank-and-file members of the SSIP there seemed from the tone of to-day's debates to be a distinct reluctance to go into partnership with the ILP affiliationists'.[28] The new League declared its object to be 'to make socialists, and to further by propaganda and investigation the adoption by the working-class movement of an advanced programme and a socialist outlook'.[29] Interim officers and a thirteen man National Council were elected. The latter greatly over-represented SSIP. It included five members of the SSIP Executive; four members of the National ILP Affiliation Committee; one, Horrabin, who had been on both; and three other 'agreed names' – Dr Alfred Salter ('the Bermondsey doctor'), F. W. Pethick-Lawrence (a member of NFRB and an associate of the Cole group) and Sir Charles Trevelyan.

THE PSYCHOLOGY OF THINGS: THE SOCIALIST LEAGUE 1932–4

What was the Socialist League's real purpose? Even at the outset its leaders were never quite clear. Nobody was able to explain why research and pro-paganda – the stated purposes of the League – should require a highly structured organisation for their promotion. Indeed if the League's official objective were taken at its full value, there was no need for the League at all. This was how it struck Fred Henderson, an old socialist whose political memory went back to William Morris's Socialist League of the 1880s. 'I feel that it would be best to let the ILP go as a separate organisation', he wrote to Cole. In one sense, however, the League would have a role: 'There does seem to be a real need for something of the kind in the psychology of things. There are large numbers of ILP members who, refusing to disaffiliate, would feel more comfortable if such a definite Socialist group were open to them.'[30]

The League started passively enough. Its leaders appeared genuinely concerned that it should not inherit the image of the ILP. Frank Horrabin was clear that the League should be 'a centre of socialist research and

48

missionary activity, but activity in and through the Labour Party, and with nothing whatsoever of the separate political machine about it'.[31] Within two years this milk-and-water approach had been tossed aside, and was replaced by an angry militancy. Writing on behalf of the National Council in December 1934, Horrabin called for a 'disciplined organisation' prepared 'as a league by means of conferences, demonstrations and agitations' to focus opinion on the vital need for resistance to fascism. 'We have passed out of the realm of programme making,' the League announced at the end of 1934, 'into the realm of action.'[32]

There was no sudden transformation. A gradual change of emphasis can be traced almost week by week in response to developing pressures. The League organised research programmes, lectures, conferences and week-end schools, and tried to build up a branch organisation. The Labour Party, meanwhile, recovered from its millenial mood of 1932, and left-wing ideas were received with increasing disfavour. The Socialist League presented policy proposals which were rejected by the NEC and the TUC General Council. Resentment grew on both sides; the League's demands became more crystallised; the party leaders' lack of interest and irritation more overt.

The League scored its greatest triumph within its first week. At the Leicester Party Conference the platform was trounced in a manner that was not repeated until 1960; and the leaders of the revolt from the floor were the men who had formed the Socialist League a few days before. Trevelyan, Wise, Cripps and Harold Clay all received massive support. The Conference committed Labour to the immediate introduction of socialist legislation on gaining office, and specifically to the nationalisation of the joint stock banks in addition to the Bank of England; it also postponed decision on the question of workers' control in the transport and electricity industries. Never again in the 1930s was the Left so successful at Conference in the face of NEC opposition.

The Left's success was mainly due to the mood of Conference, and of the trade union leadership, affected by electoral defeat and the worst months of the slump. But the 1932 conference was also unusual in another respect: the Left did not speak as an organised section. The ILP had gone. The League, though just inaugurated, had only a formal existence; its leaders spoke on behalf of various sponsoring bodies, not as members of a closely knit faction. By October 1933 the League had begun to gain a reputation as a disruptive body of middle-class intellectuals grinding a left-wing axe. Its amendments and resolutions were viewed in this light.

The League's first eight months were filled with feverish activity of an irreproachable kind. The fears which had been expressed could not have seemed less justified. The emphasis was on research, with two main purposes. First, to make socialist propaganda more intelligent and effective

49

by making it better informed. Second, 'to inform ourselves *how* we intend to achieve what we mean to do, and what steps one can take either in advance or at the time to combat opposition', when Labour had won an electoral majority.[33] For these purposes, several branches undertook to prepare local 'Domesday Books', encyclopaedias of local information on subjects like unemployment, housing conditions and education. The Leicester branch started a scheme covering among other things, 'what is to be done if the City tries to sabotage, if the House of Lords sabotages, and so on'. At the same time the League was concerned with the problem of preparing a socialist elite in the localities:

> The most urgent job of every Socialist now is to see that in his own town at any rate there is ready a group of people...who can trust one another, and who are trusted by the rank and file, people who have made it their business to see what a socialist government would require of their district, and to find out how it could be done. This is what the Socialist League is setting out to do – to create advance guards of the revolution, and to create them *now*. For when the revolution comes it will be too late.[34]

At the national level, the research and propaganda functions of the League were combined in a highly successful series of lectures delivered in London in January and February 1933, which outlined what a government with a socialist majority should do to establish a socialist system. These lectures, later published as pamphlets, provided the basis on which the League constructed its formal policy. The programme presented by the National Council to the League's first annual Conference at Whitsun 1933 contained many of the ideas and policy proposals of Trevelyan, Cripps, Wise, Horrabin, Mellor and Cole, put forward in these lectures, and of Attlee, Clay and Addison in similar lectures in March.

'These lectures', wrote the League's *New Clarion* correspondent,

> have been one of the best answers to the people who ask, "What is the Socialist League for?" The Socialist League, among its many other purposes, exists to bring home to members of the Labour Movement the necessity for a strong and determined drive towards a definite and clearly understood programme of real Socialism *and* to help in the formulation of such a programme.[35]

This statement represented the first important shift in the League's position. In describing itself as a propaganda body, the League had hitherto failed to distinguish between two kinds of propaganda. The first was beamed at 'The Movement' in the widest sense, and outside it at voters in general, and aimed to convert the electorate to a 'socialist viewpoint'; that is, to supporting Labour for the sort of sound socialist reasons that would enable a Labour Government to feel confident of national backing when it came to implement truly socialist policies. The second form was internal, aimed at all levels of the party, the unions and the Co-operative movement, and was intended to convert the party to the policies and means of implementing them advocated by the League. At the beginning, the League referred to propaganda loosely, though with its emphasis on the first interpretation. As it clarified its position on key issues, the emphasis shifted to the second.

The change created a rift on the League's National Council. Cole noted the signs almost at once: 'By the end of the year [1932] a number of us had become convinced that [the League] was heading for a disaster very like that which had befallen the ILP, by putting forward a programme of its own in opposition to that of the Labour Party, instead of trying to work for improving the official Labour programme.'[36] Arthur Pugh resigned early in the new year. Kirkwood, Salter and Pethick-Lawrence declined to stand again for the National Council in June. Cole stood and was elected, but a few days later he and E. A. Radice, the secretary, resigned.

Yet the move towards an overtly factional role was not simply a consequence of pressure from the Wise group. ILP affiliationists were in a minority on the National Council until Whitsun, and there is nothing to suggest that Cole was heading a group of level-headed SSIP men in resisting the ex-ILPers' atavistic urge for a battle. Cole's position was more ambivalent than he recalled later; after his resignation from the Council, he prepared a study guide to the sixteen policy resolutions which the League was to move at the Labour Party Conference in October – and which put forward a programme in opposition to that of the Labour Party.[37] Most of the other SSIP leaders strongly supported a more active role for the League. Mellor and Horrabin were wholly in favour; so was Cripps, who replaced Wise as Chairman in June 1933.[38] Mitchison, a close personal friend of Cole, was beaten for the Treasureship in June; but he was back on the National Council in 1934, and played a leading part in the events which led to the League's disaffiliation in 1937. Indeed the real leadership of the Socialist League rapidly moved out of the hands of the affiliationists altogether.[39]

The League's first major public clash with the official leadership of the Party was in May 1933. Walter Citrine, General Secretary of the TUC, accused the League of advocating dictatorship, and Wise of maintaining that free speech was no more one of the eternal verities than free trade.[40] Cripps responded heatedly: League policy was to bring about socialism, if possible by democratic means; moreover, the proper body to decide policy was the annual conference of the Party, not the General Secretary of the TUC.[41] Citrine replied that Cripps' constitutional proposals 'represent a very grave electoral handicap upon the Labour Party' and that 'such advocacy places a weapon in the hands of Labour's enemies which they are only too willing to use'.[42] Fenner Brockway observed with satisfaction that the League was 'beginning to get the same treatment as the ILP from Transport House'.[43]

What angered Citrine and other members of the Labour and trade union establishment was a demand which became central to the Socialist League's programme and dominated Cripps' thinking until 1935. Cripps, with others on the Left, argued that the 1931 crisis had shown that the capitalists would employ almost any means to sabotage socialist legislation. In order to forestall wrecking moves, therefore, Labour must declare in advance its unequivocally socialist policy to the electorate. Upon winning a general election, it should ensure that the King would consent to the abolition of the House of Lords before it agreed to take office. The new Government should then pass an Emergency Powers Act giving itself semi-dictatorial powers and proceed to nationalise the Bank of England and the joint stock banks. Cripps insisted that only in this way could inevitable obstruction and opposition on the part of financial interests be kept in check.

The conference of the League at Whitsun 1933 reacted strongly against Citrine's attempts to silence Wise and Cripps, and firmly set a new course. The conference 'quite deliberately resolved to concentrate on policy making and policy propaganda', which demanded the immediate abolition of the House of Lords; an Emergency Powers Act to facilitate the socialisation of industry and finance; the establishment of self-government in industry; restricted compensation only to property owners; large-scale public works as a short-term device against unemployment, and the adoption of the principle 'Work or Maintenance'; and a 'policy of planned economic development' based on the socialisation of finance, land, mines, power, transport, iron and steel, cotton, and on the control of foreign trade.[44] In the view of J. T. Murphy, who had left the Communist Party a year before joining the Socialist League in April 1933, the conference 'succeeded in making clear to itself and others that the Socialist League is not merely the rump of the old ILP carrying on, but the organisation of revolutionary socialists who are an integral part of the Labour movement for the purpose of winning it completely for revolutionary socialism'.[45]

But the League's efforts in this direction over the next few months merely angered the Executive and hardened its opposition. On 6 January 1934 Cripps delivered what came to be known as his 'Buckingham Palace' speech. 'When the Labour Party comes to power,' he declared, 'we must act rapidly and it will be necessary to deal with the House of Lords and the influence of the City of London. There is no doubt that we shall have to overcome opposition from Buckingham Palace and other places as well.'[46] The implied attack on the King raised a storm of protest from all quarters. There was uproar in the press, and official Labour Party disclaimers followed. Cripps was forced to assure the public that he was 'most certainly not referring to the Crown'.[47] As yet, Attlee was still on Cripps' side, but he was virtually Cripps' only supporter among the official leaders. What aroused most fury was the feeling that Cripps' blunder would lose votes. Dalton, especially, was apoplectic. 'I make a violent...speech [to the Constitutional Sub-Committee of the NEC] asking that his streams of oratorical ineptitudes should cease,' Dalton noted in his diary, 'or some of us who are very reluctant to enter into public controversy with other members of the Party will come to the limits of our tolerance. It is the *numbers* of these gaffes which is so appalling. Our candidates are being stabbed in the back and pushed onto the defensive.'[48]

The League was unrepentant, and approached its 1934 conference in a militant mood: capitalism, it considered, was rapidly transforming itself into fascism, and the next general election might be the last one ever. Delay in adopting a socialist programme would be disastrous. The conference therefore endorsed a document called *Forward to Socialism* as its official policy; this restated the proposals approved at the previous conference in greater detail, and in more fighting terms.

In his address, Cripps argued that Labour critics only really disagreed because of the 'supposed effects' on the electorate of formally adopting such a programme. These fears, he insisted, were misplaced.

> It is the urgent desire for active change that is forcing the younger electors into Movements like the Fascist Movement, not because they believe in its policy but because they are caught by the cheap-jack cry for action-at-all-cost. The way to counter such movements is not to seek to restrain the allegiance of youth, but to seek to divert it into the useful channel of socialist change. This will only be accomplished if the younger generation can feel assured that the Party they were asked to support is not merely talking of some vague utopia in the far-distant future but is prepared to take action, and quick action, to accomplish that change.[49]

'The urgent desire for active change', and its corollary, the desire to do something active to bring it about, were indeed motivating forces in the League as in other fringe groups. A sense of involvement in political action provided a solace and a substitute for actual results; and at the same time blinded the League to any realisation that the success of attempts to influence the Labour Party was in inverse relation to the amount of action employed to back them up. The League had been in existence for twenty months, but despite early encouragements it was becoming increasingly clear that it was losing ground.

When the NEC published its own document, *For Socialism and Peace*, the

League prepared for battle. In June 1934 it started its own journal, *The Socialist Leaguer*, edited by Frank Horrabin, and attacked the new policy with vigour; for stopping at the nationalisation of primary industries; for abandoning hope of quick nationalisation even of these; for its commitment to corporations on the model of the London Passenger Transport Board 'so dear to the heart of Herbert Morrison', rather than to workers' control and socialist planning; for its provision for full compensation to stock-holders; and for its whole approach to disarmament.[50]

The Labour Party Conference at Southport in 1934 was the watershed for the Socialist League. The League had been at pains to defend itself against the charge of divisiveness. Now it grasped the nettle firmly. The League, declared Mellor, should no longer be 'a mere umbrella for "loyal grousers" but an instrument for co-ordinating what I would call Marxist opinions and action within the wider Labour Movement.'[51] Labour's programme for the next election was to be decided. Faced with this challenge, the League tabled seventy-five amendments to the NEC document *For Socialism and Peace*. The Standing Orders Committee reduced these to twelve. The result was a series of composite amendments whose enforced vagueness added to their dangerous ring. The major amendment sought to commit the Party to fighting the coming election on the basis of a 'specific programme of action' which would give the Party a mandate 'to act with the speed called for by the situation at home and abroad in a decisive advance within five years towards a Socialist Britain'.[52] The Executive was able to demolish the League's position with ease. 'We are asked to accept [this] skeleton statement' said Dalton, 'containing three or four propositions which are not developed in any detail at all.'[53] The amendment was rejected by 2 146 000 to 206 000. Although the League continued with attacks on specific issues, none of its amendments secured more than a tiny minority of the vote, and *For Socialism and Peace* was adopted almost unaltered. An attack on the Executive's *War and Peace* statement on foreign policy did slightly better; the League opposed reliance on the League of Nations, supported close co-operation with the Soviet Union and advocated the policy of the general strike against war. The Executive's Report was adopted by 1 519 000 to 673 000 – a large minority which included substantial union backing, chiefly from the miners and shop workers.

The Socialist League resented its defeat. It considered that it had been out-manoeuvred by means of Standing Orders, and, like all minorities, it felt bitter about the power of the trade union bloc vote. Mellor, the League delegate, complained that the League was unable 'to break through the net of procedures or see fully its implications,' and that 'the anti-intellectual attack got an automatic cheer'.[54] Hitherto, wrote Frank Horrabin, the League had concentrated on policy discussion and propaganda, 'leading up to and culminating in Party Conference debates'. This was no longer possible, and in any case Labour's programme for the next election was settled. The League, he insisted, must think again, and devote itself instead to the task of ensuring 'within the wider movement, a core of convinced socialists'.[55]

A special Conference held on 25 November, described as 'a clear turning point for the Socialist League',[56] endorsed this decision.

> As a League we shall urge upon the Labour and Trade Union Movement the paramount need for immediate day-to-day activities, in order that support may be rallied to resist the onset of Fascism, and to prepare the ground so that in the event of the immediate possibility of a Capitalist or Imperialist War the General Strike may be made effective ... We shall be prepared as a League, by means of conferences, demonstrations and agitation, to focus opinion on the vital need for such resistance.

It was decided that the League should become a 'disciplined organisation', which would aim at a mass membership.

With a third turn of the wheel the League's propagandist role had taken a new form. The League had started as a propagandist body *for* the Labour Party, directing propaganda at the wider movement and the electorate. By degrees the emphasis changed so that its propaganda activities were directed against the official Party policy, with the object of changing it. Now, its propaganda was to take less notice of Transport House, and focus attention on getting more support for itself as a mass organisation within the Labour Movement.

The League's new goal after Southport was declared to be the creation of 'A Will to Power', a slogan which was kept necessarily vague. Mellor argued that '"The Will to Power" cannot be created on a diet of theory or kept alive by telling the workers to wait until the General Election comes. It must be created and kept alive by constant agitation within capitalism, and agitation harnessed to a definite socialist policy and objective.'[57] This new line offered individual Party members a chance to feel that they were actively involved in the fight for socialism. If nothing else, it provided an excuse to march and demonstrate. In 1934 unemployment was still well over the two million mark, as it had been almost continuously since 1930; the desire for action on the Left was overwhelming. Yet the Labour Party and TUC viewed all rank and file action with acute suspicion, and refused to have anything to do with the main organisation for the unemployed, the communist-led National Unemployed Workers' Movement. Horrabin summed up the frustrations of the activist Left:

> It is no good our leaders retorting that there is plenty to keep us busy in the ordinary routine work of local Party activities. Lots of us are doing our full share of that work, and fully accepting the necessity of carrying on with it. But routine activities do not satisfy the soul ... People want

to know and feel that they are engaged in a *battle*. Our leaders seem to think that a route march – strictly at attention – is a satisfactory substitute.[58]

There was a need for the League, as Fred Henderson had said, in the psychology of things.

The League's concentration on the constitutional issue was an attempt to ensure that a Labour Government really would take action once it was returned to power. The attempt had failed. Now the League's leaders, like Maxton and Mosley before them, decided to attempt to build up a power base of their own in the country with a programme of independent agitation. Where this was intended to lead was left vague. This third phase of the League's brief career, culminating in the 'Unity Campaign' which brought about the League's disaffiliation, proved no more successful than the first two.

APPENDIX: THE MEMBERSHIP OF THE SOCIALIST LEAGUE

Like the ILP and the New Party, the League's hopes for a large membership were never fulfilled. Its popular appeal was non-existent. According to A. J. P. Taylor, '[The League's] branches counted for little; its programme of ideas was all that mattered.'[59] This was not from choice. The League never claimed more than 3000 members; it was, throughout, smaller than either the ILP or the CP. Most of its branches were weak and impermanent. But this was not because they 'counted for little' in the eyes of the National Council. They counted for a very great deal, and the leadership went to great pains to try to build up an active and dedicated national organisation, particularly after November 1934, when the League set itself the task of creating a 'disciplined organisation' on the basis of a mass membership.

Intensive efforts to build up branches and membership were made from the start. By the end of March 1933 there were about 70 branches; by August there were 100; and when the League paid affiliation fees to the Labour Party in September, it claimed a membership of 2000. In 1935 this increased to 3000, at which point it remained. But even these small figures exaggerated the League's real strength. The London Area Committee conceded that the stated figure of 1112 members for the Area in 1935 included 248 in branches which had closed down, or were inactive.[60] In November 1935 the League's General Secretary, J. T. Murphy, announced that there were more than 40 active branches in the London Area;[61] but only 23 sent delegates to the Area Annual Aggregate Meeting the following July. It is probable, therefore, that the League's self-estimate for Party Conference purposes was excessive, failing to allow for moribund branches. Very few branches stayed the course. In the London Area (including the Home Counties) where the League was strongest, only 4 out of 29 active branches listed in July

56

1936 had existed three years earlier; yet in March 1933 there had been 16.[62]

What caused this rapid turnover? A rapidly changing membership was not unique to the Socialist League. That left-wing groups required, and received, a high degree of commitment from their members was of mixed value. It meant that when the policy of the leadership changed it was harder to take the rank and file, still committed to the previous policy, along with it. This was certainly true of the CP, which shed members every time the Comintern made new and fundamentally different demands of it. It was even more true of the ILP, whose excessively democratic structure tossed official policy backwards and forwards between flirtations with the Third International, the Fourth International and then the Labour Party again, losing members by the hundred with every toss. In the Socialist League much the same seems to have happened, though like the CP and unlike the ILP it managed to win on the swings what it lost on the roundabouts until its last few desperate months when membership disintegrated rapidly.

Most League branches were extremely small. In 1933, the League was claiming 2000 members and more than 100 branches; if these claims were valid, the *average* membership of each branch was less than 20. In the London Area, the average membership of *active* branches in 1935 was 35, and in 1936, 29. In July 1935, one branch had 103 members.[63] If there were others of comparable size, many branches must have been very small indeed. A branch with a handful of members could send a voting delegate to the Annual Conference; some branches were created for this purpose alone.[64]

In the provinces, the League was very weak in the Midlands and Yorkshire, and best represented in Lancashire and South Wales.[65] But for all the League's national pretensions, the London Area, with more than a third of the total membership, was dominant. At the 1936 Annual Conference of the League at Hanley, for example, only 14 out of 31 branches sponsoring motions or amendments were from outside the London Area. National Secretaries' reports provide evidence of superior organisation and greater enthusiasm in London.[66] The League was also controlled almost exclusively by London members. Between conferences, the League was constitutionally ruled by the National Council, which consisted of ten national members and a treasurer, elected by delegate vote at conference (where London dominated) and seven regional members, elected locally by regional ballot. But the full Council only met seven or eight times a year, and the day-to-day running of League activities, and most effective power, was in the hands of an Executive Committee which met weekly at the Socialist League's headquarters in Victoria Street. The Executive consisted of members of the National Council who lived in the London Area.[67] Thus the League, which complained bitterly of the undemocratic methods of the Labour Party, was run by a London-based clique over which regional members had virtually no influence. Even when a regional member of the National Council secured election as a national member, her influence was minimal because she was unable to serve on the Executive for geographical reasons.[68]

Initially the rank and file London membership probably included a high proportion of ex-SSIPers. Between July and November 1932, the ILP lost 203 out of a total of 653 branches; but in London it lost only 1 out of 89, and formed more new branches than anywhere else.[69] Fifteen of the original 16 London branches of the League were thus new creations not ILP breakaways. The SSIP, moreover, had been predominantly a London body. Later London recruits to the League may have included disillusioned ILPers as the ILP's membership shrivelled everywhere. But in London, as elsewhere, the League failed utterly to capitalise on the disintegration of the ILP, even though the ILP lost more than 12 000 members – three-quarters of its total membership – between 1932 and 1935.[70] The most important section of the League's grass roots thus cannot be characterised in simple terms as a remnant of the ILP.

6

Radicalism or Socialism?

Though the Socialist League increasingly adopted the rhetoric of marxism, its heritage included a body of ideas whose source was closer to Keynes than Marx, and which it shared with politicians of the centre and right. This it never acknowledged – and 'progressives' in capitalist parties were attacked with as much vigour as conservatives and traditionalists. Yet the links were strong.

One basis for this connection was the association of Sir Oswald Mosley and John Strachey and part of the founding group of the Socialist League in the ILP in the 1920s. In 1925 Mosley, in collaboration with John Strachey and Allen Young, an ILP organiser from Birmingham, had produced a policy statement, *Revolution by Reason*, which came to be known as the Birmingham proposals. These owed much to the direct influence of Keynes and stressed monetary policy as the key to increasing demand. The nationalisation of the banks was advocated as a first step, in order to give industry a lead by expanding national credit in order to create demand. Additional working class demand would be created through a fixed minimum wage level, to be financed by the new money, which would work by means of government subsidies to industry. Any attempt by 'the great capitalist monopolies' to restrict output to force a price rise would be met by immediate socialisation. A fluctuating exchange rate would be established. The bulk purchase of raw materials would be instituted. Finally, the danger of inflation, resulting from the injection of the new money and from the consequent increase in demand, would be met by socialist planning to ensure a greater supply and this would be carried out by an Economic Council. In this way Mosley attempted to 'weld together the socialist case with modern monetary theory'.[1]

Mosley subsequently abandoned these proposals; and in many important respects the Mosley Memorandum was fundamentally different.[2] However, they contained the idea, undeveloped, but at the time generally rejected, that the creation of purchasing power to increase production was a feasible proposition; and, quite as important, they laid emphasis on the role of planning as a means to this objective. Both ideas were at the basis of Mosley's Memorandum in 1931, of the policy of the New Party, and eventually of the economic policy of the BUF.[3] While the Treasury orthodoxy still governed the economy, they also formed the central core of the economic thought of the ILP, and after 1932, the Socialist League.

Mosley differed from the Keynesians in that he envisaged the expansion of credit as a means of increasing purchasing power, while Keynes called for an increase in production as the first step, in order to permit an expansion of credit without bringing inflation. According to Mosley:

> We part company definitely with these monetary reformers when we advocate that state banks should give a clear lead by the bold and vigorous use of the national credit. We propose first to expand credit in order to create demand. That new and greater demand must, of course, be met by a new and greater supply of goods. Here our socialist planning must enter in. We must see that more goods are forthcoming to meet the new demand. If, by socialist planning, we can ensure a greater supply of goods corresponding to the greater supply of money, inflation and price rise cannot result...
>
> We propose, in fact, to expand credit in a novel, scientific and socialist manner: to send our new emission of money direct to the spot where it is most required and will be used for the greatest economic and social advantage. As Socialists, we select for our medium of credit expansion the necessitous areas of poverty, and propose to emit our new money in the shape of consumers' credits... Producers' credits will naturally also be necessary for the production of the goods for which consumers' credits create the demand now lacking. Consumers' credits are a special expedient in time of industrial stagnation and collapse to stimulate effective demand in the right quarter and to restart the dormant mechanism of production...
>
> We propose to constitute an Economic Council vested with statutory powers. The business of this Council will be to estimate the difference between the actual and potential production of the country and to plan the stages by which that potential production can be evoked through the instrument of working-class demand. The constant care of the Economic Council must be to ensure that demand does not outstrip supply and thus cause a price rise.[4]

Thus the key to Mosley's ideas in the Birmingham proposals was planning: by means of socialist planning supply could be increased to correspond with increased demand created by credit expansion. Much of the thinking behind this planning was not Mosley's own, but that of Frank Wise, first Chairman of the Socialist League, and E. M. H. Lloyd. Mosley fully acknowledges his debt to them.

These policies were accompanied by a considerable degree of socialist planning, such as import boards, for which I was not primarily responsible. The begetters of this method were two distinguished civil servants of the First World War – E. F. Wise and E. M. H. Lloyd – who at this later period were very much associated with us.[5]

Wise, in particular, was a man of unique background. Unlike almost any other prominent political figure of the time, he combined an intimate knowledge of economics, with an extensive experience of government administration, acquired at the one time at which planning had official sanction – during the First War. He had been secretary of the Anglo-Russian Supplies Committee at the War Office from 1914–15, and became Principal Assistant Secretary at the Ministry of Food in 1917. He had thus seen the scope for government planning at first hand, and was able to see the problems and possibilities after the war-time apparatus had been dismantled in a way which was denied to his purely political colleagues.

Wise's own views fully emerged a year after Mosley's document, in another ILP policy statement, *The Living Wage*, produced in 1926 in conjunction with Brailsford, Arthur Creech Jones and J. A. Hobson, the great economist and exponent of the under-consumptionist doctrine, whose disciples included Lenin. *The Living Wage* was very similar to *Revolution By Reason*, but was more socialist in tone, and hence of the two was the policy officially adopted by the ILP. In common with most Socialists, but unlike Mosley, its authors laid greatest stress on fiscal policy. Much of the analysis, however, was along the same lines as that of the Mosley group. The emphasis was on the task of increasing purchasing power, by means of the standard Hobsonian argument for the redistribution of wealth. This was to be achieved by a major family allowance scheme, to be financed by taxation. This on its own was recognised, however, to be inadequate in a time of depression, and it was therefore advocated that, as in the Mosley document, purchasing power should be increased by means of imposing minimum wages in all industries; this was to be achieved by the printing of new money. As in the Mosley scheme, industries which refused to cooperate (in this case, by raising wages) would be summarily nationalised. Again it was argued that higher prices would be met by bulk purchases of raw materials. The Bank of England would be nationalised to facilitate credit control; and the plan would be supported by a number of additional Socialist controls.[6]

Similar proposals, with a change of emphasis and a more marxist flavour, later appeared in Socialist League policy statements. *Forward to Socialism* adopted by the Leeds Conference of the League in 1934 after Wise's death,[7] but largely formulated in the last few months of his life, contained them encapsulated as the essence of a socialist plan. The League presented a short-term plan of 'essential ambulance work', on the basis of piecemeal reforms to be carried out in the first few months, in combination with a longer-term programme of socialist planning. The policy resolution approved at the Derby Conference of the League in 1933, on which *Forward to Socialism* was substantially based, argued that a National Economic Plan of reconstruction and development should see that 'the supply of credit... be regulated by the socialised banks and distributed by a proper policy of wages and prices so as to ensure the maximum consumption of goods and services which the full employment of industrial and agricultural resources make possible; and prices must not be allowed to fluctuate from monetary causes, national or international so as to defeat this policy'. Price control would be instituted, and the Government would take control of imports and exports, in order to maintain the price of imports at a reasonable level, and to provide a basis for the planning of home production. A board of National Investment would be set up for the purpose of directing the supply of capital in accordance with the National Plan. The immediate problem of unemployment would be met by increasing unemployment benefit, and by an extensive public works programme. These measures were to be financed by increased taxation, the issue of national credit, the complete control of investment 'or by any other appropriate means until the increase of the national wealth under Socialism allows of their provision from the surpluses of production.'[8]

To this extent, socialist rhetoric apart, the League's proposals had much in common with those of non-socialist planners. But the League differed in two fundamental respects; it advocated the full-scale socialisation of the means of production within the first five years 'to secure the ownership and control of capital resources for the community and to achieve economic equality';[9] and it insisted that this must include effective provision for workers' control. It was the latter which created the really unbridgeable barrier between socialist and non-socialist planners. But the economic core of their arguments was the same.

The Living Wage proposals continued to influence Mosley's rapidly developing ideas until 1931. After 1929, the ILP economic reformers and the 'Birmingham group' became even more closely associated, in common opposition to the policies of MacDonald's government. Allen Young, co-author of *Revolution by Reason*, who later assisted Mosley in the framing of his Manifesto, 'helped to shape Mosley's ideas and instil into them much of the former J. A. Hobson – Frank Wise doctrine'.[10] The signatories of the Mosley Manifesto included Bevan, later closely involved with the Socialist League, and Frank Horrabin, an ILP Mosley supporter, who was on the Executive of SSIP, and became one of the central figures in the Socialist League, editing *The Socialist Leaguer* from 1934.[11]

There were also wide divergences between the ideas of Mosley, and those of the ILP and Socialist League. Mosley's attitude to the Empire, in particular, differed fundamentally from that of his former ILP colleagues. Whereas the Left looked to the socialist countries of the future, and in the present to the USSR, as the basis for an international economic community, Mosley saw in the Empire the markets for British products and a source for raw materials, and envisaged an economic unit on this basis which could rival the United States in self-sufficiency.

> The idea arose of an economic unit large enough to be viable in relative independence of world markets, and in my new phrase capable of 'insulation' from the 'external factors' which subsequent British governments admitted to be the cause of their downfall. It was not enough to be an island: we could only live by being great.[12]

Mosley was, in this respect, a follower of Joseph Chamberlain not Hobson; and it was partly this which led him to fascism. He had little interest in doctrinal socialism; his radicalism was aimed at dealing with specific problems, not at the creation of a socialist society. The desire for socialism was the starting point of the ILPers and the Socialist League, on the other hand. 'Remodelling their Marxism to suit modern conditions and in a modern idiom, they exposed the debility at the heart of capitalist society.'[13] Radical ideas were to them a means of achieving a socialist society; to Mosley, socialism was a political theory to be synthesised with modern economics as a means of solving unemployment.

PLANNING AND SOCIALISM

After 1931, the architects of the policies in *Revolution by Reason* and *The Living Wage* moved in dramatically different directions. Mosley became a fascist and a colourful irrelevance in British politics. Allen Young later became involved in attempts to achieve a 'centre' party alliance or a popular front, and helped Harold Macmillan write *The Middle Way* (published in 1938), which advocated a mixed economy and planning. While Wise and Brailsford set up the Socialist League within the Labour Party, Strachey, one of the strongest influences on Mosley until 1931, moved from the New Party to become the most productive and widely read British marxist theoretician of the decade.

Justifying his rediscovery of Keynes in 1938 to Communist associates, Strachey wrote that 'if, for good or evil, we have adopted People's Front Politics, we must have a People's Front economics also. If we do not, the result will be not that we avoid being involved in a Reformist economic policy, but that we get involved in a thoroughly bad Reformist economic policy.'[14] Up to this time, however, Strachey, in common with the Communists and with the Socialist League – whose ideas he did much to influence – bitterly attacked Keynesians and advocates of a British 'New Deal', pointing to the allegedly 'fascist' implications of reformist remedies to unemployment. Indeed, the Socialist League, like the ILP and the Communists, came to regard fascism as the major enemy in British society –a notion which developed after 1933 into an almost pathological obsession with the nightmarish possibility of a fascist seizure of power. It was a belief, partly derived from the 'Banker's Ramp' interpretation of the events of 1931, that the fascist tendencies of the capitalists would lead them to try by every means to prevent Socialists from gaining effective power, which accounted for the League's emphasis on 'the constitutional issues'.

At the same time, the League was especially concerned with what it saw as a sinister tendency towards the development of a 'Corporate State'. This was seen as the capitalists' final throw in their attempt to maintain their control of industry at the expense of the workers. 'In this country the Tory Party is being driven by force of circumstances from the unregulated and individualist capitalism of Victorian times, via the trusts and employers' associations of a later period, to a system of producer's corporations on Fascist lines.'[15] Examples of this were the price setting agricultural boards; iron, steel, cotton and other industries were regarded as showing similar tendencies.

This view put the League in a paradoxical position on the vital issue of planning. The League advocated economic planning; but its firm commitment to workers' control prevented it from acknowledging the merits of any form of planning short of socialism. For this reason the League toyed with the idea that Roosevelt was effectively a fascist, until Laski explained that he was actually 'mildly Progressive', carrying out the sort of mild social reform which Asquith pursued in Britain from 1906–10.[16]

The same magnanimity was not shown to planners at home. Mitchison dismissed the young Tories' 'enthusiasm for national planning' as no more than a desire for the corporate state.[17] The Liberal planners got as short shrift. 'Mr. Lloyd George,' wrote Cripps, 'who at one time boasted of his Liberalism and Democracy, is now suggesting an Economic Commission which will take a very large part of the administrative and some part of the legislative responsibility from Parliament – a commission that has a strange and unhappy resemblance to the Corporations of Italy and the organisations of Hitler.'[18] Hence the idea of an English New Deal was rejected out of hand. Murphy considered it necessary

> to warn Trade Unionists that the propagation of 'Roosevelt Recovery Plans' for Britain represents unconscious support to Fascist plans for the 'Totalitarian' or 'Corporate State'. From a continuance of such an attitude will follow, is following, the unchecked rise of the power of Finance, the power of increased rationalization, Public Corporations, which leave the claims of private property intact, class collaboration which keeps the workers subservient to the employers.[19]

Thus the League not only disagreed with non-socialist planners, but attacked them as, if anything, worse than the National Government, as the proponents of the Corporate State which was synonymous with fascism. It saw the affinity of their ideas with those of Mosley, without accepting the affinity of the ideas of all three groups, Tory planners, Lloyd George Liberals, and Mosleyites, with its own on the crucial domestic issue of the day. Cripps sternly warned the League in 'A Message from the National Chairman': 'The workers must not be led into the acceptance of the Corporate State because it is dressed up in the vague semi-socialist phraseology of planning and reorganisation.'[20]

The League, like the ILP and the CP, took for granted that capitalism was in decline and could only be saved by entering a new, fascist, phase. Lloyd George and the Macmillan group had in common with Mosley a desire to preserve many fundamental features of capitalism; consequently their planning appeared fascist in implication. The association of corporations with the organisations set up by Hitler and Mussolini was obvious and not ill-founded. Yet, while the attitude of the League was cataclysmic in theory, it never accepted that any solution to the unemployment problem short of socialism was necessarily bad simply because it delayed the coming of the millenium. It objected to corporations and non-socialist planning mainly because they seemed to constitute the very antithesis of the way in which it felt industry should be run.

The Socialist League was socialist first and radical second; like the ILP and the CP its approach was fundamentally utopian. It accepted as an article of faith that unemployment was an endemic feature of capitalism. William Mellor prefaced his proposals for a short-term programme by means of which Labour could tackle unemployment with the note: 'The plans outlined are not presented as a "cure" of this scourge of capitalism. Socialism alone can change compulsory Unemployment into remunerated leisure, with the machine as a servant, and effective demand equal to productive capacity.'[21] Thus non-socialist planning could at best – when carried out by a Labour Government with genuine socialist intentions – bring a temporary alleviation, pending the transition to socialism. At worst, when carried out by a capitalist government, it reinforced the control of industry by capitalist and financial interests, at the expense of the workers.

The latter possibility was especially abhorrent because of the strong Guild Socialist background of the League. In this respect Cole, the effective founder of Guild Socialism, was the major figure. In spite of his tactical differences with the League, his intellectual influence remained strong. He played a large part in the formulation of the League's policy document, *Forward to Socialism*; he continued to deliver lectures to, and write pamphlets for, the League;[22] and several of his former SSIP colleagues remained on the National Council. Two of these, Mellor and Horrabin,[23] central figures in the League, had a particularly strong Guild Socialist background. Both had been members of the Labour Research Department group of Guild Socialists with Cole in the early twenties. Mellor had been a Guild Socialist delegate at the Foundation Conference of the CPGB. It was therefore not surprising that the Socialist League put a very strong emphasis on workers' control, or that it put up an intense resistance to any scheme for industry which seemed to negate it.

Thus the Labour Party's own plans for industry, based on Herbert Morrison's 'public corporation' model of nationalisation, became a key target – and the proponents of workers' control achieved notable victories at the Party Conferences of 1932 and 1933. At Leicester in 1932, Harold Clay, later a prominent Leaguer,[24] attacked the NEC reports on the national planning of transport and electricity. Clay argued that the Executive's proposals for the running of these industries by public boards, for which the only criterion for appointment was to be ability, would vest control in the hands of an efficient bureaucracy with no effective public control, and would result in the exclusion of workers from power and responsibility. Morrison was constrained to withdraw the controversial part of the report for further discussion without a vote.[25] At Hastings a year later, when the matter was again raised, a NUGMW amendment insisting on statutory guarantees of direct trade union representation was passed against the platform, putting the seal on Clay's success.[26]

But this was not enough for the League, which demanded nothing less than full industrial democracy. In the eyes of the League, the issue was fundamental to the whole socialist idea, and was of deeper significance than mere economic efficiency. 'I believe in political democracy' said Clay at Leicester 'but I don't believe that can become complete until you have industrial democracy.'[27] The negation of this was the corporate state, or fascism, which reduced the workers' status to little more than that of slave labour. Reluctantly, the League accepted the necessity for Industrial Boards, but

> Socialists must see that, if industry has to be managed by Boards, the workers have a controlling place on those Boards, both nationally and locally and in every factory or other unit of industry or trade. It is not in practice sufficient that the workers' interests should be represented by one or two trade union officials on a central body. The national or local board must be built up out of similar boards in factories, mines and workshops. It is not impossible to devise means for the election by the workers of their representatives in the control of industry...
>
> Nationally, the Board of an industry must be under the direct control of some such planning authority as the economic committee of a reconstituted cabinet; and it must be answerable to Parliament.[28]

Within this framework planning was acceptable to the League. On any non-socialist basis, it meant the suppression of the workers, the bolstering of the capitalist structure, and fascism.

Thus the fear was not of jack-boots or brutality but of what Cripps called 'country-gentleman, English Fascism', a brand that could be instituted as easily by a 'corporatist' leader of the centre, a Macmillan or a Lloyd George, as by a Tory died-hard or a Mosley. Involvement with Liberals or 'liberal' Tories of a kind who advocated New Deal policies was to be avoided at any cost. Whatever the superficial attractions, Labour's parliamentary weakness was no excuse for dealings with political forces so clearly inimical to the interests of the working-class. The only possible alliance was on different lines, an alliance of 'working-class parties' – Labour, the Communists, the ILP –organisations committed to a complete transformation of the political and economic order, rather than a new attempt to shore up a decadent capitalist structure.

Part Two
United Front

7
Contests

Henderson resigned the Party Secretaryship, with great reluctance, in July 1934, his resignation to take effect from the end of the year.[1] The obvious choice as his successor was Morrison; yet many doubted the wisdom of having a prominent politician as Secretary. It was argued that the Party Secretaryship should be a full-time job, and hinted privately that Morrison would use the position to exercise a dominating influence. But it was Conference, not rivals on the NEC, which scotched Morrison's chances. The NEC confined itself to recommending that the office should not be held by anyone holding Ministerial rank in a Labour Government. This would have left it open for Morrison to be Secretary, and resign if Labour won a majority. However an amendment at the Southport Party Conference that the Secretary should be ineligible to sit in Parliament was carried against the platform by 1 449 000 to 841 000 – indicating what the trade unions felt on the matter.

The result was that the loyal but ineffective Jimmy Middleton, who had started as part-time assistant to MacDonald in 1903, was narrowly elected Secretary in December 1934. Middleton introduced few reforms at Transport House; and the tradition of staff appointments to the Secretaryship which has been followed ever since has not been the best recipe for dynamism. The 'penny farthing machine' which Wilson exposed in the fifties is one consequence of the decision of 1934.

FOREIGN POLICY AND THE LEADERSHIP

Lansbury's position as Party Leader became increasingly difficult during 1935. Until 1934 his pacifism had not been an insuperable problem. Thereafter the heightening of international tensions made it so. The Italy–Abyssinia dispute brought the issue of what Lansbury was to call his 'Dr Jekyll and Mr Hyde position' over foreign policy to a head. The majority view in the Labour Movement favoured sanctions. Lansbury was resolutely opposed to them. The question was whether the Party could continue to be led by a man who was outspoken in his denunciation of the policy advocated by most of his followers on the major issue of the day. At Southport in

1934 Lansbury had in effect offered to resign whenever his pacifism made him a liability. The problem was who should decide when this moment had arrived.

The TUC at Margate in September 1935 greatly added to Lansbury's embarrassment. Required to speak as Labour Party fraternal delegate, he pleaded with Citrine to be allowed to express his own personal attitude on sanctions.[2] The TUC General Secretary insisted that he should express the official Party position; Lansbury 'was hideously uncomfortable when delegates asked him afterwards if he had changed his opinions.'[3] His discomfort was made worse on 17 September when Lord Ponsonby, Leader of the Labour peers, wrote to him 'I cannot wait any longer!' and resigned his post on the grounds that no honest pacifist could consistently 'hold a position as leader' in the Party.[4] Cripps' resignation from the NEC on the same issue (though in opposition to 'capitalist' sanctions rather than on pacifist grounds) left Lansbury isolated.

R. T. McKenzie has described Lansbury's resignation as 'The only clear-cut instance of a Labour Leader being driven from office.'[5] Yet, whatever the pressures on him, it was in the end Lansbury's own decision. Neither the NEC, nor Conference, forced him out, and the PLP was quite ready for him to remain.

On 19 September, a special NEC meeting considered the situation. Opinion was bitterly divided. Some of the trade union members wanted Lansbury to go at once; the majority disagreed. In the end the Executive passed a resolution which was scarcely warm, but nevertheless left the matter open: 'that the question of the Leadership is a matter for the Parliamentary Party, but that in the opinion of the NEC, there is no reason why he should tender his resignation'. An amendment to delete the last clause was defeated by 8 votes to 5.[6] '[W]e decide to leave it to him and the PLP', Dalton wrote in his diary. 'We don't want the onus of pushing him out.'[7]

The Party Conference started at Brighton a week later. With all the major unions favouring sanctions, the Executive's policy was bound to be endorsed overwhelmingly. Nevertheless, when Lansbury rose to speak in the Abyssinian debate, the whole Conference, 'with the exception of two glowering trade union groups', rose and sang 'For He's a Jolly Good Fellow'.[8]

> It may be that I shall not meet you on this platform any more. (Cries of 'No'.) There are things that come into life that make changes inevitable. It may very well be that in the carrying out of your policy I shall be in your way. When I was sick and on my back ideas came into my head, and one was that the only thing worth while for old men to do is to at least say the thing they believe, and to at least try to warn the young of the dangers of force and compulsion.[9]

Delegates were deeply moved, and applause was loud and prolonged. Bevin followed. He made no concessions to sentiment. His speech was bullying and powerful.

> It is placing the Executive and the Movement in an absolutely wrong position to be taking your conscience round from body to body asking to be told what you ought to do with it. There is one quotation from the Scriptures which George Lansbury has quoted to-day which I think he ought to apply to himself – 'Do unto others'. I have had to sit in Conference with the Leader and come to decisions, and I am a democrat and I feel we have been betrayed.[10]

To those who reproved him afterwards for his savagery, Bevin replied 'Lansbury has been going about in saint's cloths for years waiting for martyrdom. I set fire to the faggots.'[11]

Bevin's speech came to be regarded as a *coup de grâce* – a cruel but necessary notice to quit, forcing Lansbury's hand. According to Bullock, 'more than any other speaker he contributed to the final result, a vote of 2 168 000 to 102 000 in favour of full support for the League,'[12] and Dalton described how Bevin 'hammered [Lansbury] to death'.[13] But an overwhelming victory for the Executive had always been inevitable; and Bevin's speech was poorly received. Lansbury had been cheered; Bevin was repeatedly booed, and his remarks were widely felt to have been unjustifiably offensive. Lansbury was upset; but Conference had passed no verdict on his leadership.

The vote on the Abyssinian debate took place on 1 October. Lansbury showed no immediate signs of intending to resign. 'Mr Lansbury will decide on Tuesday (when he meets the PLP) whether he will resign', the *Observer* disclosed on Sunday, 6 October. 'His views, I understand, remain the same as those expressed in an interview last week...he will carry on as leader of the party unless he is asked to resign.' Then he began to weaken. 'Nobody knows, not even Mr Lansbury himself, apparently, whether he will resign to-morrow', reported the *Manchester Guardian* on 8 October. 'He said only to-night that "the question of his resignation was still indefinite".' When he met the PLP that day, he made a long speech and tendered his resignation.

'AN INTERIM APPOINTMENT'

The PLP was now faced with the problem of the succession. It is possible that this had been a reason (or an excuse) for Lansbury's hesitations. Lansbury had favoured Cripps, but Cripps had already excluded himself by resigning from the Party Executive. Few could imagine Attlee as permanent Party Leader. Greenwood was the expected choice. But Greenwood was associated with the trade union opponents of Lansbury, and many MPs, feeling a deep personal loyalty to Lansbury, were reluctant to replace him with the nominee, in effect, of his chief opponents. Furthermore, supporters of claimants outside Parliament were worried that if Greenwood was chosen before the General Election the decision would be extremely hard to reverse after it. The suggestion was made – and Lansbury may briefly have been tempted by it – that he should continue to lead until the end of the Parliament, leaving Attlee to speak on foreign affairs.[14]

When Lansbury had announced his resignation, he withdrew from the PLP meeting and, for reasons which are not clear, Greenwood followed him.[15] The PLP now found itself in an embarrassing situation; should Attlee or Greenwood be elected, or should some other formula be found? There was an argument. Grenfell pleaded for unity under the old leadership; Will Thorne replied that Lansbury was now adamant, and could not be persuaded. A vote was taken, and by 38 to 7 it was decided to ask Lansbury to change his mind. When Lansbury refused, 'the Party found itself leaderless and not daring to decide upon a successor'.[16] Nominations were called for. No names were put forward. Instead it was suggested tentatively that Attlee should take over for the rest of the session. 'The suggestion was adopted – without enthusiasm',[17] and apparently with no discussion.[18] 'The trade unions wanted Mr Arthur Greenwood', commented the *News Chronicle*. 'Unfortunately for Transport House the election of the leader is the prerogative of the Parliamentary Party and in the end Major Attlee was asked to carry on as the least embarrassing way out of a bad mess.'[19] 'This is hardly more than an interim appointment', observed the *Manchester Guardian*, offering an unflattering analogy, 'much like that of Mr William Adamson as chairman and leader of the Opposition in the Parliament of 1918'.[20] Not for the first (or last) time the unpretentious Attlee, having taken a step up the ladder by default, was prematurely written off.

The General Election took place in November. Attlee's leadership during the campaign was undistinguished, and the increase in Labour representation to 154 was a disappointment to many. Nevertheless, the election focussed the attention of the press, the public, and of Labour candidates and MPs fighting in the constituencies on Attlee as never before. This background of publicity was clearly advantageous to Attlee when the PLP came to elect a leader on 26 November.

The Election had brought the other main contenders back into Parliament. But Clynes refused to stand, nobody seemed prepared to back Alexander, and Dalton decided, rather than to put himself up, to appoint himself campaign-manager for Morrison. This meant that the contest was between Morrison, Attlee and Greenwood.

Greenwood had the backing of Transport House, and of northern trade unionist MPs. Some active campaigning was, apparently, done on his behalf by MPs and officials who were members of a Masonic Lodge.[21]

Morrison, the only one of the three who was a member of the Party Executive in his own right, was probably the most widely respected in the Movement as a whole; he could still capitalise on his LCC victory in 1934; and despite a stern attitude towards the Party rebels he could command the support of left-wingers like Cripps and Ellen Wilkinson. On the other hand he had the severe handicap of four years' absence from Parliament; and he had to contend both with the enmity of Bevin and the friendship of Dalton. Dalton's busy canvassing probably hurt him most. Declaring loudly that apart from Morrison, the choice was between 'a nonentity or a drunk',[22] Dalton managed to surround Morrison's candidacy with an aura of conspiracy; and matters were made much worse by a 'secret' meeting at Dalton's flat to win over a group of MPs which was leaked to the press, to Morrison's acute embarrassment.[23] Attlee's great asset was that he was leader *pro tem*, he had led the Party for several months while Lansbury had been ill, and he was known and trusted by the veterans of the 1931 Parliament.[24] He was also – crucially – 'the neutral and *least disliked* member of the front bench', who aroused no strong feelings either way.[25]

The PLP voted at a meeting on 26 November with Attlee in the chair. On the first ballot Attlee received 58 votes, Morrison 44 and Greenwood 33. On the second ballot, Greenwood's votes swung to Attlee as a bloc – some felt by prior arrangement – and Attlee received 88 votes, Morison 48. 'I had been conscious in those last few days,' wrote Dalton, 'of a prejudice, surprisingly strong and widespread, against Morrison. There was a feeling that, if he got the Leadership now, he would keep it, but that, if Attlee got it, there might be a change later. This feeling helped to explain the swing on the second vote.'[26] Afterwards, Attlee was quietly reassuring. He said that he had been elected for one session only, and if they wanted a change later he would not complain.

Morrison then declined nomination for the Deputy Leadership – ostensibly because of his LCC work, but more probably out of pique, for he had indicated in answer to a question that he would have been prepared to combine the LCC with the far more onerous post of Party Leader. Greenwood was then elected Deputy Leader unopposed. This decision was important. It meant that Greenwood, not Morrison, led the Party in the last days before the declaration of War, when Attlee was recovering from an operation; and that Greenwood entered the War Cabinet with Attlee in 1940, while Morrison did not join until the end of 1942.[27]

There were several attempts to displace Attlee, and frequent rumours of his impending downfall. His imminent departure was predicted as early as 1936. A maladroit move to replace him by Morrison or Greenwood in the summer of 1939, when he was away sick, never got off the ground. An attempt by Morrison, in a desperate bid to pre-empt the leadership for himself, to get the PLP to insist on choosing a Leader before accepting office in 1945 proved similarly abortive. Another plot in 1947 was scotched by Bevin. Attlee passed through these crises with a calm detachment. 'Did you regard yourself as a temporary leader?' he was asked many years later. 'No,' he replied, 'I never regard these things, I just go ahead.'[28]

8

Outside Left and the United Front

If the Socialist League had done nothing else during its existence than
inaugurate [the Unity] campaign, it would have fully justified its formation.

Sir Stafford Cripps in *Tribune*

21 May 1937.

In January 1937 the Socialist League, the Communist Party and the ILP
together issued a 'Unity Manifesto', expressing a number of common
aspirations.[1] The three groups then embarked on a series of mass meetings
and demonstrations which were vigorously denounced by Transport House
and which delighted the Press, always eager to make the most of a Party
quarrel. On paper, the joint activity was directed 'against Fascism, reaction
and war and against the National Government'.[2] In practice it was closely
linked to a vigorous campaign to secure Communist affiliation to the
Labour Party.

In Michael Foot's view, the Unity Campaign was 'the most ambitious bid
made by the British Left throughout the whole period of the thirties to
break the stultifying rigidity of Party alignments'.[3] Yet the aim of 'unity' –
united action by the Labour Party and extreme left groups outside it – was
a lost cause from the start; and a tangled skein of irreconcilable views on
doctrine and tactics produced action by the Campaign's participants which
was barely linked to any consistent purpose. The main effects of the campaign were to weaken the Labour Left, destroy the Socialist League, deepen
existing divisions within the Labour Party, and queer the pitch for later
attempts to bring opposition forces together in order to bring about a
change in Government policy.

The immediate impetus was provided by events abroad. The growing
threat of European fascism; changes in the attitudes of the Labour and
Socialist International (L & SI) and the Comintern which made national
popular fronts possible; the establishment of Popular Front Governments
in Spain and France; the Spanish Civil War, which aroused more passion

on the Left than any other foreign conflict since 1918 – all these encouraged
the leaders of left-wing groups in Britain to seek an understanding on which
to base joint action. But the same factors contributed to the Unity Campaign's disaster. Each group had its own special reasons for wishing to
participate. These did not coincide, and when circumstances changed old
antagonisms rapidly reasserted themselves.

THE ILP: 'SYMPATHETIC AFFILIATION'

ILP interest in the idea had various roots. The ILP was already feeling the
debilitating effects of isolation following its voluntary disaffiliation the
previous summer – 'the worst mistake of my life', as Brockway has since
described it.[4] The ILP was making the painful discovery that separation
from the Movement's mainstream cut it off from potential Labour Party
sympathisers and destroyed any influence it might have had in Labour Party
counsels. Worse, it removed the ILP from the limelight. The Press loved a
major party split. The activities of an extremist fringe group with little
support south of the Clyde and which lacked the subversive menace of
'Moscow gold' made poor copy.

Furthermore, the ILP's decision to pull its councillors out of Labour
groups had been especially disastrous. ILP councillors were forced to
choose between public responsibility and purist impotence; many chose
the former, and left the ILP. Within the first year after disaffiliation, the
ILP lost a third of its membership.[5] The attraction of united action with
the Labour Party and with the CP lay in the prospect of spearheading a
campaign of demonstrations which would bring the ILP back into contact
with the Labour Party's mass base which it had so recently deserted.

There was more to it than this. Ever since 1918 the ILP had been struggling to find a coherent purpose. While still in the Labour Party it had
succeeded in occupying the role of left-wing conscience, generating socialist
ideas and radical solutions against an obdurate Labour Party leadership.
Its failure to influence Labour policy and the personal animosities which
developed between its own leaders and the Labour Party establishment had
made this position unbearable. But the ILP's position outside the Labour
Party, without the pricks of Party discipline to kick against, was scarcely
more rewarding. In the heady atmosphere of 1932 after Labour's massive
electoral defeat, and with unemployment at unprecedented levels, it had
been possible to believe that disaffiliation would free the ILP to become a
competitor to the Labour Party. A few months marked only by uncertainty
and decline had been sobering. It rapidly became clear that a vague commitment to revolutionary marxism and an unchannelled enthusiasm led
nowhere. The ILP was in urgent need of an ideological anchor.

The early months of lonely independence gave those in the ILP who
sought closer links with the Communists a chance to pursue their claims.

The aim of the Revolutionary Policy Committee, a pro-communist faction in the ILP which had led the campaign for disaffiliation, was a policy of 'sympathetic affiliation' to the Executive Committee of the Communist International (ECCI) – a strange misunderstanding of how the Comintern operated.

The RPC innocently imagined that if it could take over the ILP it would supersede the CPGB as the British section of the Comintern. But CPGB leaders themselves had very different plans. For them the disintegrating ILP, with a membership in 1932 two or three times that of the CP, was a new and fertile recruiting ground, and they envisaged an eventual takeover, disguised as a merger, which would have meant the demise of the ILP.

At first the Communists had dismissed ILP disaffiliation as 'a manoeuvre of the left reformist leadership to endeavour to maintain a failing hold on the leftward moving worker.'[6] But as the Comintern line changed, and the RPC strengthened its position inside the ILP, the CP began an ardent courtship. Pollitt, 'full of an infectious confidence', suggested an ultimate amalgamation which would give the ILP, as an equal partner, even greater prominence than the CP.[7]

Despite a temporary victory at the 1933 ILP Conference, the RPC soon lost influence and in 1935 seceded to join the CP – by then barely able to take a few dozen members with it. But before this happened it had done irreparable damage to any prospect of genuine cooperation between the ILP and CP. Its activities and those of the Communists hastened the ILP's disintegration, enabling the CPGB to become, by the mid-thirties, by far the most active and confident, as well as the largest, of left-wing groups. Disenchanted ILP members left in droves, branches became moribund or broke away, and these defections further demoralised those who remained. From 1932 to 1935 the ILP lost branches at a rate of over two per week;[8] total membership dropped from 16 773 in 1932 to 11 093 in 1933, 7166 in 1934 and 4392 in 1935.[9] In the twenties, the ILP had been the centre of vigorous intellectual activity, involving many of the most creative socialist thinkers. In the thirties, most of the ILP intellectuals stayed in the Labour Party; new intellectual recruits to the far Left joined the Communist Party.[10]

Those who stayed in the ILP had increasing reason to distrust Communists, and after 1934 mutual antagonism became open and acknowledged. When the Communists sought affiliation to the Labour Party, the ILP attacked them from an 'extreme left' position for betraying their socialist principles. The CP responded by calling the ILP Trotskyist, a line of attack which contained an element of truth.[11]

Yet the ILP never stopped seeking cooperation of some kind with the Communist and Labour Parties and supported a series of letters from the CP to the mass organisations of the Labour Movement in favour of joint activity. When discussions for a unity campaign were initiated, the ILP accepted the invitation to participate – but only with the deepest reservations about association with the Communists.

The attitude of the Communists towards others on the left was, if anything, even less consistent than that of the ILP. But whereas the ILP agonised over every move without any point of reference, Communist policy reflected faithfully every twist and turn of the Communist International. From 1928 Comintern policy had involved the uncompromising denunciation of all other political parties, with social democrats singled out for special abuse as 'social fascists'. The success of Hitler and the subsequent failure of German Communists to operate as an underground organisation brought a gradual change of line.

The issue of relations with the Labour Party had been a major concern of the British Communist Party from the time of its foundation. Lenin himself had written shortly before the foundation Convention in 1920 declaring himself in favour of 'adhesion to the Labour Party on condition of free and independent Communist activities'.[13] The Labour Party leadership, however, had not been convinced of Communist *bona fides*, influenced, no doubt, by the enthusiastic backing of British Communists for Lenin's dictum that they should support Henderson 'as a rope supports the hanged'.[14] In 1924 Communist Party affiliation was massively rejected by Conference, and Communists were made ineligible for endorsement as candidates. In 1925 Conference excluded CP members from individual sections of affiliated local Labour Parties. Finally in 1928 Communists were forbidden to attend Conferences even as trade union delegates.

These moves were a response to the CP's attempts to undermine Labour's organisation. Communist tactics were based on instructions issued by Lenin in 1921. These involved the taking over of an organisation by the creation of a Communist 'fraction' within it. Once control was assured, key executive positions were given to Communists, with a few non-party members retained in prominent posts as window dressing. When the Communists had gained control in this way the only method of shifting them was by disbanding the organisation. This the Labour Party was often forced to do, and in the 1920s a large number of local Labour Parties, having fallen into Communist hands, were summarily disaffiliated.

Local Labour Parties were ideal vehicles for Communist infiltration. Individual members' sections of the Labour Party were still in their infancy; in many areas they were weak or non-existent. Where there were only a handful of members, Communists could take control with comparative ease. Whether this did the Communist Party much good, or the Labour

Party much harm, is of course another matter. What it did do was to arouse great bitterness among Labour Party members and among Labour leaders like Henderson and Morrison who had close contacts with party organisation and the rank and file.

In 1926 Communist activities were extended following a Comintern instruction to all sections to build up a 'whole solar system' of apparently independent organisations which were in practice Communist controlled. The National Left Wing Movement, an organisation of this type, had already been set up after the 1925 Labour Party Conference with the object of reversing the decisions excluding Communists from constituency parties. Claiming to be a broad left-wing movement, this new body attracted dissident local Labour Parties, some Communist controlled, most merely sympathetic to the Communist case. Twenty-three local Labour Parties had been disaffiliated by the summer of 1927, including 15 in the London area, for failing to expel Communists.[15]

In 1928, on orders from Moscow, the Communist line shifted to 'Class against Class'. All cooperation with the Labour Party ceased, and Labour and social democratic parties were treated as, if anything, more dangerous than overtly capitalist bodies. This enforced change of line was a serious blow to British Communists. Communist organisations' 'bridge to the masses' had depended on good relations with non-communist left-wingers who now were lumped together with others in the Labour Party as 'social fascists'. Communist Party membership declined to an all time low by the end of 1930.

The National Minority Movement, an attempt to set up a kind of Communist controlled TUC, had met with some initial success, to the great consternation of orthodox trade union leaders; it foundered on the breach with the Labour Left. Indeed the only Communist organisation to thrive before the Comintern line began to change again in 1933 was the National Unemployed Workers Movement (NUWM). Led by Wal Hannington, this had 20000 members by the summer of 1931, and 37000 by the end of the year. The NUWM succeeded precisely because Hannington showed more concern for the unemployed than for Communist directives. It proved a major embarrassment to the TUC and the Labour Party which made no serious attempt to set up a rival body, yet refused to cooperate with it or give it recognition. The marches and demonstrations of the NUWM became a focal point for many Labour left-wingers who were dissatisfied with Labour's failure to organise the unemployed.

The 1931 crisis gave a small boost to the lagging fortunes of the CP, which had lost most of its influence in the trade union movement and almost all influence in the Labour Party. Membership doubled, though at 6279 in November 1931 it was still below the post-General Strike peak of 10730 in 1926, when many miners had joined, soon to drift away. But at the

1931 General Election 26 Communist candidates received only 74 824 votes, compared with 55 346 for 8 candidates in 1924. The average vote for each Communist candidate in 1931 was a mere 7.5 per cent – lower than at any other election for which comparison is possible before 1950.[16] With unemployment nearing 3 million, higher than it had ever been in history, and with the Labour Party in a state of confusion and disarray, the CP had little cause for self-congratulation.

The situation soon began to improve for the Communists, however. The Comintern line began to soften as early as 1931, and events in Germany in 1933 brought the beginning of a fundamental reversal of Communist policy towards social democratic parties. This reversal took place in stages, as it became increasingly clear that the Nazis constituted a major threat to the Soviet Union. Between March 1933 and summer 1935, British Communists dutifully changed their attitude to the Labour Party in a fundamental way.

In March 1933 Harry Pollitt,[17] backed by the ILP, approached the bodies of the Labour Movement with a suggestion for joint action. The TUC General Council promptly issued a circular offering suitable advice with regard to a number of bodies allegedly Communist controlled,[18] and the Labour Party produced a pamphlet entitled *The Communist Solar System*, which carefully analysed Communist tactics. Early in the following year, the CP and ILP wrote again separately, suggesting a 'united front' of all working-class organisations. This time Henderson and the Party Chairman, George Lathan, interviewed Maxton and Brockway. Trade union members of the National Joint Council were outraged. Henderson had to calm them with assurances that no negotiations had taken place, and that there could be no question of the Party associating with Communists.[19] He replied to Pollitt rejecting 'a so-called "united front" behind which intensified Communist propaganda would be carried on against associated organisations'.[20] The General Council was even more brusque. Citrine wrote that further communications from the CP would not even be considered.[21] Pollitt replied that he was not surprised. 'Your united front activities with the Federation of British Industries, and with the sectional groups of employers, must leave Mr Citrine with little time for correspondence with working-class organisations.'[22]

One of the CP's problems was over nomenclature. The Communists' old tactics of infiltration had sometimes been referred to as 'the united front from below'. What the Communists now sought was a 'united front from above' – joint action at all levels. But for many people in the Labour Party and trade unions the term 'united front' had its old sinister connotation. Their suspicions seemed confirmed by evidence that despite protestations the Communist Party was continuing to burrow away at the grass roots. A number of local and constituency parties, including Wood Green, South-

gate, Finchley, Edinburgh, Perth, Bradford and Darwen, soon found themselves in trouble for associating with Communists.[23]

Communist activities in these and other parties were designed to further
the new Communist policy, but they had the opposite effect. The NEC was
determined to prevent any drift back to the situation of the mid-twenties,
when the Communists had entrenched themselves in many local parties. In
May 1934 the Executive resolved 'That united action with the Communist
Party or organisations ancillary or subsidiary thereto, without the sanction
of the NEC, is incompatible with membership of the Labour Party, and that
the NEC seeks full disciplinary powers from the next Annual Party Conference to deal with any case or cases that may arise.'[24] Conference duly
complied, and the NEC was enabled to stamp hard on transgressors –
whether they were involved in 'united front from below' or 'united front
from above' activities.

The Communists' new line was, however, more concerned with propaganda victories than practical politics. Their appeals to the Labour
Executive were always combined with a stream of invective against everything the Labour Party stood for. They expected no response from the NEC,
and certainly did nothing to encourage one. Extending one hand in friendship while openly brandishing a knife in the other, they made the whole
performance seem like a bizarre ritual dance. In May 1934 a Communist
manifesto called for a united front but insisted that a third Labour Government would be a disaster for the working-class, because the Labour Party,
'like the Fascists, like all demagogues, will promise paradise in the future,
but advocates submission to the hellish conditions now.'[25] In August the
Daily Worker assured its readers that a Labour Government would only
govern for capitalism against the workers and that Henderson and Clynes
were no different from MacDonald and Thomas. 'There could be no greater
danger confronting the working-class than to listen to the pleas to "give
Labour another chance" etc.' Yet in the same breath it declared that its
appeal to the Labour Party and the TUC and to all working-class organisations 'initiated the most important campaign of the present period', and
announced that so serious were its intentions that it was ready 'to make
every possible concession' for the achievement of a united front.[26] In
October the Communists again joined with the ILP in writing to Henderson, this time using Spanish left-wing unity and the Spanish crisis as
their starting-point, expressing the extraordinary hope that 'you will consider this letter without allowing the differences of the past to influence
you.'[27]

The Communist tactical line was, however, in the process of a rapid
evolution. In August 1934 the *Daily Worker* had been at pains to explain
the necessity of opposing Labour candidates.[28] In November, Palme Dutt
announced that 'We are no Parliamentary fetishists,' and offered 'big con-

cessions in the electoral–Parliamentary sphere'.[29] The subtlety of the official line was now sublime. Communists must give Labour support *precisely because* a Labour victory would be disastrous. This was a version of revolutionary defeatism, but with a difference. The Communists maintained that if Labour won an election the bankruptcy of its policies would disillusion the working-class and open the way to fascism. Hence Communist support was necessary, because it would enable the working-class to turn to an alternative leadership, that of the CP, as revealed in the course of the electoral struggle. 'Wherein lies the heaviest danger?' asked Dutt. 'The return of a new Labour Government by a wide and enthusiastic Labour vote will inevitably reveal the true character of Labour policy and deal a cruel blow to the aspirations of millions of workers. The danger will then arise that the sweep to Labour will be followed by a sweep to Fascism. Against this danger only the CP can save the workers by the character of its fight already at the present stage.'[30] Communists were thus to support Labour as an insurance policy against the most dangerous possibility – a Labour success.

Willie Gallacher put it another way. A Labour victory would shatter the faith of the workers in their own organisations. 'We can out of this develop a situation that will produce a constitutional crisis and an "open confrontation of the classes".' After a big electoral swing to Labour 'such a crisis will be a practical certainty'. To help Labour along, Communist candidates should therefore only be put up where there was a definite chance of a breakthrough.[31] 'Lenin in one of his books (I think it was "Left-Wing Communism") states that the workers of this country will have to suffer the disillusion of a Labour Government before they really storm the citadel of capitalism', a correspondent wrote to the *Daily Worker*. 'Obviously the sooner they are disillusioned the sooner they will turn to the CP as the only workers' Party which will lead them to the conquest of power.'[32]

Such an approach was, of course, unlikely to be warmly received by any but the most fellow-travelling members of the Labour Party. Perhaps for this reason Pollitt was soon moderating his position yet again. In December he announced that a Labour victory was needed because it would strengthen the Communist Party, and prepare it for a *possible* crisis. There was no mention of inevitable chaos. In a sentence whose tortuousness indicated the difficulty of saying anything which did not offend against some doctrinal canon, Pollitt declared:

> It is of the utmost importance to secure a united class front at the General Election, which will sweep away the National Government and return a Labour Government, even though our exposure of the character of a Labour Government still stands, because the resultant mobilisation and victorious impetus of the united working-class will

lead to a powerful strengthening of the fighting spirit and class solidarity of the workers, the pressing forward of further demands and
advancing struggle, the strengthening of the class line, not the line of
class collaboration preached by the Labour Party leadership, and the
greater readiness to stand by the workers of other countries and prevent
intervention in the event of a revolutionary breakthrough, this [*sic*]
becomes the basis for further united advances and for the advancing
leadership of the Communist Party.[33]

In the summer of 1935 British CP delegates attended the Seventh World
Congress of the Comintern in Moscow, the first to be held since 1928. The
united front policy was firmly upheld – but it was to be an alliance of working-
class organisations only. Dimitrov warned that no quarter should be given
to Lloyd George, who was calling for a pact with Labour.[34] Pollitt made a
speech indicating the readiness of the British Party to renew its application
for affiliation to Labour.[35] It was decided, however, to delay this step until
after the Brighton Labour Party Conference in October, in order to muster
support.

The Brighton Conference was immediately followed by the General
Election. Only two Communist candidates stood. Pollitt gained a little
ground against Labour at Rhondda East, and Gallacher won West Fife,
apparently taking votes from the Tories as well as from Labour.[36] Elsewhere,
despite NEC efforts to prevent it, Communists were active in many constituencies in support of Labour candidates. The Communist Party manifesto declared simply:

> The only guarantee of peace is the crushing defeat of the Government
> and the election of a Labour Government pledged to a policy of peace
> and armament reduction.
>
> The Communist Party calls upon all working men and women to vote
> down this wage-cutting Government, and to return a Labour Govern-
> ment pledged to improve the conditions of the masses.[37]

CAMPAIGN FOR COMMUNIST AFFILIATION 1935–6

When the election was over, Pollitt wrote to the NEC applying for affiliation
to the Labour Party. The Communist Party, he stated, was prepared to work
'honestly and sincerely' as part of the Labour Party, 'not as a manoeuvre or
for any concealed aims, but because it believes that this would unite the
working-class and make it better able to fight against the National Government, against Fascism, and imperialist war'. But he went on to declare that
the CP was and would remain a revolutionary organisation.[38] A week later
the CP defended itself against an ILP charge that it had sold out by an-
nouncing that its purpose was to change 'the present character of the
Labour Party and transform it into a real broad federal organisation in spite

of the intentions of the most reactionary Labour leaders'.[39] It was thus scarcely surprising that the NEC should reply by saying that 'affiliation is sought not for the purpose of promoting the Labour Party's declared policy and programme but, on the contrary, to utilise party facilities on the platform, in public conference, and in the party press, to displace their essential democratic and Socialist character and substitute a policy and programme based upon Communist Party principles'.[40] This, after all, was what the Communists had claimed themselves.

A number of developments were, however, encouraging a feeling that Labour might benefit from Communist affiliation. Soviet opposition to Nazi Germany and support for the League of Nations convinced many people that the Communists' conversion to cooperation with social democrats was genuine. The successful formation of popular front governments in France and Spain seemed to provide further evidence of this. Mounting difficulties of the Republican Government in Spain had won the sympathetic attention of the whole British Left. The civil war which began in July 1936 seemed temporarily to erase sectarian differences. Soviet support for the Republican forces took the form of military aid from September. This was warmly approved, not only on the extreme Left, by people who viewed the prospect of a Fascist victory in Spain with horror. Shortly before the Spanish War broke out, Gollancz launched his Left Book Club, strongly sympathetic to the Communists, and pressed the case for a Communist–Labour alliance to a large, enthusiastic membership. Communism suddenly became fashionable among people who had had little interest in the tactics of industrial permeation of the twenties. The Labour Left was able to gain strong support in the rapidly expanding constituency parties for Aneurin Bevan's view that Communist affiliation 'would lead to the spiritual reawakening of the British Working-Class Movement'.[41]

On the other hand, established Labour Party and trade union leaders, in control of the big majorities, were not prepared to share the CP's amnesia about past conflicts. Herbert Morrison in particular, had bitter memories of the termite-like activities of Communists in the individual members' sections of the London Labour Party. 'The issue involved' he wrote in June 1936, 'is the issue as to whether the Labour Party is to become Communist or not, for the Communists within our ranks would give us no peace until that were done, if it could be done'. Affiliation would mean a return to the constant friction, splits and troubles of the years before Communists were excluded. 'Local party after local party was weakened, good men and women were discouraged by the organised activities of Communist fractions stirring up trouble for the Movement in accordance with their duplicated instructions'.[42]

Trade union leaders shared Morrison's anxieties. They also had very immediate reasons for fearing any strengthening of the Communists' posi-

86

tion. As the depression receded prices had begun to rise. At the same time mechanisation had brought increases in productivity in many industries. These changes had not been accompanied by corresponding wage rises. Discontent had arisen, not across industries, but factory by factory, and this had brought an increasing number of unofficial strikes in single establishments. Communists were often involved, and even more often got the blame – from trade unions as well as from employers. A National Council of Labour pamphlet issued in July 1936 which denounced the CP roundly for its political tactics included an important industrial section:

> On numerous occasions the executives of unions have been faced with
> unofficial strikes, deliberately fomented by Communists and directed
> not so much against the employers as against executive authority and
> the unions themselves. When the mischief has been done and the men
> have been victimised, the Communists have promptly deserted them
> leaving the trade unions to deal with the difficult situation created by
> their pernicious intervention in union affairs.[43]

The Communist aim was to win a vote on affiliation at the Labour Party Conference at Edinburgh in October 1936. Throughout the spring and summer Communists worked inside affiliated organisations in an attempt to build up enough support to secure this objective. There were some notable successes. In April the South Wales Miners' Federation (where the Communists had been strong since the General Strike) voted 2 to 1 for affiliation, and elected a Communist, Arthur Horner, as President. By August the *Daily Worker* was claiming the support of the MFGB, ASLEF, the AEU, the Furnishing Trades Association, the National Union of Clerks, the Socialist League, the Fabian Society, the Scottish Socialist Party and 60 Divisional Labour Parties.[44]

In July the *Daily Telegraph* estimated that both the pro- and anti-Communist factions in the trade union movement could count on over a million Conference votes, and reckoned Communist success as a possibility.[45] The *Morning Post* expected the affiliation motion to fail, because the remaining big unions to make up their minds, which included the TGWU, could be relied on to oppose. Nevertheless in its view 'a close vote is inevitable, and upon that vote will depend consequences hard to calculate'. At least three-quarters of a million Conference voters would support affiliation.[46] The *New Statesman and Nation* predicted 'a platform victory against affiliation, but so large a vote and so strong a feeling for working with Communists that the virulent anti-Communist attitude of the *Daily Herald* and Transport House will in practice have to be modified after Conference'.[47]

But, as so often in the past, changing events in the Soviet Union helped to sabotage Communist efforts in Britain and turn away wavering sympathisers. The first great show trials in Moscow took place in the summer of 1936, and presented the world with the spectacle of Zinoviev, Kamenev and an array of other old Bolsheviks confessing to an implausible range of crimes. Many on the left in Britain, not only in the Communist Party, accepted the substance of the charges. Walter Citrine, who had made a six-week journey to Russia and had written a shrewd account of his experiences,[48] was one of those who did not. In August he signed a request from the L & SI and the International Federation of Trade Unions (IFTU) pleading for mercy for Zinoviev and his fellow prisoners and urging that they should have a proper defence. The *Daily Worker*, whose general attitude was summed up by the headline SHOOT THE REPTILES, carried another story headed CITRINE SIDES WITH TRAITORS.[49] This approach scarcely reassured those in the trade unions and Labour Party who were still wondering whether the CP would make a comfortable bed fellow.

By the time of the Edinburgh Conference between 850 000 and a million voters seemed to be committed to affiliation. But when a card vote was taken, only 592 000 votes were cast in favour, with 1 728 000 against, out of a total Conference voting strength of about 2½ million. What had happened to the missing pro-affiliation vote? In the event, big unions supposedly behind the Communist bid split their votes. A minority of the 145 000 AEU vote went to the opposition. Only 325 000 of the miners' 400 000 vote was cast for affiliation.[50] Dalton calculated that only 150 000 Divisional Labour Party voters, 'at most', supported the Communists.[51] ASLEF voted in favour, but it was the only other major union to do so. Hopes of obtaining the large distributive workers' vote were not fulfilled.

A subsequent vote on an AEU motion in favour of a meeting of 'representatives of all working class bodies to bring about a United Front' was voted down by 1 805 000 to 435 000. This time the miners, whose delegates had been opposed both to affiliation and to the united front but had felt mandated to vote for affiliation, voted against, while the AEU, whose mandate was more definite for the united front than for affiliation, voted more solidly in favour. The Communists derived some comfort from the calculation that a third of the Conference had voted for one resolution or the other, but they had little reason to do so.

9
Labour and the United Front

Support for a united front with the Communist Party developed gradually among Labour left-wingers, as tension between the Socialist League and the NEC increased, the international situation deteriorated and the Communist campaign gained momentum. The Socialist League backed Communist overtures to the NEC from the start. As early as April 1933, Cole, Tawney and Wise signed a letter to the Labour Movement calling for a united front.[1] While the Socialist League was still in its early 'loyal grousing' stage, however, it was not prepared to make a definite stand on the issue in the face of official hostility. A resolution at the League's first Annual Conference in 1933 favouring joint action by the League with the Communists and the ILP was defeated.[2] For the next two years the Socialist League continued to approach the issue cautiously: although it supported a united front in principle, as late as June 1935 it refused to be 'directed into activities definitely condemned by the Labour Party which will jeopardise our affiliation and influence within the Party'.[3] This attitude soon changed.

FASCISM AND THE LABOUR LEFT

As the domestic economic situation stabilised, and from 1934 began notably to improve, the Socialist League's cataclysmic message lost much of its relevance. Hitherto the most telling argument for a fully socialist policy, as against a gradualist one, had been that the capitalist system was on the point of collapse. Now it appeared that 'we have seen that the system has more kick in it than we had thought; we have seen that it will not die of its own accord'.[4] Partly for this reason, the League's attention shifted to the sphere in which the situation appeared unmistakably to be deteriorating – international affairs.

To the Socialist League, Dollfuss' takeover in Austria in 1934, the Abyssinian crisis in 1935, and most of all, the Spanish Civil War in 1936 seemed to point to a rising tide of world fascism, and to threaten an imperialist war which would enable the National Government to implement fascism at home. The League, unlike 'rearmers' in the Labour Party, did not single out

Hitler as a particular menace to peace; it regarded Germany as no more than a part of an international imperialist system whose inherent competitive strains would lead to war. As Cripps explained to the Bristol Conference of the Socialist League at Whitsun 1935:

> Fundamentally our problem is a simple one. We loathe and detest the whole idea of Imperialism, its fierce competition built upon the greed of capitalism, its exploitation of subject peoples and its selfish approach to all problems of foreign policy. Whether the imperialism is British, French, German, Italian or Japanese, it is equally wrong and equally certain in the long run to plunge the world into war.[5]

And the Conference concluded that 'In the attempt to perpetuate the territorial and economic maladjustments of the Peace Treaties the victorious capitalist powers are seeking by show of force to suppress the rapidly developing imperialist ambitions of Germany'.[6]

Consequently, the League of Nations, mainly composed of capitalist nations, did not and could not offer any security. As long as states remained dependent on the capitalist system, they would inevitably retain the right to defend the interests of the private owners who controlled them; and disinterested cooperation for the sake of peace was inconceivable. Hence any war undertaken against an 'aggressor' in the name of the League was to be resisted for two reasons. Because it would inevitably be an imperialist war which would solve nothing; and because it would help the ruling class to exploit and coerce the workers.

The Socialist League therefore opposed rearmament, opposed sanctions against Italy, and advocated a policy for the Labour Movement of preparing for 'the mass resistance to war', by which it meant a general strike, and perhaps a seizure of power by the workers. The latter was presented as the Socialist League's alternative to rearmament as a deterrent, but aimed at deterring the National Government.[7] The League's position was not pacifist, although it often found itself allied with Lansbury and the pacifists. Against official party policy, it supported the supply of arms to the Spanish Government. Its attitude, like that of the Labour Party until July 1937, was that only a socialist government could be trusted with the possession of armaments. But unlike the Party leadership, it took this position to its logical conclusion, and opposed any use of arms by the National Government, even in conjunction with the League of Nations. If Britain became socialist before other countries, it would be necessary to organise defence in association with other socialist states.

The Socialist League clashed repeatedly with the NEC on these issues. At Southport its amendments (which amounted to a redraft) of the NEC's document *War and Peace* demanded close relations with the Soviet Union as a substitute for reliance on the League of Nations, and called for the adoption of the policy of a general strike against war. Before the Brighton Conference in 1935, Cripps resigned from the NEC in order to present the Socialist League's case against sanctions more effectively.

At the Edinburgh Party Conference in 1936, the League both made ground and lost it. On rearmament, a confused debate in effect left the matter open, and paved the way for a coup by Dalton on the issue in the Parliamentary Party in July 1937. On Spain, an initial resolution backed by the National Council of Labour supporting non-intervention was withdrawn, after Spanish fraternal delegates had made an impassioned plea for aid. A new resolution was presented, demanding that the British and French governments should sell arms to the Spanish Government if other powers could be shown to be violating the Non-Intervention Pact. On Cripps' motion, this was strengthened with a phrase placing on record the Conference's view that the Fascist powers had already violated the Pact, and the whole resolution was carried unanimously.

Thus by the autumn of 1936 the Socialist League had some reason for encouragement, but at the same time the Party's attitude to rearmament was causing concern. Meanwhile, the Left felt its own impotence when it compared its position with that of French and Spanish comrades. Reports from members of the International Brigade, in particular, appeared to present a shining example of the possibilities open to socialists if they were able to forget their differences and act together in the struggle against fascism.

After the decision in November 1934 to become a 'mass organisation', the Socialist League embarked on a programme of demonstrations and agitation. The results were disappointing. New recruits on the Left went to the Communists. The Socialist League, like the ILP, was outflanked and ignored. This was in spite of the League's new General Secretary, J. T. Murphy, whose energy and enthusiasm were combined with a solid training in the organisational techniques of the CP. Murphy tried to create the atmosphere of a fighting unit, advancing with marxist commitment and determination towards its goal. He made strenuous efforts to tighten organisation by bringing Area Committees and branches more under the direction of the Executive. But it was a losing battle.

The November 1934 Conference had optimistically halved the subscription, in the belief that a consequential increase in working-class membership would more than compensate for the loss of revenue. It did not do so. A permanent deficit necessitated heavy dependence on the munificence of Sir Stafford Cripps.

The general election of October 1935 gave rise to a temporary truce between the Party's leadership and its left-wing. But once this was over, the Left was quick to draw a moral from the result. 'Socialism will not come in this country by democratic means through the Labour Party unless we learn the outstanding lesson of this last election, that our propaganda and policy must be so framed as to leave no doubt in the mind of any worker that we are determined to get rid of Capitalism and Imperialism'.[8] The National Council decided to make the League an even more autonomous body, following the decision of November 1934 to its logical conclusion. The League was to become a fully fledged political party, comparable with the ILP and CP, and differing from them only in that it was determined to remain affiliated to Labour. From now on, wrote Murphy, 'the League has to function more as an affiliated organisation of the Party than as an organisation of individuals diffusing Socialist League literature within the Party'.[9] The National Council launched a campaign consisting of 40 or 50 conferences and 'mass meetings' during February and March 1936, to 'challenge most clearly and boldly the reascendency of "gradualist views" within the Party and the whole Movement', and with the aim of doubling Socialist League membership.[10] In June, the recruiting drive was acknowledged to have failed, the 'mass meetings' had been poorly attended, and the subscription was restored to its 1934 level.

An independent role benefited the Socialist League no more than the ILP. At a time when events seemed to demand bold action more than ever, the League found itself isolated and ignored. The temptation to remedy the situation by means of united action with the Communists and the ILP was great.

The League's enthusiasm for a left-wing alliance was increased by the Blum Popular Front in France and by the outbreak of the Spanish Civil War. Like the ILP, however, the Socialist League opposed a 'Front Populaire' kind of grouping which included Radicals or Liberals. A broad popular front 'may be considered effective for the immediate purpose of opposition to reaction', wrote Cripps in March, 'especially when the forces of reaction are in power, but they carry with them the seeds of their own disintegration unless the working-class parties are prepared to abandon the class struggle as the basis of their political action'.[11] The only possibility was a united front of *working-class* organisations – which in Britain meant the ILP, the CP and the Labour Party. For the moment the CP agreed, because the Comintern could not as yet stomach an alliance with Lloyd George, architect of anti-Soviet intervention in 1919; but the Communist attitude soon changed to support for an open grouping of all 'progressive' forces.

Cripps' own attitude to the Communists typified that of many of the more credulous on the non-marxist Labour Left: the Communist change of heart should be taken at its face value; it would be foolish and unworthy to turn away a penitent prodigal with so many fine qualities. 'Up till recent times it was the avowed object of the Communist Party to discredit and destroy the social democratic parties such as the British Labour Party,' he wrote, 'and so long as that policy remained in force, it was impossible to contemplate any real unity'.[12] But things were different now. The Communists had 'disavowed any intention, for the present, of acting in opposition to the Labour Movement in the country, and certainly their action in many constituencies during the last election gives earnest of their disavowal'.[13]

Meanwhile the Left Book Club was forcing the pace with its local groups, bringing together socialists of all tendencies into a *de facto* united front which delighted the CP and highlighted the failure of the League to arouse the Labour rank and file. Socialist Leaguers and others on the Labour Left felt increasingly frustrated by the constraints of official Labour Party rulings. 'It is of paramount importance,' said Bevan in September, 'that our immediate efforts and energies should be directed to organising a United Front and a definite programme of action'.[14]

Leading left-wingers became increasingly involved in the Communist Party's campaign for a united front and for affiliation. By the autumn of 1936 the Socialist League was joining the CP, the ILP and various trades councils and trade union branches in the organisation of a large-scale Hunger March. 'Why,' asked Bevan, 'should a first-class piece of work like the Hunger March have been left to the initiative of unofficial members of the Party, and to the Communists and the ILP... Consider what a mighty response the workers would have made if the whole machinery of the Labour Movement had been mobilised for the Hunger March and its attendant activities.'[15]

An increase of fascist violence also met with a united response from the Left, again in the face of NEC opposition. The League was becoming increasingly open in its defiance of Party Conference and NEC directives. On 31 October the League itself called an anti-fascist Conference in the Whitechapel Art Gallery. The speakers 'were as representative as the delegates themselves', and the views of the Labour Party and Trade Union rank and file, of the CP, the ILP, the League of Youth and various Jewish organisations together with those of the Socialist League were put before the Conference.[16] A Committee of 25 was elected to carry on the work of controlling Mosley in the East End.

The Edinburgh Party Conference's rejection of Communist affiliation, and of the united front, had merely increased the Socialist League's determination to defy the official leadership and act on its own initiative. An open breach between local parties and the trade unions and NEC, sharpened by a bitter clash at the Edinburgh Conference, seemed to give added justification for this defiance. The League gave full support to the constituency parties' movement, and Cripps became chairman of the newly founded Constituency Parties Association, no doubt hoping to gain local party sympathy for his activities. Relations between the minuscule League and the big battalions of the trade unions and the NEC were rapidly moving towards a state of open war.

NEGOTIATIONS

It was against this background that Cripps had initiated a series of 'long and difficult discussions'[17] in the summer of 1936 with representatives of the ILP and CP with the object of launching a Unity Campaign. These negotiations demonstrated the divisions which separated left-wing groups as much as the common ground between them.[18]

The League was represented by Cripps and Mellor, the Communists by Pollitt and Dutt, and the ILP by Maxton and Brockway. Tension quickly arose between the ILP and the CP. This reflected a backlog of suspicions and antipathies, and found expression in an important difference of policy. A year earlier the Communists had rejected the possibility of having anything to do with the Liberals. Now their view had changed. They wanted to include in the Unity Campaign's manifesto a demand for a full Popular Front, on the French or Spanish model, including all opponents of the National Government. The purist ILP refused to accept this; Maxton and Brockway were not prepared to have any dealings with capitalist parties and insisted on a 'Workers' Front' of proletarian parties alone. The Socialist League adjudicated, and since Mellor agreed with the ILP on this issue, the campaign was limited to the pursuit of an exclusive united front of 'working-class' parties.

Nevertheless, the discussions almost broke down on the exceedingly academic question of which countries a socialist Britain should seek as allies. The Communists wanted these to include capitalist countries as well as Russia. The ILP demanded a pact with working-class governments alone – but with Russia excluded. That the Campaign manifesto's formula on this point would have no conceivable bearing on Britain's future international alignments was apparently not regarded as relevant. In the end Cripps found a solution, in an ILP agreement to differ. These differences were on a theoretical level, but they masked a deep mutual distrust which excluded any real unity of purpose. The CP and ILP were still licking wounds from a fratricidal conflict which had much more reality, and contained much more personal animosity, than the struggle with the remote Labour Party leadership or even more remote National Government.

The newest supporters of the idea of a Unity Campaign were the representatives of the Socialist League – and especially Cripps. Cripps was the key figure, because of his standing in the Labour Party and in the country; both the ILP and the CP saw the value of associating with him. Brockway felt that making use of Cripps for Communist ends was Pollitt's main motive:

> [Pollitt] wooed him assiduously; playing up to him in committees, staying on for chats with him after committees. I was fully aware, of course, of Pollitt's moves in the struggle going on underneath the superficial

> unity of our committee, the struggle as to whether the Popular Front
> view of the CP or the Workers' Front view of the ILP should win the
> allegiance of the Left in the Labour Movement.[19]

Brockway regarded Cripps during the negotiations as something of an
eager child, and referred to his 'simple enthusiasm'.[20] Cripps appeared 'at
sea' in the theoretical discussion,[21] which was scarcely surprising of one who
admitted that he had never read a word of Marx.[22]

Cripps, ever open to the influence of a new *guru*, especially a conspicuous-
ly working-class one, had indeed fallen under Pollitt's spell. For the time
being Mellor, who had become Chairman of the Socialist League, prevailed
on the issue of whether to pursue the united front or the popular front.[23]
But Cripps had already moved further than many of his colleagues in the
League towards the Communist position and Pollitt exploited this situation
to the full, leading him on with great skill, careful to restrain his impetuosity
and his impulse to follow through his principles to their logical conclusion,
regardless of consequences. The splits in the Labour Party from 1936 to
1939 owed much to Pollitt's adept management of Cripps.

AGREEMENT

According to the eventual agreement, the objective of the Unity Campaign
was 'unity of all sections of the working-class movement within the framework of the Labour Party and Trade Unions in common struggle against
Fascism, Reaction and War, and for the immediate demands of the worker,
in order to develop the strength and unity of the working-class for the
defeat of the National Government'. This was to be 'built upon the basis
of day to day struggle for immediate limited objectives by mass action, industrial and political, and through the democratisation of the Labour Party
and Trade Union Movement.'[24]

Only the Socialist League, and particularly the undevious Cripps, had
accepted this objective as it was stated. The CP's aim was to further its
own campaign to affiliate to the Labour Party – or at least to win sympathy inside the Labour Party through its attempt to do so. The ILP
joined partly to end its own debilitating isolation and partly as a matter
of principle. Maxton, who was opposed to the reaffiliation of the ILP,
was highly sceptical about the whole operation.[25] Brockway, though he
had come to the conclusion that the ILP must reaffiliate or fade away,[26]
later justified his support for the Campaign entirely negatively. Acknowledging that the Campaign was a disastrous failure, he asserted that
'if I am asked whether the ILP made a mistake in entering the campaign,
my answer is "No". The effect would have been disastrous if we had
refused the invitation of the Socialist League to participate in an effort
to realise what was in the heart of every class-conscious worker – the

need for the unity of the working-class.'[27] Cripps, on the other hand, felt that an injection of extreme left blood into the Labour Party would be regenerative:

> The Communist Party and the ILP may not represent very large num-
> bers, but all of us who have knowledge of militant working-class activities
> throughout the country are bound to admit that Communists and
> ILPers have played and are playing a very fine part in such activities...
> Just as unity has wrought wonders in Spain, inspiring and encouraging
> the Spanish workers with a heroism past all praise, so in our, as yet,
> less arduous struggle it can give new life and vitality.[28]

For Brailsford, similarly, the Campaign was an effort to bring 'new and vital forces' into the official movement.

> [T]he Labour Party has ceased to be the natural vehicle for the emo-
> tions and aspirations of the masses – their anger, their hope, their
> impulses of humanity and gallantry. It tends to become a mere elec-
> tioneering machine. My case is, in a sentence, that this jealous boycott
> of the Left impoverishes and narrows the Party.[29]

The international situation provided the imperative. 'The parties to the agreement realise that unless the National Government is brought down,' wrote Mellor, 'and virile Labour placed in power, the working class will be massacred in the most appalling imperialist war of all time, and that soon.'[30] But how could the Unity Campaign ever have achieved this? The view that marches, rallies and demonstrations could even win over Labour Party Conference or the NEC ignored the big trade union bloc votes, firmly in the hands of leaders implacably hostile to Communist affiliation.

The reality was that the Unity Campaign partners were involved in a private game based on long traditions and complicated rules which had no relevance to the shaping of major events, or to the factors which influenced real electors as opposed to an idealised image of the working class. 'Instead of realising that it is not only the faults of Labour policy but also the sheer facts of "prosperity" which are maintaining the National Government in power', wrote Richard Crossman,

> they dilate on the need for Communist affiliation and a strong policy
> with regard to Spain, as though these items were of the slightest interest
> to any save the minority of politically conscious electors. Such critics
> frame their propaganda to satisfy their own tastes and neglect the simple
> fact that it is not they but the Tory voters who must be converted. Their
> busy activity is self-intoxicating, but millions of people still read the
> racing page, because, on the whole, conditions are not bad enough to
> drive them to politics, and they have not seen a Labour canvasser for
> five years, far less seen any signs of practical activity by the local
> Labour Party.'[31]

In the League, enthusiasm for the Campaign was largely confined to the leaders. The final details of the agreement were worked out by mid-December, after months of intense 'secret' negotiations which had been the subject of general gossip. But the rank and file were not told about the decision until it was a *fait accompli*. This angered many people in the League's local branches. The *News Chronicle* (which favoured progressive alliances) predicted that the League's leaders would face a split when the proposal was put to a Conference of Socialist League delegates on 16 and 17 January 1937, 'for a substantial section of Sir Stafford Cripps' followers are indignant at the bargain which has been concluded behind their back.'[32] The Labour Executive had met on 8 January and indicated that disaffiliation was likely to follow if the League's plans became operational; on 13 January it issued a stern warning in the form of a circular letter entitled 'Party Loyalty – An Appeal to the Movement'. The probability of being thrown out of the Party did not appeal to those who had joined the Socialist League precisely because of its commitment to affiliation.

The special Socialist League Conference was held in a West End tea room. It was scarcely an advertisement for the Unity which the League's leaders hoped to propagate. There were bitter clashes. Eventually the Unity document was accepted by a narrow margin and on a minority vote – 56 in favour, 38 against, with 23 abstentions.[33] This majority was only obtained because a number of provincial delegates mandated to vote against were persuaded by Cripps that disaffiliation was unlikely, and broke their mandates to abstain or vote in favour.[34] Even so, it appears that the decision to participate in the Campaign was supported by representatives of a few hundred members of the League at most.[35]

After the Conference, dissenting delegates, including some from Lancashire, Cumberland and South Wales, held a private meeting to express their angry opposition. '[T]he Unity agreement,' wrote one who was at this meeting, '...is a complete desertion of the principles governing the League's constitution. Disintegration has already set in. In the end, what will remain of the membership is more likely to be absorbed by the Communist Party.'[36]

The *Daily Telegraph* commented with some justice that 'What has been announced in the fashionable phrase as a "united front" might be better styled in the terms of an older fashion, the "divided skirt", embarrassing the staider members of the Socialist community.'[37]

10
'Unity'

The Unity Manifesto was issued immediately after the Socialist League Conference. It demanded a massive fight against fascism, unconditional opposition to rearmament and recruiting, a pact between Great Britain, France and Russia and 'all other States in which the working-class has political freedom', nationalisation of the arms industry and democratisation of the armed forces. It called for national work plans, the forty hour week, pensions of £1 per week at 60, increases in income tax on higher incomes, heavier death duties, control of 'stock exchange gambling' and of private profiteering, nationalisation of the mines, higher wages, holidays with pay and the abolition of the Means Test.

There were, however, notes of reservation which pointed the way to future difficulties. The ILP held back from affiliation to the Labour Party 'until democratisation has taken place'. All parties agreed to abstain from any general criticism of the Soviet Union and its Government – a hard pill for the ILP to swallow – and while the CP was allowed to demand that the National Government should adopt a pact with France and Russia, the Socialist League claimed the right to emphasise the need for a change of government before such a policy could be implemented.[1]

The campaign opened officially with a large meeting at the Free Trade Hall in Manchester on 24 January. Cripps, Mellor, Maxton and Pollitt spoke. 3763 'pledge cards', pledging support for the aims of the campaign, were signed. Even the hostile *Daily Herald* described the reception of the speakers as 'enthusiastic'.[2] Harry Pollitt, in particular, received an ovation. The Campaign, he said, was not directed against the Labour Party: 'On the contrary, the whole central aim was directed to strengthening the Labour Party, the trade unions, and the co-operative movement so that the Labour Party in Great Britain would become the real united expression of the whole of the political thought and development of the working-class.'[3]

Three days later the Labour Executive disaffiliated the Socialist League, making nonsense of the declared aim of increasing 'unity' by gaining affiliation for the CP and even the ILP.[4]

After this, the 'Unity Committee' organised a series of demonstrations at which Socialist Leaguers, ILPers and Communists spoke from the same platform, and which captured the headlines. 'We marched in demonstrations to Trafalgar Square and Whitehall to hear men like Stafford Cripps, Aneurin Bevan and the Communist leaders Harry Pollitt and William Gallacher...denounce the National Government, and call for a united front, nationally and internationally, against fascism and war,' Lord (Ted) Willis, who was on the extreme left in the Labour League of Youth, recalls in his memoirs. 'With clenched fists held aloft we chanted as we marched: "Red front, red front, red united fighting front!"...It was all fine heady stuff, and we returned home with our enthusiasm renewed, confident that we had that day significantly advanced the cause of socialism and anti-fascism.'[5]

Michael Foot maintains that 'week after week the Unity Campaign held its massive demonstrations'.[6] Yet in the first four weeks, the Campaign's eight 'mass demonstrations' rallied a total of only 12 000 supporters, even by the Unity Committee's own estimates.[7] This compared sadly with the success of the Left Book Club, which was able to muster 7000 members at one rally in the Albert Hall early in February.[8] On 24 March the Unity Committee issued a progress report. Nearly 100 local committees were in action, it announced proudly. 'Pledge card signatures' numbered 18 000 and collections at 41 demonstrations had brought in more than £1200.[9] But the League had itself claimed to have more than 100 branches; the combined membership of the three bodies exceeded 15 000 (on paper at least) and a total of 205 000 pledge cards had been distributed. After ten weeks of the Campaign, the Committee's figures were scarcely impressive.

SPAIN

Meanwhile behind the scenes 'Unity' was rapidly degenerating amid wrangles between the League and the NEC on the one hand, and between the ILP and the CP on the other. Within a fortnight of the start of the Campaign, an issue which had been bothering the ILP (and some members of the League) for some time began to cause serious friction with the CP. Certain aspects of the Moscow trials were becoming a major worry and embarrassment to more open-minded left-wingers. Cripps was inclined to regard the trials as an internal matter for the Soviet Union. D. N. Pritt gave them his enthusiastic support. But there were others in the Socialist League who spoke out against them; and the ILP demanded an international commission to investigate the question. This annoyed the Communists, who asked that speakers should refrain from discussing the trials at United Front meetings.[10] The issue was decisive in killing the Campaign in the autumn.[11] Before then relations between the Communists and the ILP had deteriorated beyond repair because of developments in another country – Spain.

The ILP had associated itself with POUM, a revolutionary party which had come increasingly under attack from Spanish Communists. In December 1936 Andrés Nin, a POUM leader, had been manoeuvred out of the Catalan Government. By March 1937 POUM leaders were being denounced as 'agents of Fascism'; in May clashes between Communists, Anarchists and POUM supporters resulted in hundreds of dead and wounded. In June POUM was declared illegal and its leaders were imprisoned, including Nin, who was tortured by the Communists and finally murdered by the International Brigade.[12]

In all these events the ILP, which had sent a contingent to serve with POUM, and the CPGB, which organised the British end of the International Brigade, had an intense practical and emotional involvement. Members of the ILP contingent[13] on leave in Barcelona at the time of the May riots were hunted down by the Communists, and Bob Smillie, grandson of the famous miners' leader and son of Alex Smillie, a Scottish ILP leader, was arrested as he tried to slip across the frontier. He died in a Communist gaol in Valencia. Bob Smillie had been Chairman of the ILP Guild of Youth, and Brockway wrote of him 'Without exception, he was the finest lad I ever knew.'[14]

While all this was happening the *Daily Worker* kept up a steady barrage of vilification against POUM, which British sympathisers of the Republican cause in Liberal and Labour circles, reluctant to think ill of the dominant group on the Government side, were inclined to accept. Thus Kingsley Martin refused to accept a series of articles by Orwell favourable to POUM. 'I did not love the Communists, but I knew that the Spanish Government was compelled to give them too much power because no country except the Soviet Union was aiding the Republican cause. I probably underestimated the Communist atrocities.'[15]

Bitterness between the ILP and the British Communist Party reached a pitch never before known. Members of the two groups may actually have been killing each other in Catalonia. Yet in Britain the pretence of 'Unity' was not interrupted. Brockway suggested to the Unity Committee that he, Cripps and Pollitt should go to Spain with the noble but absurd aim of seeking to re-establish unity in the anti-fascist ranks. Cripps was sympathetic, but Pollitt, not surprisingly, refused. 'We had to leave the matter with my declaration that despite the Unity Campaign, the ILP considered it its duty to vindicate its Spanish comrades', wrote Brockway: 'The Campaign went on; Pollitt and I spoke together from the same platform and were both scrupulously careful not to reflect our Party differences, but the inner spirit of unity was dead.'[16]

SCOTTISH SOCIALISTS

Meanwhile the ILP was involved in a much more petty quarrel – with the Scottish Socialist Party (SSP). When the ILP disaffiliated in 1932 the affiliationists had at first intended that the Socialist League should include breakaway Scottish ILP branches. Instead a leading Scottish affiliationist, P. J. Dollan, persuaded Scottish branches to form a separate body, which like the League affiliated to the Labour Party. The SSP survived until 1940, engaging (unlike its English equivalent) in local election battles with the ILP, and propagating a staunch pacifism.

Its relations with the official Scottish ILP were bad from the start. The central issue between them concerned not policy but money. The ILP claimed that property and funds held by branches split by disaffiliation should revert to itself. The SSP's position was summed up by Dollan at a Glasgow conference of affiliationist branches in August 1932: 'Whoever may claim to be the ILP, we in this hall are the ILP.'[17] A protracted legal wrangle followed, in which the Labour Party Executive gave the SSP financial support. The SSP, meanwhile, kept in close touch with the Socialist League, and in March 1936 negotiations for an amalgamation were initiated; the plan was for a federation which would give each organisation national autonomy.

At first the SSP refused to go along with the League in its support for Communist affiliation;[18] however, when the proposal for a Unity Campaign began to be discussed, the SSP did not want to be left out and changed its mind.[19] But an obstacle to the SSP's inclusion in the Campaign remained – its continuing dispute with the ILP. The outstanding problem was a sum of £200 which had been accumulated by former members of the Hamilton branch of the ILP, now in the SSP. A court decision had awarded this money to the ILP; the matter was due to come up again before the Edinburgh Court of Session; the ILP had every reason to expect that the previous decision would be upheld. At the end of 1936 the SSP wrote to the Scottish Council of the ILP suggesting that the long dispute over funds and property should be settled in an amicable way as an indication that both sides favoured socialist unity. But the Scottish ILP, with a dwindling membership and in chronic financial difficulties, was not prepared to buy SSP support for the Unity Campaign at this price. It therefore rejected the SSP's suggestion, and insisted that the legal proceedings must take their course.[20]

The SSP did not join the Unity Campaign; and negotiations for amalgamation with the Socialist League petered out. An SSP Conference in March 1937 rejected a pro-Unity Campaign motion by 114 to 76[21] – a majority which in friendlier circumstances might have gone the other way. The Scottish ILP saved a few pounds, but missed a chance to embarrass the NEC by forcing it to disaffiliate two socialist societies instead of one.

COLLAPSE

'Unity' was, however, already doomed. The Labour Executive soon began to take sterner disciplinary measures than mere disaffiliation. The 'hawks' on the Executive, led by Arthur Greenwood who reflected the point of view of Transport House officials, had favoured outright expulsion for the rebels from the start.[22] Such a step had been widely expected. 'If [Cripps] really seeks that alliance he will have to withdraw from the Labour Party' the *Manchester Guardian* had commented on 22 December. Next day the *News Chronicle* predicted that 'If the plan is persisted in it is certain that the Socialist League will be expelled and Sir Stafford Cripps will cease to be a member of the Labour Party.' But a majority on the Executive preferred to play a waiting game. Many were reluctant to drive men of the ability and stature of Cripps, Mellor, Bevan, Brailsford, Strauss, Pritt and Laski out of the Movement, and were inclined to hold fire until the reaction of the rank and file could be gauged. There was, moreover, strong pressure from Labour leaders who did not endorse the Campaign, but strongly opposed expulsions. Some of them, including Cole, Lansbury, and several other Labour MPs wrote to the NEC late in January urging it not to start a 'heresy hunt'.[23]

Cripps, meanwhile, needled the Executive with outrageous speeches. In November 1936 he told a Stockport audience that he 'did not believe it would be a bad thing for the British working-class if Germany defeated us. It would be a disaster to the profit-makers and capitalists, but not necessarily for the working-class'.[24] The NEC immediately dissociated itself from this speech, and carpeted Cripps. But Cripps refused to turn up to a special sub-committee of Dalton, George Dallas, Lathan and Middleton formed to reprimand him.[25] Though furious, the Executive dared not act against him. His standing in large sections of the Party was too high. The constituency parties loved him. The PLP respected him as one of its two or three most effective spokesmen on any subject, and his fine service during the 1931 Parliament had not been forgotten. The miners also backed him, partly because of his brilliant advocacy, free of charge, on behalf of the North Wales Miners' Association at the Gresford Colliery inquiry in 1935 (and also because of the strength of the Communists in the miners' leadership). Even those who attacked Cripps most fiercely recognised his value to the Movement.

Yet reaction against the Unity Campaign was strong. 'I saw Mosley come into the Labour Movement,' thundered Bevin, 'and I see no difference in the tactics of Mosley and Cripps'.[26] Morrison forbade London County Councillors from contributing to the Communist press under threat of the direst penalties – a move clearly aimed at G. R. Strauss.[27] The expulsion of Cripps, and perhaps others, was widely predicted for the NEC meeting at the end of February, though it was clear that the Executive was sharply divided. 'It looks about twenty to one that Stafford will be expelled from the party,' Laski wrote privately in mid-February, 'about five to one that I shall be too...We shall know next week when the Executive decides.'[28]

A loyal defender of Cripps was, however, the Party Leader himself. 'I shall of course do all that is in my power to oppose disaffiliations [*sic*] though it will not be easy as Stafford and Co. have played into the hands of every Right-wing influence in the party besides offending a vast mass of members who are not Right-wing but who will not stand for the flouting of Conference decisions', Attlee wrote to Laski on 22 February.

> This is the real folly, due, I fear, to a lack of understanding of the move-ment . . . The real difficulty will be in meeting the argument that the offenders against party discipline are prominent and for the most part middle-class people and that they should not be treated differently from rank-and-file members who offend and are dealt with by their local parties for infractions of discipline. I fight all the time against heresy hunting, but the heretics seem to seek martyrdom.[29]

Cripps, indeed, seemed to be relishing the role of St Sebastian. 'This may be one of the last speeches I shall make as a member of the Labour Party', he told Oxford undergraduates on 19 February,[30] before getting onto a train to Glasgow where he announced happily 'I am hanging by the skin of my teeth, but I propose to hang on as long as I can.'[31]

What saved him was a brilliant speech in the House of Commons on 23 February. By chance, the Report of the Royal Commission on the Gresford Mining Disaster was the subject of debate. Cripps was the inevitable choice to lead; his outstanding performance was an embarrassing reminder of the loss the Movement would suffer by ejecting him. The next day the NEC held an eight hour meeting at Transport House. It postponed a decision on Cripps and the League. 'How could we use an axe on Sir Stafford after his Gresford Colliery speech of last night?' said one member afterwards. 'It would be most inopportune while the London County Council Elections are on', said another.[32]

This proved to be more than a stay of execution. Cripps and his associates were preserved from outright expulsion. Nevertheless further disciplinary action was to follow soon. Once the LCC elections were over, and had resulted in a second Labour victory, the NEC felt freer to tie the matter up.

Twelve members of the Labour Party Regional Organising staff had already been canvassed for their views. Most demanded the sternest possible measures against the rebels. 'It must be our discipline or the Communist Party discipline', wrote one. Hinley Atkinson, London organiser and Morrison's right-hand man, expressed concern at Socialist League efforts to take over constituency General Committees. One woman organiser claimed that there was a move 'to get the wives of Communists to join the Women's Sections so that they can get their point home, and get the Sections to send delegates to the various Conferences'. She asked for 'a

definite ruling on these matters'. These were the noises Transport House
wanted to hear.[33] The organising staff at Transport House was set on taking
a tough line. It produced a private memorandum claiming that the Campaign was controlled by the Communists, pointing to a link-up with Ben
Greene's 'disruptionist movement',[34] and hinting darkly about large-scale
financial backing. It concluded that 'we are really confronted with the
necessity of either declaring once more our complete independence of the
Communist Party or completely changing our policy towards it'.[35]

DISSOLUTION

The NEC moved at last on 24 March, declaring that members of the Socialist
League would be ineligible for Labour Party membership from 1 June.
Morrison, though widely regarded as a hard-line party disciplinarian, tried
with Attlee's support to postpone a decision yet again, and leave the matter
to Conference. His amendment to this effect was, however, defeated by 14
votes to 6, and the main motion banning League membership was passed
nem.con.[36] The Socialist League now had to decide whether the pursuit
of 'Unity' was worth the price of excommunication.

Cripps decided that it was not. Backed (and perhaps persuaded) by
Pollitt he decided to jettison the League. Many members were taken aback.
Up to this point Cripps had seemed to be seeking precisely this kind of
confrontation. Now he and Pollitt advanced the elaborate argument that
by dissolving the League the NEC would have to deal with individuals, and
this would widen the resistance by bringing in a considerable number of
influential Labour MPs and trade union officials who were not members of
the League.[37]

Mellor disagreed strongly. He emphasised 'the importance of the
League as an organised unit in the Labour Party'.[38] But the League had
become a unit outside it; and as membership of the Labour Party had
always been the central justification of the League, there was never any
real possibility of its continued existence. So although Mellor was the more
consistent, Cripps' position was more realistic. In any case, the League was
falling apart. When the Campaign started, a large section of the membership had seceded;[39] more members drifted away in the weeks that followed.
Between January and May, the League's membership slumped from 3000 to
1600. Without wealthy patrons, the League's national organisation would
have collapsed completely. In May it was revealed that members' subscrip-
tions for the past year had amounted to a mere £198; a special appeal for
£1000 to meet the deficit had raised a paltry £24. As before, rich supporters
had come to the rescue, donating the huge sum of £1807 between them. No
names were given, but Cripps was known to be by far the most generous
contributor.[40]

This had been causing the League some embarrassment. Dalton taunted the League with being 'little more than a rich man's toy' and suggested that Cripps was getting tired of paying to keep it alive. 'The so-called Unity Campaign was being financed by one or two rich men. If it were deprived of these plutocratic props, the whole agitation would speedily collapse'.[41] Middleton spoke of 'large sums of money, the sources of which are not disclosed, being spent on the Campaign'. Mellor denied this hotly. 'No rich men are subverting the Campaign. There is no Moscow gold'.[42] This was doubtless true. But Mellor was not able to deny that the Socialist League was kept going by rich backers, or that Cripps and Strauss were paying heavily to keep *Tribune* afloat. Yet the attacks were ungenerous. As the *New Statesman and Nation* pointed out, the wealth of Cripps and Strauss was not a matter for complaint by Dalton when they subscribed to Labour Party funds.[43]

The dissolution Conference of the League was held in Leicester on 17 May. Only half the surviving branches sent delegates. A ten hour private session was heated and acrimonious. A telegram from H. N. Brailsford in Spain was read out at the start. Bráilsford had heard of League disbandment intentions. As this would be a 'political blunder of the first magnitude' he wished to resign from the League altogether. A minority agreed, and wanted the League to carry on. But most accepted Barbara Betts' formula that dissolution was 'not a funeral but a conscious political tactic', and voted for disbandment, though also for the continuation of the Unity Campaign.[44]

The latter was effectively dead, but Cripps was still trying to resuscitate the corpse. 'My own position I want to make clear', he told *Tribune* readers after the Conference: 'I regard the Unity Campaign and all it means and stands for as the one real hope for the working-class movement of this country to-day, and whatever comes I shall stick by that campaign'.[45] The Campaign now consisted, in theory, of a partnership between Labour Party individual members and the ILP and CP. This did not last long. A few day later the NEC warned Strauss that if he appeared on the same platform as Communists and ILPers at an advertised meeting in Hull he would be expelled. Strauss wanted to take up the challenge. But Cripps, with Pollitt's support, decided to retreat yet again. The National Unity Campaign Committee dissolved itself, claiming absurdly that it had 'conducted one of the most successful campaigns in the history of the Labour Movement'.[46]

Labour members of the Unity Committee now set up a separate Labour Unity Committee, with separate local unity committees, in order to keep within the letter of the NEC's directives. These finally wound up after the Bournemouth Party Conference in October. Long before this, the quarrel among the parties in the Campaign over Spain and the Moscow Trials had become embarrassingly public. Even Cripps commented on the irony of holding unity meetings at which members of two of the parties supposedly seeking unity were selling literature at the door bitterly attacking each other.[47]

At Party Conference, Cripps made a fine speech about unity, almost managing to avoid mentioning the Communist Party entirely. But the major bloc votes were already mandated in support of the Executive, and those delegates whose minds were still open found Morrison more persuasive. 'Would Mr Pollitt appear on a platform with Socialist, Working-class Trotsky?' he asked. 'He would not. If some of the leaders of the POUM in Spain, a Working-class Party, came to London, and the ILP wanted another United Front platform with them and Mr Pollitt, Mr Pollitt would not appear'.[48] The reference back of the Executive's rulings on the Socialist League was rejected by 1 730 000 to 373 000; the Executive's position on the United Front was endorsed by 2 116 000 to 331 000 – far more decisively than in 1936.[49] Faced with these decisions Cripps ended the Campaign.

What had it achieved? 'Its result was the destruction of the Socialist League, the loss of influence of Cripps, Bevan, Strauss and other "Lefts",' wrote Brockway, 'the strengthening of the reactionary leaders, and the disillusionment of the rank and file'.[50] Yet its consequences were much more far reaching than this. The Unity Campaign had been concerned with an exclusive alliance among 'working-class' parties. By the end of the Campaign many of its supporters (and especially those in or close to the CP) were also supporting the idea of a 'Popular Front' of all opponents of the National Government. Others were moving in that direction. 'Before we adopt a Popular Front,' Brailsford had said, expressing one view, 'the working-class must show a unity within itself'.[51] But the truth was that the campaign for 'unity' went far to discredit all alliances, whether to the right or to the left. The bitter antagonism created by united front activities tainted any other policy favoured by the Left – especially if it received enthusiastic Communist backing. When the Left switched to the practical politics of a progressive electoral alliance which should include the Liberals, its arguments fell on deaf ears.

At the same time, those in the party who had been suggesting for a long time that the only way to beat the Government was through a centre alliance with Liberals and progressive Tories, had been inhibited by the Left from pressing their case. It was embarrassing to attack the Left for associating with other socialist parties while themselves associating with capitalist ones. Consistency required an exclusiveness which cut the Labour Party off from contacts with the centre as well as the Left. As early as 1936, when Conference rejected a United Front it also rejected 'any attempts to "liberalise" the Labour Party by watering down its policy in order to increase its membership' – a move against those who sought a programme aimed at winning Liberal support.[52]

APPENDIX: TRIBUNE

The Socialist League's most enduring legacy was the weekly paper *Tribune*, launched on 1 January 1937. Conceived after the 1936 Edinburgh Party Conference as an independent paper which 'would advocate vigorous Socialism and demand active resistence to Fascism at home and abroad',[53] it replaced the Socialist League organ the *Socialist* and aimed at a wider public. Inspired by the recent success of the Left Book Club, its backers convinced themselves that it would be possible to establish a 50 000 sale for a twopenny weekly 'in a matter of weeks on the crest of the enthusiasm guaranteed by the Unity Campaign'.[54] The editorial board included Bevan, Ellen Wilkinson, G. R. Strauss, Laski, Brailsford and Mitchison, with Cripps as Chairman and Mellor, who had once edited the *Daily Herald*, as editor.

Tribune became a permanent part of British political journalism, a spring-board for a variety of distinguished writers, and the established house journal of the Labour Left. In its earliest days, it was also a training ground for a couple of young socialists who were to emerge after the War as two of the most effective left-wing leaders: the close association of Barbara Castle (then Barbara Betts) and Michael Foot with Aneurin Bevan, which lasted the rest of Bevan's life and profoundly affected post-war British politics, began in *Tribune*'s offices in 1937. Betts (who had written for the *Socialist Leaguer* and the *Socialist*) and Foot were both members of *Tribune*'s original staff; Bevan wrote a weekly column for the paper on events in Parliament.[55] Possibly as important as the association of these three was the close involvement of all of them, especially Foot and Betts, with William Mellor, 'the granite-like socialist conscience of the Socialist League'.[56] Barbara Betts, youngest member of the League's National Council since 1936, formed a close relationship with Mellor, 'one of the principal influences in her life'.[57]

Mellor's editorship was brief. This was because of the political vagaries of Cripps, and the power his money gave him. Whatever encouragement *Tribune* provided to the Labour Left, the first few weeks showed that the paper's founders had made a serious financial miscalculation. The Unity Campaign, on which they had pinned their hopes, failed to provide a circulation which approached the level needed for solvency. Sales figures were so bitterly disappointing that the paper nearly collapsed. It was rescued by a massive injection of funds, principally from Cripps and Strauss, who put up £20 000 between them,[58] and over the next few years, *Tribune*'s financial problems necessitated an identification with its chairman which belied its claim to independence.[59]

When, in 1938, Cripps switched from support for an exclusive working-class 'united front' to support for a 'popular front' of all progressive forces, he wanted *Tribune* to change its policy too. Mellor dug in his heels. Cripps, influenced by the Left Book Club triumvirate of Gollancz, Laski and Strachey, and moving closer to the position of the Communists, forced Mellor's resignation. Cripps thereupon offered the editorship to the young Michael Foot. Foot, disgusted by the shoddy way in which Mellor had been treated, refused. H. J. Hartshorn was appointed instead, and for a time *Tribune*'s analysis closely reflected that of the *Daily Worker*. In 1940, however, the idiosyncratic Cripps ejected Hartshorn for sticking too closely to the Communist line. *Tribune*'s early history, indeed, fully justified the derisive nickname 'Cripps's Chronicle'.[60]

Part Three
Rank and File

14

Repression

11

Repression

The activities of Sir Stafford Cripps made good copy. Reporters flocked to the meetings of 'the red squire' who took delight in embarrassing his staider colleagues, and who could usually be relied upon for remarks of outrageous subversiveness. Cripps' Socialist League was not, however, the only Labour Party pressure group battling against Transport House. Out of the lime-light, local activists were involved in another, far more representative, skil-ful and successful assault on entrenched Executive attitudes. Unlike the Socialist League, the unofficial 'Constituency Parties Movement' was a genuine outgrowth of local feeling. Unlike the League, it obtained massive support within the Party. Instead of tackling the leadership on the whole range of policy, it concentrated on a few, attainable, demands. Greatest contrast of all, it achieved its main objective – a fundamental change in the Party Constitution and in the balance of membership on the National Executive.

The real influence of the NEC has varied – depending on the strength of the Parliamentary Party, on the relationship between the trade unions and the Party leadership, and on whether Labour has been in or out of office. Yet, in spite of fluctuations, the National Executive has always been the most powerful body in the Labour Party outside Parliament.[1] Constitutionally the sovereign body in the Party is Annual Conference. But between Confer-ences it is the National Executive which is in charge of all aspects of Party organisation, discipline and policy; it is the Executive which submits policy resolutions, and detailed policy declarations, to Conference for approval; and it is the Executive, in conjunction with the Cabinet (when Labour is in power) or the Shadow Cabinet (when it is not) which determines the content of Labour's election manifesto. Hence for the Labour Party and for the British political system the composition of, and method of election to, the National Executive are of the highest significance. It was these that the Constituency Parties Movement sought, successfully, to alter.

The Constituency Parties Movement achieved this in spite of the backing of the far left. Cripps and Labour's left-wing stood to gain from an achieve-ment of the local parties' demands – and the change has helped the Labour

Left ever since. Yet it is significant that this one successful movement was not led by left-wingers. Its key leaders wisely sought to avoid identification with ideological factions. When, as the movement seemed to be making progress, the Left joined in, its support was more an embarrassment than an asset. Maladroit attempts by left-wingers to widen the area of conflict with the Executive very nearly sabotaged the whole enterprise.

The Constituency Parties Movement was in no sense a rival to the Labour Party: it *was* the Labour Party. It was firmly based on the local bodies it claimed to represent; with no individual members, its leaders were accountable to accredited delegates of the official organisations of the Labour Party rank and file, which, by 1936, included the vast majority of constituency parties active enough to be represented at Annual Conference. Its success marked the coming of age of Labour's growing non-union membership, ending a period of nearly twenty years in which the extra-Parliamentary Party had been answerable only to the trade unions. It also showed how pressure *could* be effectively exerted on the party leadership – providing a contrast between the 'instrumental' approach to politics of its main leaders, and the 'expressive' approach of left-wingers who supported it.

THE PARTY CONSTITUTION AND THE RANK AND FILE

Constituency activists had been nurturing a major grievance for a long time. They resented their absolute exclusion from the decision-making process of the Party at national level. 'Party democracy' did not take them into account. Local parties[2] had no direct representatives on the National Executive. Their vote at annual Party Conference was tiny, and their ability to affect Conference decisions was negligible. In the twenties, individual members had been able to feel that they had some influence because the number and proportion of MPs sponsored by Divisional Labour Parties had steadily increased.[3] The outcome of the 1931 election destroyed this link between the PLP and the constituencies. The atrophied Parliamentary Party contained only 13 members sponsored by constituency parties. In the 1930s the expanding individual membership felt a new sense of isolation and impotence.

Non-unionists had originally been granted a very high status in the political wing of the Labour Movement. When the Labour Representation Committee (LRC) was founded in 1900, the socialist societies were treated generously. Total membership of the societies – the Independent Labour Party, the Social Democratic Federation (SDF) and the Fabian Society – was barely a twenty-fifth of the membership of affiliated trade unions. Yet the keenness of the socialists and a trade union attitude of 'casual benevolence' produced a twelve man Executive with five socialist society representatives and seven trade unionists.[4]

Repression

In the early days most local activists worked through the branches of the ILP, which in many areas constituted the only Labour political organisation. By 1918 there were some 657 local ILP branches, with 35000 members.[5] Local Labour representation committees had, however, been set up from the start, and by the outbreak of war in 1914 there were LRCs and trades councils doing party work in 158 areas.[6] When Henderson reformed the structure of the Labour Party at the end of the War, it was these, and not the myriad ILP branches, which became the basis of Labour's local organisation.

The new local Labour Parties retained the federal structure of the old LRCs, but with individual members' sections grafted on. For the first time, it became possible to be a direct member of the Labour Party without being a member of an affiliated society or trade union. This change undermined and soon destroyed the traditional role of the ILP as the main body responsible for political activity in the constituencies. It also raised the question of representation for the new individual members of the Labour Party at Conference and on the National Executive.

LOCAL PARTIES AND THE NEC

The trade unions, long suspicious of the activities of the socialist societies, were not enthusiastic about Henderson's scheme for individual sections. To help make it acceptable, therefore, Henderson proposed as part of his reforms a National Executive of 21 members: 11 nominated by affiliated organisations (mainly trade unions, but including socialist societies), 5 by Local Labour parties, 4 women and a Treasurer – all, *including members nominated by local parties*, to be elected by the whole of Party Conference. In other words, for the first time trade unions were to control the entire membership of the Executive. This was to be the price for letting Henderson have his way on constituency organisation. But even this price was not high enough. Henderson was forced to concede two extra places to the trade unions' section, bringing the total to 23.[7]

The pre-war imbalance was thus reversed. The 1900 Constitution had given political activists a representation quite out of proportion to their numerical strength; the 1918 Constitution denied them true representation altogether. The socialist society places on the NEC were abolished.[8] Local parties were merely allowed to *nominate candidates* for 5 out of 23 places – to be elected or rejected as the large unions saw fit.

From the outset this arrangement caused resentment. Local parties accepted that the trade unions' financial contribution, and their ability to speak for the mass working-class movement, gave them a right to the largest share of places on the Executive and a predominant voice at Conference. But there was a strong feeling that hard-worked local activists should count for

TABLE A *Constituency party membership 1928–40*

Year	Constituency and central parties no.	Total individual membership (official figures)
1928	535	214 970
1929	578	227 897
1930	607	277 211
1931	608	297 003
1932	608	371 607
1933	612	366 013
1934	614	381 259
1935	614	419 311
1936	614	430 694
1937	614	447 150
1938	614	428 826
1939	614	408 844
1940	614	304 124

Source: LPACR.

more per head in the counsels of the Party than the mass affiliated membership which played no part at all.

The matter was raised at Conference as early as 1920, when Herbert Morrison, Secretary of the London Labour Party and not yet an MP, proposed an amendment to the Constitution which would give local Labour parties direct representation on the NEC. He argued that the existing system was undemocratic, and excluded local men who were not well known MPs. The NEC opposed, and the amendment was narrowly lost.[9]

Thereafter, the claim of the local parties to a greater voice became more compelling year by year. Trade union votes at Conference solidified into fewer and more massive blocs, as the major unions came together in the great amalgamations of the early twenties.[10] The local parties themselves expanded rapidly. In 1918 there were 389 Constituency and Central Parties; by 1928 there were 535; by 1934, 614. Individual membership had reached an official figure of 215000 in 1928 – more than six times as many as had been affiliated through socialist societies (with three reserved NEC places) in 1914. By 1931 this total had risen to 297000 and by 1935 to 419000 – a total which probably represents as large a 'true' membership as in the early 1970s.[11] Yet this expansion was given no constitutional acknowledgement.

The frustrations of the rank and file found various expressions in the twenties. Many activists were drawn into the battle of the ILP against the Labour Party leadership. Others took part in the National Left Wing Movement, a Communist controlled body founded in 1925, which caused the

NEC to disaffiliate 23 local Labour parties over a period of eighteen months.[12] But until the mid-thirties there was no organised attempt to increase the influence and status of constituency parties which received the backing of more than a tiny minority of general committees.

12

Revolt

In September 1932 an article on 'The Local Labour Parties' appeared in a new journal published by the Society of Labour Candidates. This was the first shot in a campaign which reached its culmination five years later. The author was Ben Greene, who was soon to initiate, organise and lead the Constituency Parties Movement. Greene argued that local parties lacked influence because they were unorganised. 'As long as four to five hundred local party units are free to fling into the Party Conference a host of commonplace expressions of opinion and a medley of new half baked ideas, the influence of the political section of the Party will remain small. But with proper organisation, the varied products of their wonderful political energy could be digested, considered and presented in an orderly responsible manner to the Party Conference'.[1] He proposed a national organisation which could convert and form constituency party opinion, and thereby give it a chance against the trade union bloc vote at Conference. The following summer he made a first attempt to give this idea a solid basis.

Ben Greene was a six foot seven extrovert with an abundance of charm and confidence, an infectious energy and a great talent for organisation. He came from an affluent Quaker family, was educated at Berkhamstead and Oxford, visited Russia just after the Revolution and travelled widely on the Continent in the twenties. In 1931, describing himself on his nomination papers as a 'works manager' he stood as Labour candidate for Gravesend.[2] In 1935 he held the job of a deputy Returning Officer for the League of Nations plebiscite in the Saar. He seems to have had no permanent employment or profession.[3]

Greene's political views were a bizarre and explosive mixture. He was a sincere supporter of intervention on the Republican side in Spain after 1936; yet he held an equally sincere belief (reinforced by his Saar experience in 1935) that socialists had much to learn from the Nazis. 'There is more socialism than nationalism in the Nazi Movement', he told friends to their embarrassment. On one occasion he urged some left-wing comrades to accompany him on a visit to Germany as guests of the Hitler regime. Apparently he also seriously contemplated setting up an information office for the Nazis in London.[4] In the end, Greene's pro-Nazi sympathies destroyed him. But until 1938 they did him remarkably little harm.

In June 1933 Greene sent a circular to constituency parties inviting them to help form an association. In July he launched an 'Association of Labour Parties'. His main associate in this venture was Lieut.-Col. L'Estrange Malone.[5] The new Association elected Malone as Chairman and Greene as Secretary. Hector Hughes KC was made treasurer.[6] C. G. Amman, a former junior minister, and Major J. Milner (constituency-sponsored MP for Leeds South East) were among those elected to the Association's organising committee. After the inaugural meeting Malone and Greene insisted that there was 'no question of opposition to the leaders of the party, and no sort of contest with industrial elements', but there was strong feeling that the non-trade union element should have 'a greater voice in the councils of the party'. Hence constituency party representation on the NEC should be increased, and the method of electing it changed. However, they added with emphasis (lest anybody should suspect them of sympathy with the Crippsite left) 'they were strongly opposed to such views as had been put forward by freak sections, such as the establishment of dictatorships and so on'. Finally, it was announced that the first general meeting of the new body would be held during the Hastings Party Conference in October.[7]

The same day the NEC held its monthly meeting at Transport House. Arthur Henderson drew attention to Greene's circular. It was decided to issue a counter letter to constituency parties asking them to defer decisions on the subject 'pending the opportunity for discussion of the subject at Annual Conference'.[8] But soon afterwards the NEC changed its mind. There was no discussion of this matter or of constitutional amendments at Hastings in October. Several weeks before Conference, the Executive accepted the recommendation of its Organisational Sub-Committee and of C. R. Shepherd, the National Agent, to oppose the Association. Another circular was issued to constituency parties informing them of the new decision.

The cause of this *volte face* was a misunderstanding. Before summoning the first general meeting of the Association in October, Greene consulted Transport House officials and gained the impression that he had their tacit approval. This was evidently not intended. The NEC considered that he and Malone were acting without its authority. On NEC instructions, Middleton and Shepherd interviewed both of them, and Greene confessed that they had not asked the NEC directly for fear of being turned down.[9] The incident put Greene in bad odour with Transport House and the NEC, which thereafter regarded him with deep suspicion.

The NEC ban was effective. The new Association was stillborn. Nevertheless, the Hastings Conference showed that the need for such an organisation existed. A number of DLPs had tabled amendments to the Constitution on the issues of local party representation to Conference and on the Executive. But neither question was debated, and Arthur Henderson asked that all such amendments should be remitted for consideration by the NEC – the standard procedure for a committee burial. This provoked a chorus of angry protests from constituency delegates.

'I want to ask the Conference and the Executive to consider whether it is not throwing people into the arms of other Parties,' complained one, 'or out of politics altogether, to ask them to join an organisation in which they know that anything decided purely by the Trade Unions goes through, while the proposals of others are sent back for consideration.'[10] Several others mounted the rostrum in his support, or shouted from the floor.

The NEC was unmoved by this demonstration of rank and file discontent. Its report to the Stockport Conference in 1934 was predictably negative about amending the Party Constitution. It accepted a few minor changes, including provision for the Chairman of the League of Youth to become an ex-officio member of the NEC. But constituency demands for a larger vote were flatly rejected. Proposals for changes in the nomination and election of the NEC were unacceptable, because 'they do not guarantee changes which would lead to improved representation or greater efficiency'.[11]

'To talk about democratic representation to your Executive is an absolute farce', declared one delegate at Stockport. Shepherd replied disingenuously:

> The remedy, if I may say so, for all the claims that have been made, is in the hands of the Constituency Parties themselves. Every member elected for that section of the Executive Committee by the whole Conference was nominated by a Constituency Party. If it becomes possible for him to be elected by the whole Conference to the Executive it is only because he was nominated by a Constituency Organisation.

The section of the report dealing with Constitutional amendments was then adopted by the massive majority of 1 721 000 to 347 000.[12]

THE HOME COUNTIES LABOUR ASSOCIATION

For Greene, this decision was the signal for the start of a new campaign. This time he tackled the problem differently. In 1933 he had assembled a handful of Westminster-orientated minor politicians in an attempt to start an unofficial national organisation from scratch. Now he decided to work from the grass roots up. Operating from within his own area, the prosperous home counties, where there were no Labour MPs but there were large,

restless and vocal constituency parties, he set about establishing a regional organisation for local parties created by the constituency parties themselves.

The first step was taken by the Surrey Labour Federation, with which
Greene was closely in touch.[13] Shortly after the Southport Party Conference,
the Federation issued a circular convening a conference for February 1935 to
consider the establishment of an Association of Constituency Parties for the
Home and Southern Counties. Transport House reacted swiftly. The
Federation's Secretary, E. R. Simmons, received an angry letter from
· Shepherd complaining of lack of consultation;[14] and a few days later the
NEC decided that it was not prepared to give recognition to any new organ-
isation of the kind contemplated.[15]

On 12 January the Federation considered the NEC's reaction and decided
to ignore it. 'The Surrey Federation was of course fully aware of the attitude
of the National Executive Committee to the proposals which were raised
before the Hastings Conference for the formation of a Constituency Labour
Association', Simmons wrote to Shepherd.

> Since that time it has become increasingly evident that those proposals
> were supported to a much wider extent than the National Executive
> seemed to appreciate. In order to elucidate the position the Surrey
> Federation, after a great deal of lengthy discussion, has decided to call an
> unofficial Conference to find out what the real views of local Parties are.
> To make the conference as unofficial as possible and to save any embar-
> rassment that might arise, this Federation felt that it would be to the
> mutual advantage of all not to inform the National Executive of its
> decision till after the Conference had demonstrated whether or not the
> proposals had the support of local Parties.

However, since the NEC had found out, they were welcome to attend.[16]

The Executive refused the invitation and issued a peremptory note
to DLPs condemning the proposed Conference and castigating the
Surrey Federation for having called it surreptitiously. As for a new associa
tion:

> The National Executive Committee does not believe that any organisa-
> tion within the Party should be created without responsibility for some
> electoral function. The Party's resources, both nationally and locally,
> are far too limited to spend on machinery which has no reference to
> elections to some Public Authority.

Simmons responded with a counter circular quoting at length from
speeches by Morrison and Shepherd at the 1920 Conference in favour of
direct constituency representation.

The Federation was right not to be cowed by Transport House sabre rattling. Few divisional parties were intimidated. The 16 February Conference was held in London at the Browning Settlement, near the Elephant and Castle. 200 delegates were expected; 315 came, sent by 49 Divisional Labour Parties and some 40 local parties in the southern and home counties.[17] This compared with a total of 336 delegates from 329 DLPs in the whole of Great Britain at the 1934 Party Conference at Southport.[18]

The meeting was an outstanding success – and for the NEC it was highly embarrassing. A motion expressing dissatisfaction with the existing method of electing DLP 'representatives' to the NEC was passed by 311 to 3. Ben Greene's party of Hemel Hempstead then proposed that an unofficial Home Counties Labour Association should be set up. 23 divisional parties agreed, with 11 against and 15 abstaining.[19] Finally it was decided to hold another conference in June.

The NEC was in a difficult position. The Executive had hoped that, as with the 1933 Constituency Parties Association, admonitory circulars would ensure the Conference's failure. Now it was faced with the prospect of a new organisation set up by authorised delegates from a large number of active and politically reputable divisional parties. An outright prohibition at this stage would create resentment. The NEC therefore confined itself to appeals for loyalty and veiled threats. '[The Executive] asks me to urge the Surrey Labour Federation to reconsider its action in the matter and agree to take no further action', Shepherd wrote to Simmons at the end of February. 'The views of the National Executive Committee have not been lightly taken. Only the best interests of the whole movement forces it to show so much concern about the proposed establishment of an Association that can only succeed in dividing the movement into sections.'[20]

The Home Counties Labour Association (HCLA)[21] was formally established in June, at the Friars Hall, Blackfriars Road. The new Association declared that its main objects were:

> To secure such alterations in the constitution and method of election of the National Executive Committee of the Labour Party as may be necessary to provide satisfactory representation of local constituency organisations on that body.
>
> To provide Constituency Parties with a medium for the preliminary consideration of Resolutions intended for inclusion in the Agenda of the Labour Party Conference with a view to organising support for those finding general approval, thereby ensuring discussion at Conference itself.

The second objective worried the NEC quite as much as the first. Greene's aim was a local party 'bloc vote' at Conference. Party leaders were alarmed at the prospect of a body representing the rank and file and undercutting its own pronouncements on policy. They also feared that a constituency bloc vote would be controlled by the Left.

The Friars Hall Conference elected Ben Greene as Secretary. The chairmanship was filled by Charles Garnsworthy,[22] an insurance agent from Reigate, whose steadiness was to be a valuable counter-weight to Greene's ebullience. Malone and the other prominent people involved in the 1933 Association had no part in this one.

The Brighton Party Conference in October provided a vindication of the Surrey Federation's action. The 1935 NEC Report tried to shelve the constitutional question once again: 'In view of the near approach of the General Election, no attempt ought to be made to make further changes in the National Executive Committee position at present.'[23] The only straw of comfort was a promise to report to Conference on the whole subject when the election was over. This did not mollify Greene, who regarded it simply as a delaying tactic. He also objected to what he considered to be the blatant stage management of Conference – an old grievance. 'In view of the present conditions at Annual Conference, it can hardly be a matter of surprise that more and more local Parties feel that representation at the Annual Conference has become an expensive futility, especially as visitors' tickets can be obtained on application free of charge.'[24]

Greene did not, however, improve his own personal standing at Brighton by a speech, the first of the whole Conference, in which he called for the reference back of the paragraph in the Executive's Report advocating the boycott of German goods. He argued that the likeliest sufferers were Jews; he compared the boycott with the Tory embargo on Soviet goods; he questioned the *bona fides* of the World Non-Sectarian Anti-Nazi Council; and he suggested that the best way to influence the Nazi Government was by adopting the policy towards it of the Society of Friends. Greene said nothing which was directly sympathetic to the German regime. But his speech made no concessions to the sensitivities of Conference. It was not well received. Indeed, his motion failed to find a seconder.[25]

A NATIONAL MOVEMENT

In November, the General Election interrupted the activities of the new Association. Greene contested Gravesend for the second time, again unsuccessfully. Labour made extensive gains in the London area, but made little progress elsewhere in the South of England. Constituency parties now faced five years of Opposition with no clear idea of what part they were supposed to play in the Movement during the interval before the next election. Constituency activists could feel little sense of achievement. A mood of frustration was helpful for Greene's campaign.

After the election HCLA consolidated its position. Greene tried to define the Association's role in a way which would not antagonise the party leadership. He insisted that HCLA itself must not become involved in ideological conflicts: 'it must be definitely recognised that the Association cannot under any circumstances become identified with any particular policy. Party policy is an issue solely to be decided by the Annual Conference of the Labour Party.' Nevertheless, 'the Association offers means whereby... discussion can be done *inside the Party* on a wider basis than the present Party machinery allows for'.[26] The NEC, fighting off assaults on its authority from Labour's left-wing, was not prepared to appreciate such distinctions. To the Executive, HCLA was unofficial, a rival and a threat.

In the spring of 1936 Greene set about convening an Assembly to be held in May, at which parties were to be asked 'to co-operate in sending forward selected resolutions in identical words so that they appear on the Conference agenda not as the views of one Party but as the considered views of a large collection of Parties'.[27] Transport House regarded this as mutiny, and issued yet another circular condemning the Assocation. An angry correspondence between Greene, Shepherd and Middleton brought a further deterioration of relations. In September, at Greene's suggestion, over a hundred DLPs petitioned the NEC recommending a change in its representation.[28]

Meanwhile help was emerging from other quarters. In March 1936 R. St John Reade, a Bristol school teacher and local councillor, had set up the Bristol and District Labour Association on similar lines to HCLA. Reade had also fallen foul of Transport House. A few months earlier he had tried to arrange a conference of local Labour Parties to discuss the possibility of sending party workers out of Bristol to take part in a rural campaign in neighbouring counties. Party headquarters had disapproved: 'we found ourselves up against the strenuous opposition of Transport House and the National Executive Committee, who actually circularised all divisions in the area urging them to take no part in the conference. However our conference proved a great success and resulted in the formation... of the Bristol and District Labour Association of Constituency Parties.'[29] Reade's bitterness against Transport House 'obstructionism' was intense. This made him at times an embarrassing ally. However, the establishment of his association indicated that the movement could be extended nationally.

The involvement of Bristol had another significance. Cripps was MP for Bristol East. The Bristol branch of the Socialist League was one of the largest in the country. The Socialist League had a long-standing resentment of the trade union bloc vote; now it began to see the potential of the local parties' campaign. In May 1936 the League's Annual Conference at Hanley passed a resolution urging effective democratic control and government within the Labour Party.[30] This was the start of a connection with Cripps which was to be a mixed blessing to the Constituency Parties Movement.

The 1936 Edinburgh Party Conference was the decisive turning-point in the campaign for constitutional change. The anger of local delegates at their treatment by the Executive could no longer be contained. Suddenly Greene's campaign, hitherto restricted to the South and South-West, became a major talking point throughout the Movement.

The NEC, which had used the election for postponing discussion of the constitutional question at Brighton, included in its 1936 report a blanket rejection of all the constituency parties' demands. This had been predictable. But what infuriated delegates most was a recommendation that constitutional issues should only be discussed every three years. Acceptance of this would rule out any debate on the local parties' grievance until 1939.

After consulting Reade, Greene called a meeting of divisional party delegates, to be held under the joint auspices of HCLA and the Bristol Association, for the Sunday before Conference opened. Seventy delegates attended. It was decided to move the reference back of the Arrangements Committee's report, which had relegated discussion of the Party Constitution to the last day, and to organise an active canvass of other delegates at Conference.

The reference back was heavily defeated. This in itself was good propaganda. 'As vote after vote was announced at Edinburgh in which the forest of cards with 1 or 2 were defeated by the few cards held up with 100s on them, the ironical cheers of the delegates of the constituency Parties became more and more marked', Greene wrote afterwards. 'The result was to bring about a very definite revulsion of feeling among the delegates of the constituency Parties against the present constitution of the Labour Party.'[31] In the circumstances it was scarcely tactful of George Lathan, the new Party Treasurer, to remind local parties that their financial contribution was really very small.

By Wednesday it was clear that the vast majority of DLP delegates were ready for strong action. A meeting was called for the following night, and Cripps agreed to take the chair. It was a dramatic occasion. More than 200 delegates attended – out of a total of 280 accredited delegates at Conference. Feeling was almost unanimous that any attempt by the NEC to force through its report would be intolerable; and it was agreed *nem. con.* that local parties must act at the Conference to show their determination. A Provisional Committee of Constituency Labour Parties was set up with regional representation, to 'devise and take such steps as they may deem necessary to inform constituency Parties of the present conditions and to bring these parties into consultation with one another, so that proposals may be put forward unitedly of such remedies as will lead to the Labour Party constitution becoming a great democratic instrument.'[32] The constituency parties' campaign had become a national movement, and could no longer be ignored.

Ben Greene became Secretary of the Provisional Committee. Other members included Charles Garnsworthy (Chairman of HCLA), St John Reade from the Bristol Association, F. G. Bowles,[33] Sara Barker[34] and Aneurin Bevan.[35] The most notable member of the new Committee was Sir Stafford Cripps, who agreed to become Chairman.

Cripps had a large following in the constituencies, even among those who rejected his more extreme views. His participation gave the local parties' campaign prestige, and for the first time focussed the attention of the national press upon it. It also provided cash; Cripps gave the Committee £300, which paid Greene's out of pocket expenses over the next year.[36] But the snags outweighed the advantages. At the end of 1936 Cripps was preparing for the Unity Campaign, to be launched in January. The NEC had an almost paranoid suspicion of organisations identified as 'Crippsite'. So, too, had trade union leaders – upon whom any change in the Party Constitution depended. With Cripps as Chairman, it was not surprising that the new Provisional Committee should soon be accused of being a vehicle for Cripps' ambitions. Cripps, to his credit, drew attention to the dangers of involving him. He told the meeting that it would be much better to select someone who was 'less of a Bolshevik and more respectable'.[37] But delegates were not in a respectable frame of mind.

Nevertheless, the Party leadership could no longer fall back on the idea cultivated by Transport House that the constituencies' campaign was merely the creation of a handful of politically suspect malcontents. The suggestion in the 1934 NEC report that 'one or two organisations may feel aggrieved' had been shown up as absurd. The NEC was now in an unprecedented situation. It faced an organised rebellion by the vast majority of those constituency parties which were strong enough to send delegates to Conference. It could use the trade union bloc vote to steam-roll Conference, if it chose; but to do so would be to risk open war. Such a response would also play straight into the hands of Cripps and the Socialist League, who could only gain from the increasing alienation of local activists from the Executive.

The Executive therefore decided on a strategic retreat. On Friday morning George Oliver MP announced on behalf of the Conference Arrangements Committee that debate on the constitutional question must be postponed for yet another year because discussion about Spain had taken up so much of Conference's time. Delegates were outraged at this evidence of brazen collusion between the Arrangements Committee and the Executive in order to get the NEC off the hook. There were shouts of protest. F. C. Watkins MP (Railway Clerks' Association)[38] demanded that the Executive show its good faith by declaring that 'the whole position will be very carefully and sympathetically examined in order that the feeling of frustration which undoubtedly exists among the Divisional Parties can be dealt with and a remedy proposed at the next Annual Conference'.

At this point Hugh Dalton, Chairman-elect of the Labour Party, rose on the platform.

> I am authorised to say, and I say it with complete sincerity, that the NEC, if its proposal to leave these matters over is accepted, will be quite prepared to go into the whole matter very carefully, and so far as I am personally concerned – if I may add a personal undertaking – I will be happy, if it should be part of my duties to do so next year, to have friendly consultations with some, at any rate, of those who have proposals to put forward on this point with a view to removing those disharmonies and those sources of ill-feeling … of course, what I am saying now must not be taken to commit the National Executive to the acceptance next year of any particular proposal which has been made. But I do give an undertaking that we will consider the matter in the most friendly and the most co-operative fashion.[39]

Delegates were taken aback. Many were uncertain how to react. Were they being offered a conciliatory hand, or was this a clever attempt to disarm them? They had come to the Conference Hall spoiling for a fight. Now the NEC was trying to avoid a confrontation. A Manchester delegate, Councillor Tom Larrard,[40] defiantly moved the reference back of Oliver's report:

> This matter had already been considered carefully and unsympathetically by the Executive Committee [Laughter]. There was virtually no change on the Executive Committee and only the same unsympathetic consideration was to be expected. Every constituency Labour Party delegate was dissatisfied with the treatment received, and it was the constituency parties that won elections.

> It is no joy [replied Oliver] for the Standing Orders Committee to come and suggest postponement of this question.

> It is no joy for us to come and waste a week like this [Larrand snapped back, midst loud cries of 'Order']. We got a promise that this should be considered.

When Oliver tried to say that if there had been no Spanish trouble there would have been no difficulty, his words were drowned with cries of 'That's an excuse', and he retorted angrily, 'Very well, if you want to sit to-morrow and on Sunday say so definitely.' Another delegate shouted 'I am prepared to sit until next week if we can have a discussion', and Larrard called back, against more shouts of 'Order', 'You are cutting out a session in order to shirk this question. If other delegates want to go home let them go. We were called here to do conference business.' The protests continued, but eventually the Arrangements Committee's recommendations were accepted.[41]

13
Struggle

GREENE, THE LEFT AND THE EXECUTIVE

The year's postponement was wholly to the advantage of the advocates of reform. A snap vote on Friday morning could only have supported the NEC. Dalton's commitment gave the local parties' movement a year in which, first, to convince the NEC that its case was substantial and that constituency feeling was not ephemeral, and second, to gain enough trade union support to carry a change. Greene had no illusions about the difficulty of the task. He did not see any chance of achieving it 'unless great pressure can be put upon the Executive'.[1]

Greene had to be careful. He needed to rally support wherever he could find it. Yet those most willing to give active help were people already hostile to the Party leadership for other reasons. The Unity Campaign opened in January 1937 with a great burst of publicity centering around the position of Cripps. There was a serious danger that the Executive's attitude would be hardened by an association between the local parties and the Left. And there was also a danger that many constituency parties would be persuaded that the regional associations pioneered by Greene were front organisations for attempts to disrupt the Party.

Above all, the attitude of the trade unions was crucial. Greene had no dealings with the trade unions. His movement was, indeed, aimed at breaking what he considered to be the stranglehold of the unions at Conference and at Transport House. If trade union leaders became convinced that Greene's campaign was aimed at extending left-wing power they would close ranks firmly against it. Hence Greene had to fight a war on two fronts: against the Executive, and any NEC temptation to back-pedal or to imagine that the problem would disappear; and against the over-enthusiasm of some of his own associates.

The link with Cripps and the Socialist League was the hardest to manage. Cripps did what he could for the local parties' campaign and tried to keep his other activities separate. At the end of November he advised Bristol East DLP not to submit to an unofficial Conference of South Western Constituency Labour Parties a resolution expressing confidence in himself and disgust at recent attacks on him, because 'it was undesirable to mix up that matter with this conference'.[2] Nevertheless he was an ally who needed to be kept at arm's length.

This was most clearly demonstrated when Greene became involved with *Tribune*. HCLA had been considering setting up its own paper since February 1936. Sir Stafford Cripps was approached as the obvious financial backer. Cripps made a counter proposal: that the constituency parties should associate themselves with *Tribune* which was to be launched in January 1937. It was a tempting offer, and the Executive of the Home Counties Association accepted.

> 'The Executive felt that it was reasonable that the efforts of the Association and those of Sir Stafford Cripps should be combined on a basis where the Association, in return for representation on the management of the paper, should throw its whole weight into getting member Parties and those Parties outside the Association to take up the paper and assist in building up a strong and virile circulation.'[3]

Ben Greene was accordingly appointed to *Tribune*'s Board of Directors. William Mellor, editor of *Tribune*, attended the Annual General Assembly of HCLA early in 1937 and made a strong appeal for support.[4]

It was a short-lived and unhappy arrangement. Greene had little sympathy for the Socialist League, and less for the Unity Campaign, which *Tribune* backed. The last issue of the *Socialist* (the organ of the Socialist League until *Tribune* replaced it) carried an article by Greene in which he made his reservations abundantly clear:

> I adhere to the line I took at the inaugural Conference [of the Socialist League] at Leicester with a greater conviction than ever. The first thing I think the Socialist League should realise is that the day of affiliated socialist societies is past. I do not suggest that the League should be wound up, but I do suggest that if it proposes to play a real part in the Socialist Movement it must adjust itself to the fact that the only place for Socialists in this country is inside the local Labour parties as active members. The League must recognise that the Constituency Labour Parties' organisations represent the national organisation of British Socialism; and we of the Constituency Parties are bound to have a deep suspicion and resentment of any organisation that tends to take away members from active constituency work with another parallel loyalty.[5]

The first issue of *Tribune* demonstrated to Greene that he was involved in an enterprise which was utterly incompatible with his local party activities. 'I am very disappointed in the *Tribune*', he wrote to Garnsworthy the day it was published. 'This is not what I had in mind. I shall have to see what I can do about it even if it does mean personal difficulties'.[6] At the February meeting of the HCLA Executive, he asked to be instructed to resign from the Board, but was persuaded merely to write voicing the Association's disquiet at *Tribune*'s policy.[7] But the situation did not improve, and on 8 March he resigned. *Tribune* had given its unconditional support to the Unity Campaign without any formal decision of the Board of Management, he explained to the Association. 'It appeared that the Editor considered Ben Greene's presence on these boards as purely personal whereas both he and the Executive understood that he was there in a more or less representative character'.[8]

Nevertheless, the Constituency Parties Movement continued to suffer the embarrassment of support from *Tribune* and the Socialist League. In December 1936 the ILP, partner in the Unity Campaign, had added its unwelcome embrace. The ILP declared loftily that 'we are now prepared to say that if this revolt develops to a point which gives reasonable hope that it will succeed in bringing about the democratisation of the Labour Party and the adoption by it of a challenging Socialist policy...the ILP would be prepared to reconsider the question of affiliation'.[9] This was an endorsement which the local parties' campaign could have done without.

Inside HCLA Greene had to exercise a restraining hand. Despite his eccentric interest in Nazi Germany, policy questions interested him comparatively little, and he never indicated a predilection for any political tendency within the Party. He showed no sympathy for those who used HCLA's meetings to express ultra-left views, and he succeeded in containing the tactical extravagances of some of the more extreme participants. When one delegate at the November 1936 Assembly of HCLA suggested that Party Conference should be boycotted, turning it into a second TUC, 'until...reactionary officials at Transport House could see the force of [the local parties'] arguments', Greene pointed out that for local parties to challenge the trade union bloc vote 'would be to chase a shadow with which they would never catch up'. What mattered was to raise the moral quality of constituency organisations within the party.[10]

After Edinburgh, HCLA continued to operate as the hub of the Constituency Parties Movement. At the same time, working through the Provisional Committee, and with Cripps' financial backing, Greene established similar regional bodies in other parts of the country. In February a Yorkshire regional conference was convened by Sara Barker at Leeds. Lady Mabel Smith (an ex-member of the NEC) presided, and Cripps, Greene, and Garnsworthy attended. 28 DLPs were represented by 93 delegates. A Permanent Regional Committee was set up, with Miss Barker as Secretary and Lady Mabel Smith as Chairman, after an attempt to oppose Cripps' Chairmanship of the Provisional Committee had been crushed.[11] East Anglian Labour Parties set up a regional committee at Norwich on 6 March; a resolution requesting the dissolution of the Socialist League, moved by the convener, was withdrawn after discussion. In the North-East,

Arthur Blenkinsop,[12] Secretary of Newcastle North DLP, became Secretary for the area and was co-opted on to the Provisional Committee. Committees were also set up in the Midlands, the North-West and the West Country. The Provisional Committee became the committee of a new national Constituency Parties' Association.

To coordinate this activity, Greene rented an office in Great James Street near Gray's Inn, and hired a secretary recently made redundant by the No More War Movement, 'in consultation with Sir Stafford Cripps' – who may have paid the bill.[13]

By February Greene could report dramatic progress and widespread support, but 'the present United Front Campaign...has rather complicated the work of this Committee and has tended to confuse the issues, and I have had to make it clear that this Committee has no connection whatever with the Unity Campaign'.[14] Nevertheless, Greene did not discourage HCLA from setting up a 'Labour Spain Committee' to take independent action in support of the Spanish Government; and he had to accept an incautious resolution recommending parties to refuse to operate NEC decisions on the Socialist League and the Unity Campaign, and offering support to those parties which defied NEC rulings in these matters.

Meanwhile Dalton, as NEC Chairman, had been carrying out his pledge to Conference. At the end of November the NEC decided to hold a series of its own conferences of DLP representatives to sound out local feeling. Greene suspected that this was a move to outflank him. He need not have worried. Though maintaining a public neutrality, Dalton had come round to the view that constitutional reform was desirable, and he became the constituency movement's most valuable ally. Between January and Whitsun 448 DLPs sent delegates to NEC area conferences.[15] 'When the reports of these Conferences were collated,' Dalton recalled in his memoirs, 'we found that there had been an almost universal demand by the Constituency Parties to elect their own representatives on the Executive'.[16] Such had been the success of Greene's campaign.

Greene, however got little of the credit. Indeed, most Labour leaders, including Dalton, continued to regard him with extreme distaste. Greene's pro-German sympathies were partly responsible for this. When Greene wrote to Dalton complaining that the Party Chairman had been making speeches in which 'you either state or strongly imply that I am fascist or have fascist tendencies', Dalton rejected the accusation, but added that Greene had 'made it clear on several occasions that your attitude towards the Nazi regime in Germany is not that generally adopted in the Labour Party'; and he reminded Greene of an article he had written comparing Nazi brutalities with atrocities allegedly committed by German Social Democrats. Greene replied furiously 'I happen to have had a very close and intimate knowledge of German politics since the War and if I disagree with the Labour Party's attitude to Germany now, and if I consider this attitude deplorable and dangerous then I have not only a right but a duty to express my opinion based upon my own intimate experience'.[17] It was not a promising position to take.

Meanwhile Greene was providing the Executive with other evidence that he was a trouble-maker. In February 1937 he was the subject of an embarrassing NEC inquiry. He was accused of conspiring to force the early retirement of his former agent at Gravesend. In the course of the investigation, the agent brought up the question of Greene's pro-Nazi sympathies. Stanley Hirst, conducting the enquiry on behalf of the NEC, decided that the case was unproven and it was dropped.[18] But it was an unsavoury and ill-timed affair.

For some time Transport House had been compiling a dossier on Greene's activities. An opportunity now arose to use it. In the spring, Greene was adopted as Labour candidate for Hull South West, a seat which had been held by Labour from 1929 to 1931. Greene's candidature needed the NEC's endorsement; Transport House was able to produce grounds for withholding it. The Organisation Department prepared a lengthy memorandum listing Greene's misdeeds since 1933. These included the holding of a Press Luncheon at the Criterion Restaurant in Edinburgh in 1936; the publication of a paper called *Revally* which 'not only attacks the Executive, Headquarters and the Annual Party Conference, but singles out the Leader of the Party and the Chairman of the National Executive for personal criticism'; a circular denouncing the NEC for calling for a boycott against German goods; and organising 'a competition on literature production' arising out of criticism of NEC publications.[19]

Yet, in spite of everything, it was Hugh Dalton who rescued Greene. Greene was interviewed by the NEC Organisation Sub-Committee on 25 May. Dalton was in the chair. Greene answered his accusers well. Dalton, carefully disguising his own preferences, persuaded the sub-committee to recommend to the NEC that a delegation from the HCLA should be received, but that Greene's candidature should not, meanwhile, be endorsed.[20] Dalton had, in fact, used the question of Greene's endorsement as a lever for giving the Home Counties Association the right to be heard.

Greene was only half aware of the progress he had made. 'The NEC think that only a little firmness is necessary and we shall fade away', he wrote to Garnsworthy. 'Walker[21] thinks we are a fly by night affair which can be put down with a strong hand as with the Unity Campaign'.[22] The attitude of most of the Executive was 'that we had no right to usurp Executive authority and the democratic way was for us to put a resolution down on the annual conference agenda'.[23] However, 'Dalton has seen a little of the light and is rather dazed and dazzled by it, but apparently willing to learn more as he has invited me to an informal talk to-morrow'.[24]

In fact, Dalton had decided to back the constituencies almost all the way. A week later the Organisation Sub-Committee accepted the Constituency Parties Movement's main proposals lock, stock and barrel. Demands that voting at Conference should be based on a local party's affiliated membership not its individual membership, and that regional associations should be officially recognised, were rejected. But direct representation in all divisions of the NEC except division IV (Women); proxy voting by Constituency Parties not represented at Conference; and an increase in the local parties' representation on the NEC from five to seven – all these were recommended to the Executive.[25] By the time that Greene and Garnsworthy, representing HCLA, met the Sub-Committee on 16 June – the first official contact between the NEC and any of the organisations of the constituency movement – the essence of their case had already been accepted.

This was not victory. Dalton had carried with him the NEC Organisation Sub-Committee, of which he was by far the most influential member.[26] Winning over the Executive itself was another matter. 'It was a stiff and prolonged battle in the Executive', Dalton wrote later. 'Some of the Trade Union Section were strong in opposition and so, fearing for their seats if they had to face this new and unknown electorate, were one or two in the Constituency Parties' section'.[27] The latter included George Dallas and Joseph Toole, the two least known and therefore most vulnerable. The recommendation to increase constituency representation from five to seven was, ironically, as much a device to calm their fears of exclusion as a concession to the constituency parties, though it pleased both.[28]

The NEC discussed the matter at the end of June. Dalton was able to report the massive support for change that had been demonstrated at the NEC area conferences of DLPs earlier in the year. He stressed the need 'to conciliate many of our most active workers'. Various objections were raised. 'Some thought the change would play into the hands of the Party Agents, who had their own organisation and special interests...What would you do, I was asked, if the Constituency Parties elected seven Agents to the Executive'?[29] Finally Dalton made a strong personal appeal from the Chair. It was necessary, he said, 'to remove a rankling grievance which was hindering unity'.[30] A vote was taken, and the Sub-Committee recommendations were narrowly accepted.

CONFLICT

But success in the NEC was not a victory in Conference. Many leading trade unionists saw the proposals as a serious threat. Strongly suspicious of Cripps and his middle-class, intellectual Socialist League, resentful of left-wing jibes at union power, above all procedurally conservative and wedded to precedent as their best safeguard, they felt little inclination to give way to local party demands which might turn out to be the thin end of a powerfully disruptionist wedge. Moreover, developments between June and September seemed to confirm their worst fears.

The extent of opposition was not realised at once. In July *Labour Organiser*, the party agents' journal, felt that while some of the NEC's proposals 'seem revolutionary and surprising' in view of past decisions, 'one presumes that they will be able to carry the Trade Union vote with them'. But this reckoned without the activities of some of the local parties' more irresponsible – or disingenuous – supporters. 'It is clearly of the highest importance for everyone who is working for the revival of the Labour movement that those leaders of the Labour Party who have stood for the unity of the movement should be elected to the National Executive', John Strachey wrote archly. 'Amongst the nominations are Sir Stafford Cripps, Professor Harold Laski and Mr G. R. Strauss. If these three are elected, as should certainly prove possible, to the National Executive on the local Labour Party list, an immense gain will have been effected. Members of the Left Book Club have surely no greater concern than the election of these three candidates to the National Executive on the local Labour Party list'.[31]

The pro-Communist Left Book Club had no connection with the Labour Party, and the suggestion that its members should use constitutional reform to secure the election of Communist sympathisers to the NEC naturally made good propaganda for the opponents of change. But this was less damaging to the campaign for reform than moves from within the Constituency Parties Movement to influence the results of the NEC elections. A central objective of the campaign had been to get proper rank and file representation on the NEC – so that the constituency parties section would not be restricted to national figures who could get the backing of big unions. With success in sight, Greene and his associates decided that changing the Party Constitution might not be enough. DLPs, many of which mandated delegates, might be as unwilling to vote for men of merely local prominence as great unions. Thus, while the NEC worried about the possibility of a constituency section of seven agents, the Constituency Parties Committee was concerned about the prospect of a constituency section composed of seven well-known MPs.

The Committee therefore decided to hold a mini-conference of DLP delegates the day before the October 1937 Bournemouth Party Conference opened – similar to the pre-Conference meeting at Edinburgh in 1936. 'The qualifications of many of our best members are unknown outside a very limited circle,' it was argued, 'and the [Constituency Parties] Committee feel that the arrangements for the meeting on Sunday, 3 October, should aim as far as possible to overcome this present but temporary difficulty'.[32] Ben Greene himself was a candidate for the NEC, and he hoped to benefit personally from pre-Conference exposures of this kind.

The NEC, suspecting a left-wing ploy, promptly condemned this move. Cripps ridiculed the Executive's fears:

> It is being suggested that somehow or other the Constituency Parties Association is being used by certain corrupt and irresponsible people – such as myself!! – to wangle a vote in the election to the Executive. The suggestion... that a particular panel of members was to be put forward is of course entirely false and has only been made as an excuse for actions which may be taken by the Trade Unions at Bournemouth... What we want is to have seven representatives who will be able to put the views of the constituency parties and who will feel that their loyalty to the constituency parties is the determining factor in their election.[33]

But a day earlier the *Manchester Guardian* had carried a report of a circular issued by the North-West Committee of Constituency Labour Parties which seemed to undermine such protestations. This called for support in the election for a panel which included Cripps, Laski and Greene. Herbert Morrison, by now in favour of reform, hit back with a warning: 'It has not unnaturally been assumed that the intention is to promote the election of particular persons to the Executive by something in the nature of a pre-arranged block vote... Some of the influential trade unionists are now beginning to wonder whether they should agree to the change'.[34] The *New Statesman and Nation* noted rumours of mounting trade union opposition and a growing threat that the reforms would be rejected. 'If this happens – as we earnestly hope it will not – it will be because the Trade Union leaders have been annoyed by attacks from the Left into taking up an unreasonable stand-pat position'.[35] When regional Constituency Party Committees in the Midlands and North-East issued their own panels as well, the *Manchester Guardian* commented that if the reform failed, this would be largely because of such efforts.[36]

14
Revolution

The DLP pre-Conference meeting was held on Sunday, 3 October. The tactics of some of the regional committees were strongly criticised by moderate supporters of reform. Frank Bowles, a member of the Constituency Parties Association Executive, condemned them as deliberately provocative, and said that they were bound to create suspicion in the trade unions. John Wilmot – himself a leading candidate for the NEC –protesting strongly against canvassing for the Executive, said that the proposals had been put in jeopardy by such 'foolish and tactless manoeuvres', and called for the disbandment of the Constituency Parties Association.[1] The discussion among the supporters of reform reflected a growing uncertainty about the fate of the proposals.

When Conference opened next day, with Hugh Dalton in the Chair, the issue seemed to hang in the balance. 'Some of the big unions will openly oppose, others will plead for delay, and the result at the moment is in doubt', commented the *Manchester Guardian*. 'The exact course of the debate cannot be forecast, but even if the main changes should be carried there is a strong presumption that their operation will be deferred'.[2] The Railwaymen (with 215 00 votes), the General and Municipal Workers (242 000) and the two textile workers unions (170 000) were definitely opposed – making a total of 627 000 against. The miners (400 000),[3] the distributive workers (137 000) and the Railway Clerks (49 000) had come out in favour of reform; in addition the proposals were likely to have the support of almost all the DLPs themselves with some 500 000 votes between them – making a total of about a million votes for constitutional change. However, both the engineers (71 000) and the Transport Workers (301 000) went to Conference with their delegations uncommitted. The preference of the majority of smaller unions, wielding over half a million votes, was not known. Thus, with about 450 000 'committed' votes separating the two sides, the decision turned on the behaviour of the 900 000 'uncommitted' (or unknown) votes – and the single bloc vote in the hands of Ernest Bevin and the TGWU assumed a critical importance.

The debate on the Party Constitution was taken as the first item of the Conference. Dallas opened for the Executive. This was a clever move on Dalton's part. Dallas was a member of the constituency parties section of the NEC, but he was widely regarded as primarily a trade unionist. He was also known to have had doubts about the proposals. By getting him to speak in favour of reform, Dalton hoped to bring a few extra DLP votes his way and, more important, help win over wavering trade union delegations. Dallas made a cogent case. He stressed the strength of feeling that had gathered in the localities on the side of reform. 'It is no exaggeration for me to say that when the Executive Committee received the reports from these regional consultations which we had during the past 12 months, without a single exception of any description, however varied some of the suggestions were, this one suggestion [direct representation on the NEC] came up from every one of the regional consultations.' He discounted recent 'unfortunate incidents'. 'The Local Labour Parties are growing in power, and, we hope, in influence. There has been a feeling of frustration...We will take that away'.[4]

When he sat down, Dalton, who made little pretence of being an impartial chairman, called John Wilmot to speak. 'He, I knew, would be persuasive, and would be likely to turn some hesitant Trade Union votes our way. Also he was a candidate for the National Executive, and I hoped to have him as a colleague'.[5] Wilmot made a bitter attack on the leaders of the Constituency Parties Movement (in which he had taken no part) – an attack which was echoed by almost every speaker in the debate, and which seemed to be regarded as a touchstone of responsibility and Party loyalty: 'I do appeal to the delegates...not to allow this important issue for the Party's future to be prejudiced because some stupid, ill-advised and disruptive manoeuvres have been made from certain quarters...I do beg of you to believe that the demand for these reforms comes, not from a group of disgruntled disruptionists, but comes from the great mass of responsible Constituency Parties'.[6]

The next speaker, Charles Dukes of the NUGMW, ignored Wilmot's plea. 'There are certain elements in the Conference who believe that they can get on to the Executive by that method who cannot do so by the straightforward method of election that now obtains in the Conference'.[7] Then came an attempt to smear the local parties' leaders: 'Is it, after all, so strange that the main promoters of this method have always been those elements opposing the Executive's policy...? I sincerely hope the delegates, regarding this matter as one of domestic policy, will look dispassionately and strictly at the arithmetic of this matter'.[8]

The last speaker before lunch was Ernest Bevin. Constituency delegates had been waiting for his speech with eager anticipation. He started with a jibe at Cripps: 'It was the vote of my Union, I believe, which on one occasion resulted in Mosley going on the Executive. God forgive them! Now look where he is. At least we did it quite constitutionally. I believe we put another gentleman on, who did not stay very long, and who is still with us and is now trying to reform us'.[9]

But this time Bevin was not at the rostrum to bully. He was there to manoeuvre. He played his hand skilfully: 'Now we are pretty evenly divided and our votes not decided. It is going to be determined by the course of events to-day, so you will not accuse us of having a bloc vote all ready. It depends to a large extent on the Local Labour Parties and the Executive.'[10]

What Bevin offered was a deal. He was prepared to concede direct representation to the Executive; but in return he demanded that the proxy vote should be dropped ('it leads to jiggery pokery business'); that there should be no increase in the size of the constituency parties section; and that the change should not come into operation until next Conference – which, as the date of Conference was to be changed from October to Whitsun, meant waiting eighteen months ('I do fear, and my Union fears, rush tactics in the Labour Party'). It was a typical Bevin speech – heavily spiced with illogicalities, ambiguities and obscurities, but with the central message unmistakable.[11]

The NEC retired for a lunch-time of horse-trading with the Transport Workers. It now seemed likely that the AEU would oppose. If so it appeared that the whole issue would be decided one way or the other by the TGWU vote. Bevin had made it clear that this could be bought – at a price. So the NEC conceded the proxy vote, the least popular of the proposals, and the immediate operation of the reform. On the increase in the size of the constituencies' section from 5 to 7, the NEC held firm, and got its way.

In the afternoon session, Ben Greene was called. Greene defended himself and his organisation which, he declared, 'is a perfectly legitimate and perfectly right organisation, and any reference made to it has been made in ignorance... If there is any idea that the Constituency Party organisation that has sprung up is in any way connected with policy proposals, that idea is completely and absolutely wrong... The only object we have in mind in getting Constituency Party representation on the National Executive is to make sure that there is someone on the National Executive acquainted with the problems and work that face us in the Constituency Parties.'[12]

George Ridley MP wound up for the Executive – making the concessions that had been thrashed out in the lunchbreak: 'since Mr Bevin's gesture was of a very substantial kind, it would be an unfortunate thing if the Executive did not recognise the substantial character of it and go some of the way, at least, in order to meet Mr Bevin's point of view'.[13] In other words, as the *Manchester Guardian* put it, constituency parties were told that they deserved more recognition, but were not good enough children to get it until they were a little older.[14]

Then came the voting. First, a delegate moved the (now shelved) proposal for proxy voting. This was defeated overwhelmingly on a show of hands – a poor omen, some felt, for the major reforms. The next issue was the increase in the constituencies section from 5 to 7; this had been accepted by the TGWU, and so it was the first critical test. A card vote was taken. The reform was carried by 1 408 000 to 1 134 000 – a majority of 274 000. This margin justified the Executive's deal with Bevin, for without the support of the 301 000 TGWU bloc vote the decision would have gone the other way. The most important proposal – direct and separate election to the constituencies section on the NEC – came next. Here Bevin's support proved unnecessary. 1 814 000 votes were cast in favour, and only 658 000 against. The minority consisted almost entirely of the textile workers, the NUR and the NUGMW.

The biggest surprise came with the last vote. This was on the immediate operation of the reforms, which had been dropped by the Executive at Bevin's insistence. Moved and seconded from the floor, it was carried massively, by 1 886 000 to 466 000. 'This,' wrote Dalton, 'was Dukes and Marchbank getting their own back on Bevin.'[15] It had been assumed that unions hostile to reform would favour postponement as a second best. Instead they seemed to say to Bevin and the NEC: since you have asked for it, you can have it, and suffer the consequences, now.[16]

When this final result was announced, a great cheer broke out from the constituency delegates in the Hall. 'The Chairman, very happy, tried to look solemnly impassive.'[17] The local parties had won on all the central issues – the increase in representation, direct election, and the immediate implementation of the changes, losing only on the proxy vote. And in the last vote they had carried Conference without the aid of Executive patronage.[18]

The result of the first direct election to Division III (Constituency Labour Parties) was announced two days later. One member of the old Local Parties section, Arthur Jenkins, did not stand. Morrison replaced Dalton at the top of the poll, with 348 000 to Dalton's 306 000. Otherwise the voting both confirmed and refuted the fears of Executive and trade union Cassandras. Dallas was re-elected, though he came sixth. Joseph Toole was forced off and relegated to a humiliating thirteenth place. The remaining four places were filled by Philip Noel-Baker and a trinity of left-wingers, Cripps, Laski and Pritt. Ben Greene, attacked by name or by implication in almost every major speech in the debate, received 84 000 – disappointingly far from the number needed for election, but more than any other candidate who was not a well-established political leader of national standing.[19]

The changes had not resulted in the election of seven party agents, nor of seven left-wingers. Nor had they produced genuine representatives of the rank and file, as Greene had hoped. As the disgruntled Alderman Toole

pointed out, the local parties section was in this sense even less satisfactory than before. Of the seven elected, only Dallas was a true provincial.[20] The rest 'all live in London and they do not understand the
problem of working men and women who live in the North and are members of the Labour Party... It is no good giving the Labour movement only
the views of Bloomsbury, Chelsea, the Café Royal, and the smart set in
society.'[21] Labour's 447 000 individual members found themselves represented by seven men only two of whom could claim to be working-
class. The other five all went to public school, two to Winchester and one
to Eton. Two were rich barristers; the other two were dons. It was scarcely
a cross-section.

Nevertheless the consequences of the change were great. In 1937 the only
visible effect may have been to add to the NEC a few intellectuals, mainly
left-wing, who were 'largely prisoners of the National Executive majority',[22]
at a Conference which, on other issues, gave the Left its usual drubbing. Yet
neither Cripps nor Pritt behaved like prisoners – indeed within three years,
offences against Executive rulings had earned both expulsion from the
Party; Laski later became a highly controversial Party Chairman. But the
real importance of the change did not become clear until after 1945. Dalton
felt that the new method 'worked up to a point, rather conservatively';
he chose not to go into post-war developments: 'the rise of the Bevanites is
a later story'.[23] After the War, and especially when Labour was again in
Opposition after 1951, the change assumed great significance in intra-
party conflicts. The annual battle for places in the constituency parties
section became a recognised barometer of the relative strength of warring
factions. Those elected by local party delegates could claim a special
authority. Both in the 1950s and in the 1970s, the existence of the constituency parties section substantially increased the leverage of the Left.[24]

Before 1937 the NEC had been an extremely powerful body. Yet it had
been made up, broadly speaking, of mediocrities. Trade unionists on it
were second rankers, whose political knowledge and experience was often
small. Women members were, on the whole, undistinguished. The constituency section usually included only two or three leaders of national
importance. Including the Party Leader (on the Executive *ex-officio*) there
were seldom more than three or four NEC members who had held, or
seemed likely to hold, major ministerial office. Links with the PLP were
weak. After the 1935 election the number of MPs on the Executive rose from
2 to 11 – but they were still a minority.

The 1937 reform provided a greatly needed injection of talent; it also
powerfully reasserted the position of parliamentary leaders on the Executive. Since 1937, MPs have always held a majority of NEC places, and the
Party Executive has tended to reflect (though not always with an identical
balance) the attitudes and divisions of the PLP.

AFTERMATH

The constituency parties' organisations continued to operate after Bournemouth, though with declining vigour. Their main purpose had been achieved. What finally killed them was a recognition by the Executive that existing regional organisation was inadequate, and the establishment of official regional councils on which DLPs had representation.

Attempts to organise a constituency party bloc vote at the 1939 Southport Conference failed. With the outbreak of war, the Constituency Parties Association rapidly disintegrated. Long before then, both Cripps and Greene had ceased to be involved. Cripps was asked to resign by the Association of Constituency Labour Parties at Bournemouth. Garnsworthy told Cripps that as the local parties' Executive did not support his attitude towards the Communists, his chairmanship had become a liability. After the major reforms had been passed, Cripps resigned, explaining to a meeting of the Association that he felt that his position in it would be better filled by somebody who was less of an embarrassment.[25]

Greene stayed as Secretary for a year. But his views on Germany were creating increasing difficulties. Shortly after Munich, Greene made an animated speech in defence of Germany to a meeting of the Association's Executive at the Trade Union Club in London. Nobody present shared his sympathies, which could no longer be overlooked. He was asked to resign. Afterwards, Garnsworthy joined Greene at the Lyons Corner House. Greene was deeply upset. Garnsworthy told him that if he did not change his ideas, he would be thrown out of the Party. The two never met again. With the declaration of War, Garnsworthy entered the forces. Greene was sent to Brixton Prison under Regulation 18B as a Nazi sympathiser.[26] In 1945, Hull South West, the seat for which Greene had been adopted, returned a local Labour councillor as its MP.

Greene received no recognition for his achievements. Speakers who had clambered onto the local parties' bandwagon at the 1937 Conference had dissociated themselves from him. The Press largely ignored him. The Executive consistently treated him as a trouble-maker. After Bournemouth, Transport House invented the myth (which no account has ever refuted) that the NEC 'generously and spontaneously'[27] initiated the reforms. Later, Dalton characteristically tried to take all the credit himself; Greene and the organisations established by him are not mentioned in Dalton's memoirs.[28]

Yet without Greene's activities, the issue of constitutional change would never had come to a head at Edinburgh in 1936, and there would have been no decision on the question in 1937; reform might well have been delayed indefinitely. Greene's success owed little to the Left – Cripps's support was as much an embarrassment as a help, and pressure from left-wingers within the Constituency Parties Movement was largely destructive. The Movement's most valuable ally was Dalton, who saw the issue as distinct from ideology – and who also saw a chance to increase his own popularity. But the main reason for the Movement's victory was that Ben Greene's organisations succeeded in doing what no other group or faction has ever managed – mobilising the great army of fundamentally loyal constituency activists in a *united* campaign against the discipline imposed by the general staff at Transport House. Party officials tried to dismiss HCLA and its imitators as disruptionist splinter groups. This tactic failed: Greene had shrewdly limited his demands to those which reflected a universal grievance. It was Transport House, not the constituency parties' associations, which was shown to be out of touch with rank and file feeling.

At Bournemouth in 1937, Ernest Bevin had commented on organisations of the type set up by Greene: 'We have seen them come and we have seen them go in the past.'[29] The Constituency Parties Movement was short lived. But it brought a revolution in the Labour Party of far greater importance than anything achieved by noisier and more glamorous factional groups which captured the headlines, and claimed, with no mandate whatsoever, to speak for the rank and file.

Part Four
Alliance

15
Popular Front

In England the Popular Front is only an idea, but it has already produced
the nauseous spectacle of bishops, Communists, cocoa-magnates,
publishers, duchesses and Labour MPs marching arm in arm to the tune
of 'Rule Britannia'.

George Orwell, 17 February 1938.[1]

The adoption of the 'Popular Front' tactic by the Communist International
at its Seventh Congress in July 1935 reflected Soviet concern at Germany's
growing power and indicated a desire to work with non-communist parties
against the rise of fascism. In France and Spain, the 1935 decision led to
the establishment of Popular Front governments based on alliances
between Communist, Socialist and Radical or Liberal Parties. In Britain,
Communists had initially placed a primary emphasis on the achievement
of a united front of 'working-class' parties only – the aim of the abortive
Unity Campaign. The collapse of this campaign enabled the CPGB to con
centrate on a broad Popular Front calling for a grand alliance of Socialist,
Liberal and dissident Tory opponents of the National Government.

Yet while it was the Communists who gave the tactic its name (and who
helped to give it a bad reputation), the idea was not pioneered on the far
left, nor was support for it restricted to Communist sympathisers. Indeed
a progressive alliance of some kind was a frequent subject for discussion in
the 1930s, and at one time or another leaders of every party or faction who
wanted to change Government policy considered it seriously.

The idea developed gradually with roots on the right as well as the
left. Initially, the only support inside the Labour Party for cooperation
even with the tiny group of Lloyd George Liberals came from within the
small and over-worked PLP, whose effectiveness as an Opposition was
restricted not merely by numbers but also by its own lack of expertise and
Parliamentary skills. Outside Parliament (and especially on the exclusivist
Labour Left) resistance was, for the time being, strong – with all talk of
alliance with non-socialists identified as 'MacDonaldism', and treachery.

Certainly those who spoke loudest about realignment in the early days after 1931 were 'National' Labour men still hankering for an eventual reunion. The Labour Party must remain 'a mere Parliamentary group fettered to antiquated and now purposeless sectional interests', Lord Elton warned in February 1932, unless it broadened its appeal and became a national party based on 'a revived national Socialism'.[2]

There had been rumours that MacDonald was seeking a return to Labour to make this vision a reality. A few weeks earlier the *Clarion* reported an exchange between Lansbury and the Prime Minister in the corridors of the House of Commons. 'Well George', said the PM triumphantly, 'I'm coming back'.[3] Clifford Allen, old ILP comrade and close confidante of MacDonald, had meanwhile been circulating a document attributing to the Prime Minister 'the courage and realism of Lenin', and stressing MacDonald's determination to return to the Labour Party.[4] It was scarcely a tactful, or a hopeful theme. 'It may well be that Mr MacDonald may dream of some such future for himself,' considered the *Manchester Guardian*, 'the future of a national leader, attaching himself to the moderate elements of Conservatism, the remnants of Liberalism, and the less extreme sections of his old party', but, it concluded, the prospects of this were remote.[5]

Nevertheless, talk of new alignments was by no means all wistfulness and nostalgia. The 'remnants of Liberalism', and especially Lloyd George, shared a great deal of common ground with Labour. Before the election Henderson had spent hours in consultation at Lloyd George's bedside, and the Lloyd George group had apparently modified its attitude to Labour during the election as a result.[6] As soon as the election was over, Lloyd George made his own position clear. 'There is a fruitful belt of territory that Liberal and Labour, without touching the regions of divergence, could cultivate together for the benefit of the nation' he told an interviewer. 'But I hope the effort at co-operation will not be confined to Labour or Radicalism. There are many progressive minds outside these parties...I trust that no partisan exclusiveness will prevent all these elements from coming together'. Moreover (he claimed) the Liberal proposals *How to Tackle Unemployment* were so similar to *Labour and the Nation* that there were disputes over copyright in ideas between the two parties.[7]

There were rumours of an impending alliance between Liberals and Labour throughout 1932. In January Dalton noted 'G. L. toying with idea of L. G. coming into the Party. Cripps and I both strongly against this.'[8] In April, Lansbury had to deny a newspaper story that the formation of a 'Radical–Socialist bloc' was imminent – insisting that he had not seen Lloyd George since the election.[9] In September, with the Samuelite Liberals on the point of deserting the Government and going into opposition on the issue of protection, the *Morning Post* reported 'persistent rumours of a new working alliance with left-wing Liberals', and suggested that Henderson might be about to make an announcement to this effect.[10]

Eighteen months later the *Manchester Guardian* reckoned that the best chance of an alliance had been in the earliest days of the Parliament, when there had been

> a good deal of informal talk between certain Liberal and Labour men about the possibilities of coming together on an agreed programme. It was the most favourable movement toward common action we have seen, but it passed. Any movement of the kind from the Labour side would seem to be foredoomed to failure for the reason that it is mainly sponsored by 'reformist' Labour elements often recruited from Liberalism itself, and therefore afraid of coming out into the open for fear of what 'root and branch' Socialist orthodoxy might say.[11]

THE NEXT FIVE YEARS GROUP

It was not 'reformist' Labour elements but a Labour renegade and a Tory who sponsored the first organised attempt to coordinate the forces of the centre. In February 1935 Lord (Clifford) Allen, ill but apparently indefatigable, working in close cooperation with the young Tory MP for Stockton, Harold Macmillan, set up the Next Five Years Group, composed of leading people 'of all parties or of none'.[12]

The Group was supposed not only to be non-party, but to be non-political as well. This created difficulties. Early in 1935 Lloyd George presented to the Government a *Memorandum on Unemployment and Reconstruction*, containing proposals for a British 'New Deal'. A Cabinet Committee discussed it, civil servants scrutinised it, and the Cabinet politely rejected it. Lloyd George then looked around for allies. The Next Five Years Group had just been launched, and shared many of his views; it gave him a cautious welcome. He was allowed to help with the drafting of a book which the Group was about to publish – Allen insisting that Lloyd George should be given 'special rights of dissent because of his importance'.[13] But Lloyd George was not concerned to be non-partisan; he was looking for ammunition to use in the forthcoming general election. In July he announced the establishment of his 'Council of Action for Peace and Reconstruction'. In the same month the Group's book, *The Next Five Years – An Essay in Political Agreement*, appeared – without Lloyd George's signature, and with no indication that he had been involved.

The Next Five Years presented 'a programme of action for a number of years to come; which is reasonable enough to justify the hope that it will enlist the support necessary to secure its adoption.'[14] Half of the book dealt with foreign policy, and advocated a more vigorous pursuit of the 'collective peace system' through the League of Nations. The other half, mainly the work of Sir Arthur Salter and Geoffrey Crowther, dealt with domestic policy and stressed the need for planning in all aspects of economic affairs. It called for a small Government Planning Committee including the Prime

Minister and several Ministers without portfolio 'of the highest rank', which would work in conjunction with an Economic General Staff of non-political experts. It advocated the 'complete socialisation' of transport, electricity supply, some forms of insurance and the manufacture of armaments, and with measures of control 'without disturbing ownership' for the joint stock banks.[15]

An important feature of the book was that it elevated the idea of a mixed economy to a principle: it regarded public ownership neither as an end in itself, nor as a necessary evil.

> The historic controversy between individualism and socialism – between the idea of a wholly competitive system and one of state ownership, regulation and control – appears largely beside the mark, if regarded with a realistic appreciation of immediate needs. For it is clear that our actual system will in any case be a mixed one for many years to come: our economy will comprise, with great variety of degree and method, both direct State ownership and control, and management by public and semi-public concerns, and also a sphere in which private competitive enterprise will continue within a framework of appropriate public regulations.[16]

At the front of the book were listed the names of 153 members of the Group who wished to be associated with the ideas it put forward. These included a glittering array of well known people, with a heavy bias towards Bloomsbury and the universities, creating the impression that here was a book which reflected the collective wisdom of the intellectual and literary establishment – rather than a manifesto to make Parliamentarians join hands.[17] The list included 17 MPs – 10 Conservatives, 5 Liberals, 1 National Labour and 1 Independent. But although there were several Labour candidates and ex-MPs, and two prominent trade unionists (both ex-chairmen of the TUC)[18] the list did not include a single sitting Labour MP.

This was partly because the tiny post-1931 PLP contained few thoughtful people with the freedom of the backbenches. But there were other reasons. Harold Macmillan has described the economic section as 'a compromise between Socialists and anti-Socialists; but it was a compromise very much to my taste. On looking through it again, it must have seemed at that time to lean rather more to the Left than to the Right.'[19] To the Left, however, there were a number of features that were disquieting. The Group's readiness to allow industry a great measure of autonomy in its own reorganisation seemed suspiciously close to Italian corporatism. More than anything the Group's refusal to include the Bank of England among its candidates for nationalisation – and its insistence that the position of the Bank's Governor should be as independent as that of a judge[20] – was taken as proof of the gulf which separated this solution from a socialist one.

The Group remained divided about its political role. Was it to be a 'neo-Fabian Society', as Crowther suggested,[21] or a new political party? The possibility of joining forces with Lloyd George's Council of Action was considered, and rejected. The Group took no collective action in the 1935 election. Once it was over, Macmillan began to press for a more actively political stance; Allen insisted that the Group should remain academic and propagandist. The controversy became personalised. '[M]uch of the trouble during the last $2\frac{1}{2}$ months has been due to one man, Macmillan,' complained Allen to the Group's Executive in June 1936, 'functioning on every committee and attempting the guidance of practically all our activities.'[22] It was essentially the same conflict which had arisen on the Left, within SSIP and then the Socialist League – should a group aiming to change national policy on a broad front concentrate on educating and winning over an influential or powerful elite, or should it seek the backing of a wider, public audience?

Finally Macmillan decided to strike out on his own. In June 1936 he revamped the Group's journal, *New Outlook*, as a glossy and expensively produced magazine – independently of the Group. *New Outlook* presented a five point programme: a clear policy of collective security; the abolition of the means test; strong action in the distressed areas; the reduction of tariffs; and the extension of public control over industry – including, in some cases, public ownership.[23] Macmillan wanted a centre party based on the kind of people who were in the Next Five Years Group, but with a large part of the Labour Party added. He suggested Herbert Morrison as the leader of a great popular political party: 'but he [Morrison] would have to achieve a fusion of all that is best in the Left and the Right and it would have to be a Left Centre rather than a Right Centre'.[24] Unfortunately most of Macmillan's supporters looked unmistakably Right Centre. And there was no answer to Hugh Dalton's criticism that members of the Next Five Years Groups and of similar undertakings were 'like officers without rank and file, better known to each other than to the general public, moving in select and narrow circles, carrying almost no electoral weight'.[25] Macmillan continued his campaign into 1937 – but at the end of that year both *New Outlook* and the Next Five Years Group were finally abandoned.

FOREIGN POLICY AND THE POPULAR FRONT

In one sense the November 1935 election provided little encouragement for advocates of an inter-party alliance. The previous summer Lloyd George had suggested a deal between Liberals and Labour – involving the general withdrawal of Liberal candidates in return for a free run for Liberals in a hundred seats. This came to nothing, despite concern on the Labour Left at 'mysterious conversations between Labour and Mr Lloyd George'.[26]

Lloyd George gave up the attempt in disgust, dismissing Labour's attitude as 'It is not victory that matters; it is the dug-out and the doctrine.'[27]

The election result did not suggest that an electoral pact would have been especially productive. The truth was that a great reduction in the number of Liberal candidates – from 513 in 1929 to 161 in 1935 – left little room for electoral bargaining. The Conservatives won only 31 seats on minority votes, and it is by no means clear that most of these would have been Liberal or Labour if the weaker of the two had withdrawn.[28]

Yet the election strengthened the case for an alliance of some kind because it seemed to show that a 'progressive' Government was unforeseeable without one. Labour had obtained an even higher proportion of the popular vote than in 1929 (37.9% compared with 37.1%) with fewer candidates (552 compared with 571) but obtained little more than half as many seats (154 compared with 288). In 1929 Labour had seemed to be on the brink of an absolute majority; in 1931 it had lost disastrously, but in exceptionally unfavourable circumstances. Now, after an election fought in 'normal' times, a majority seemed a remote prospect indeed.

Furthermore, the changing international situation was creating a sense of urgency – on all sides – which the domestic crisis had failed to provide. Foreign policy was becoming a subject which transcended normal political behaviour, divided friends and brought together traditional enemies. Eleanor Rathbone, an Independent MP, suggested in September 1936 that there were already in existence two 'Popular Fronts':

> unorganised, largely unconscious, perhaps undesired. Both stretch
> from extreme Right to extreme Left. Both think they are seeking
> peace... Popular Front No. 1 seems to include the Rothermere
> press, *The Times* and several other Conservative organs, a large
> section of City opinion, probably a considerable proportion of the
> Conservative party in Parliament, Lord Lothian, the ILP, Mr
> Lansbury, and all pacifists who are 'absolute' whether on Christian
> or on revolutionary grounds. All these want to emasculate the
> League by removing all its coercive provisions...
>
> Popular Front No. 2...includes, on the Right, Mr Winston
> Churchill, the Duchess of Atholl, an unknown but probably large
> number of the more far-sighted Conservatives, probably most –
> certainly the best known – of the National Labour and National
> Liberal groups, the whole of the Labour and Liberal parties except
> the sections already included on the other front, the Communist
> Party, the opposition press, the best of the press outside London.
> All these...perceive that Fascist ambitions will grow by what they
> feed on... Hence all these uphold collective security through the
> League and oppose its emasculation.[29]

148

Attempts to turn 'Popular Front No. 2' – the disparate political groups and interests increasingly anxious that Britain should meet German claims with firmness – into an organised political reality started to gain momentum after Hitler's march into the Rhineland in March 1936. For the time being, the Labour Left rejected the Popular Front, and stuck to 'working-class unity' as its objective. Nevertheless, among Socialist League supporters there were some who favoured a wider alliance. Aneurin Bevan was one; in September 1936 he remarked that by bringing Communists and Liberals together 'we shall be making the centre more solid'.[30] The League's General Secretary, J. T. Murphy was another. So strong, indeed, were Murphy's sentiments that in the autumn of 1936 he resigned his post, and joining forces with Allan Young (a former Mosley associate, now working with Macmillan on *The Middle Way*)[31] he set up the People's Front Propaganda Committee which became a rival to Cripps' Unity Committee, launched shortly afterwards.

Murphy's Committee (described by Macmillan as 'almost wholly left-wing and not very business-like')[32] organised meetings to show that support for the Popular Front came from men of all shades of opinion. One such meeting brought together Robert Boothby, John Strachey, G. D. H. Cole, Richard Acland (a Liberal MP) and William Dobbie (a Labour trade unionist MP). All went well until Cole declared that a major objective of the People's Front must be to smash the Government. Boothby stormed off the platform. 'I dissociate myself from this Movement from now on. I am through with it' he told the press afterwards.[33] The *Manchester Guardian* could not resist the comment that the developing political alliance of two Magdalen men, Boothby and Strachey, close personal friends for twenty years, had been destroyed by a former fellow of the same college.[34]

LABOUR AND REARMAMENT

The 1937 Bournemouth Party Conference brought Labour more closely into line with other Government critics. Conference dealt summarily with the United Front tactic and placed association with Communists more firmly out of bounds than ever. 'Fronts' of any kind emerged with a bad name. Yet, at the same time, Dalton and Bevin persuaded the Party to accept a resolution which demanded a big armaments programme as a regrettable necessity. The PLP had already decided to abstain on the Defence estimates (instead of opposing them, as had been its normal practice) and the NEC had produced a document which called for a Government 'strongly equipped to defend this country, to play its full part in collective security, and to resist any intimidation by the Fascist Powers designed to frustrate the fulfilment of our obligations'.[35] Endorsement of this statement was carried massively by Conference.

The *New Statesman and Nation* saw this decision as the climax of a develop-

ment which 'could be traced from the "never again" stage after the war...
to something which in practice seems very little different from preparation
for a military alliance against the Fascist Powers'. The electorate would
gain the impression 'that in the event of a war crisis the Labour Party would
be at least as ready to co-operate with the National Government as Social
Democracy everywhere proved ready to co-operate with capitalist Governments in 1914'.[36]

In *The Troublemakers*, A. J. P. Taylor has suggested that this view of
Labour's development was false. The notion that the Left 'moved gradually
towards a more realistic, tougher policy in the usual English way' is a
legend: 'Until 22 August 1939 the Labour movement from Right to Left
retained its old principles or, if you prefer, its old illusions. It still held the
outlook of Keir Hardie and E. D. Morel, of Brailsford and J. A. Hobson...
Two simple sentences expressed it all. Imperialist capitalism was the cause
of war. Socialists should oppose both war and capitalism.'[37]

Against this, it may be said that the retention of old principles, old ideas
about the origins of war and its significance, did not preclude the acceptance of new necessities. It was possible to believe in the fundamental
corruption of an international system which produced wars, and at the same
time to see a need for national defence which involved no break with that
system.

Labour had many doubts and many uncertainties and by no means
purged itself of earlier attitudes. Those who spoke in favour of rearmament
or collective security continued to do so in traditional language and with
traditional invocations. Labour contained in its ranks a small group of uncompromising pacifists and a very much larger group who believed that
a capitalist government could not be trusted, under any circumstances, in
international affairs. But after 1937 it was the view of the Party establishment, the trade union leadership, and increasingly, after the collapse of
the Unity Campaign, of the Labour Left as well, that in order to ensure
peace, abnormal measures, including the acquisition of a realistic military
deterrent, would be necessary; and on this the Party was increasingly
united. The position expressed by Dalton at Bournemouth was to gain the
support of a growing majority in the Party and the Movement: 'In this
most grim situation, not of the Labour Party's making, our country must
be powerfully armed. Otherwise we run risks immediate and immeasur-
able. Otherwise, a British Labour Government, coming into power to-
morrow, would be in danger of humiliations, intimidations and acts of
foreign intervention in our national affairs, which it is not tolerable for
Englishmen to contemplate.'[38]

Both Left and Right opposed the making of concessions to the Dictators —
and suspected the Government of a greater willingness to come to terms
with fascist than with socialist governments. Where the Left differed from

Dalton's view was in disputing the wisdom of supporting the rearmament of an unreformed National Government lest 'we...put a sword in the hands of our enemies that may be used to cut off our own heads'.[39] For this reason, though both Left and Right regarded the ejection of the Chamberlain government from office as a first priority, the Labour Left saw this as a matter of desperate urgency and was prepared to contemplate previously unimaginable compromises to bring it about. For the first time since 1931, there were people on both wings of the Party ready to seek a tactical alliance with non-socialist 'progressive' forces.

TORY REBELS

Meanwhile major divisions had appeared within the Government. In February 1938 Eden resigned as Foreign Secretary, objecting to Chamberlain's personal diplomacy, and in particular to his pursuit of an understanding with Italy. In March, Hitler moved out of his backyard and invaded Austria. In the new crisis, the suggestion began to be heard that the Government should be broadened to include leaders of other parties.

This appealed to members of the Government, and also to its backbench Tory critics – though for markedly different reasons. The idea of extending the 'national unity' concept of 1931 had long attracted orthodox Conservatives who saw it as a means of muting criticism. Baldwin had wanted Bevin in the Government as early as February 1934.[40] Tom Jones, Deputy Secretary to the Cabinet, recorded in his diary at the end of 1936 'a growing opinion in many quarters in favour of a *genuine* National Government which would bring in Herbert Morrison, etc.'[41] *Anschluss* in March 1938 strengthened this feeling. Rumours spread that the Government was actively seeking a deal with the Opposition. Churchill told Harold Nicolson on 16 March that he was biding his time 'in the hope that the negotiations which are now going on between Chamberlain, Attlee and Sinclair for a formula of policy that will command the assent of the whole House have either failed or come to fruition'.[42] According to the *News Chronicle*, unofficial feelers had been put out to discover whether Labour leaders would be willing to accept ministerial offices under Chamberlain in order to present to the world a united national front.[43]

For Tory rebels, the attraction of a new Governmental formation was that it might bring in people ready to press for a stronger line against Hitler. 'At this time I should like to see a widening of the national basis of the Government by the introduction of some of the Liberals who left it before and some of the Labour leaders', Harold Macmillan told Tory ladies in Stockton on 18 March. 'I should also like to see the inclusion of a great outside figure like Mr Winston Churchill.'[44]

For several days there was some active if hopeless plotting by Conservative dissidents, with talk of changes more dramatic than this. 'The

H. of C. is humming with intrigue today', Chips Channon, a keen Chamberlain supporter on the Tory benches, noted in his diary on 17 March, 'and the so-called "Insurgents" are rushing about, very over-excited. They want to bring back Anthony Eden and their Shadow Cabinet is alleged to include Lloyd George, Winston and Eden.'[45] A day earlier, Churchill had boasted to Harold Nicolson that if Chamberlain's alleged conversations with other party leaders did not lead to 'a clear statement', he would 'refuse the whip and take some fifty people with him'.[46] Ronald Cartland, a young Tory rebel, told Dalton a few weeks later that about forty Conservative MPs had been prepared to vote against the Government after the Austrian affair 'in favour of some alternative combination'.[47]

Claud Cockburn's (frequently accurate) scandal sheet *The Week* later claimed that the Tory rebels had actually drawn up a list of an alternative Government, known as the '12-10-2 Government', to include 12 Conservatives, 10 Liberals and 2 Labour leaders; this had foundered because Labour refused to respond.[48] Kingsley Martin gave Dalton (who had been absent at the time) a similar account – suggesting that Attlee, Greenwood and Morrison had been briefly interested in a plan for a new Government under Churchill and Eden:

> The Labour Party and Liberal Party would be strongly represented in the Cabinet. It was said that Bevin would be willing, if offered the Ministry of Labour. It was calculated that there would be so large a break away from Chamberlain in the Tory Party that this breakaway plus Labour plus Liberal would command a majority in the House of Commons.[49]

The *Manchester Guardian* reported, however, that when Herbert Morrison spoke rather circumspectly in favour of Labour joining in forming a Progressive Opposition to the Government 'he suffered a private snubbing' from colleagues.[50]

How much was reality and how much inflated rumour is hard to judge. In the immediate situation it came to nothing. When the Commons debated the Austrian crisis on 24 March, one of Churchill's finest speeches had little effect on the House. There was no vote, no Tory breakaway, no change in the composition of the Government, and no change of policy. Nevertheless, the talk and manoeuvrings in Parliament had repercussions outside it. They created a new upsurge of interest in the possibility of a Popular Front.

POPULAR FRONT AND THE LEFT

Shortly before the Commons debate, Sydney Elliott, editor of the Co-operative paper *Reynolds' News*, announced a new popular front campaign for a 'United Peace Alliance'. Unlike earlier campaigns, the Alliance avoided any substantial proposals in the domestic sphere (where politicians remained deeply divided), and concentrated on the international situation. It aimed to strengthen the League, guarantee Czech independence 'by force of arms if necessary', combat fascism in Spain, and operate 'a complete scheme of Air Raid Precautions' in this country.[51]

The Alliance was principally concerned with tactics. The problem was how to get the Government out. Elliott pointed out that 150 Tory seats were held either on a minority vote or with majorities of less than 5000, and claimed that on the basis of the Alliance, 340 seats and a clear Parliamentary majority were obtainable. In addition, 20 sitting Tory MPs could probably be persuaded to join.[52] Small Conservative majorities could be wiped out by a progressive alliance which, as the Liberal *News Chronicle* argued, 'would give the "floating voters" something worth voting for'.[53] This involved waiting until a general election, which need not be held until 1940. Dalton had pointed out eighteen months earlier that 'not even if a Popular Front were formed and clamoured loudly for a new election, is there any reason to suppose that the Government would oblige its opponents'.[54] But by the middle of 1938 the next election had become an event which could be held at any time.

Within a few days of the launching of the Alliance, the idea had received the enthusiastic backing of the *Yorkshire Post*, the *New Statesman and Nation* and the *News Chronicle*, which reminded readers of its prediction a few months earlier 'that if a Popular Front in Britain was not established in peace-time it would come "with blood and tears" in a time of grave national peril'.[55] Delegates representing 60 DLPs at a joint meeting of unofficial London and Home Counties Labour Associations and the 'Labour Spain Committee' supported it.[56]

The Labour Left, which a few months earlier had had no time for dealings with capitalist politicians, quickly rallied behind this new initiative.[57] Constitutional changes of the previous autumn which had strengthened the Party's left-wing now allowed the Popular Front to become a central issue on the Executive. Cripps, Ellen Wilkinson, Pritt and Laski confronted their colleagues at the end of April with a broad demand for a Popular Front, and specifically for a Special Conference on the international situation.

The press was delighted. 'A first-class row has developed in the Socialist Party executive over the proposed Popular Front against Mr Chamberlain', declared Trevor Evans of the *Express*.[58] The *Daily Mail* announced that Labour was 'split from top to bottom'[59] and the *Telegraph* that it faced a 'grave internal crisis'.[60] The *Daily Herald* – the party's own paper – indicated the concern of Transport House over the controversy by devoting its leading article to condemnations of the Popular Front every day for a week.

Early in April, the NEC had issued a strong statement on *Party Loyalty*

153

reaffirming past decisions and asserting that 'so far as the Labour Party is concerned there can be no association in any way whatever with either "United Front" or "Popular Front" Movements. This decision is definitely binding on all members of the Labour Party.'[61] Now, under strong pressure, it moderated its position in another statement, *Labour and the Popular Front*. While dismissing any supposed electoral advantages of a Popular Front as imaginary, it allowed that 'a new situation might arise, of course, if any considerable number of Members of Parliament now supporting the Government were to rebel against the Prime Minister's authority. At the present moment, however, there are no signs of such a rebellion.' And it added that 'we shall go forward in no spirit of Party exclusiveness. We appeal to all that it best in the nation – to all men and women of goodwill – to make a victory for democracy and peace possible while there is still time. We shall welcome their aid. We offer them our fellowship.'[62]

These phrases suggested to the *New Statesman and Nation* that the statement 'may even have been written by someone with sympathy for the proposals it rejects'. The truth was that it reflected the divisions in the Executive – and indicated the real position. The possibility of an alliance was no longer excluded. But Labour leaders would not make the first move; and any overtures would be treated suspiciously and with ambivalence.

16
Labour and the Left Book Club

A major reason for the NEC's hesitations on the Popular Front was that the Communist Party had been agitating vigorously for one since 1936. The Communists did not make a fundamental distinction of principle between the united front and the popular front – the first was seen as a preparation for the second. The Labour Party Executive was therefore inclined to regard both with equal suspicion as tactics designed principally to increase Communist influence in the Labour Party. This suspicion was not diminished by the linking of united and popular fronts with the situation in Spain.

Closely associated with the Communist Party, and providing a prolific propaganda backing for Communist campaigns for aid to Spain and for united and popular fronts, was the Left Book Club. 'The Club devoted all its efforts to the explanation and advocacy of a People's Front', recalls its leading official.[1] The Club certainly printed more on the subject than anybody else, was responsible for getting the idea widely discussed in political circles in Britain – and created a firm association in the minds of most people between the Popular Front and Communism.

The Club was the brainchild of Victor Gollancz, pacifist schoolmaster turned successful publisher. The basic scheme of the Club was simple. For 2s 6d members received a 'Left Book of the Month', chosen by the Selection Committee – which consisted of Gollancz, John Strachey and Harold Laski. Left-wing books could be guaranteed a high circulation without risk to the publisher, while members received them at a greatly reduced rate.[2]

LEFT BOOKS AND THE POPULAR FRONT

The first monthly 'choice', *France To-day and the People's Front*, by Maurice Thorez, the French Communist leader, was issued in May 1936.[3] Thereafter, no month passed without the offer of a book on the Popular Front, Spain, or the Soviet Union. 'That we launched the Left Book Club within weeks of Franco's arrival on the mainland was by no means accidental', wrote Gollancz.[4] The timing was certainly important; it enabled the Club both to stimulate and to provide for a colossal demand for knowledge about the civil war – and to link this with resistance to fascism worldwide by means of a Popular Front. 'The aim of the Left Book Club is a simple one', ran its prospectus. 'It is to help in the terribly urgent struggle for world peace and *against* fascism, by giving, to all who are willing to take part in that struggle, such knowledge as will immensely increase their efficiency.'

In one sense the Club was an immediate, overwhelming success – as a publishing venture, mass movement and crusade rolled into one. Gollancz had hoped to recruit 10 000 members in the first year.[5] Instead he found himself with 30 000 after six months, 45 000 after twelve months and 58 000 by March 1938. By the end of 1937 the Club had 730 local discussion groups, and it estimated that these were attended by an average total of 12 000 people every fortnight.[6] Local groups discussed the monthly 'choice', raised money for medical aid for Spain, distributed leaflets and organised political meetings. Groups soon sprang up all over the world. There were groups in Jugoslavia and Chile, China and South Africa, Norway and Ceylon; Australia had 17; one of these, in Brisbane, had 450 members in 1939.[7]

The growth of the Club was partly spontaneous, partly a consequence of imaginative organisation. From the start, giant Club rallies were held in large halls all over the country. In attendance and in drama, the Club's biggest meetings outdid any organised by the Labour Party. People came to a Club rally as to a revivalist meeting, to hear the best orators of the far left – Laski, Strachey, Pollitt, Gallacher, Ellen Wilkinson, Pritt, Bevan, Strauss, Cripps, plus the occasional non-socialist, such as the Liberal, Richard Acland, to provide Popular Front balance.

Gollancz regarded the social side of the Club as crucial: he stressed the importance of the 'drafting through the Club, and particularly through the groups, of formerly "unpolitical" people into active, political work',[8] and succeeded in providing a social life which in many areas local Labour Parties were clearly failing to offer. In April 1937 he launched the Left Book Club Theatre Guild with a full-time organiser; nine months later 200 theatre groups had been established, and 45 had already performed plays. Sporting activities and recreations were also catered for. As *Tribune* commented solemnly, 'walks, tennis, golf and swimming are quite different when your campanions are "comrades of the left"'.[9]

Technical, professional, vocational and special interest groups were also encouraged. The writers' and poets' group contained many of the best talents of a fertile decade.[10] The Poetry group had seventeen branches, a Youth section, and a journal – *Poetry and the People*. There were also groups of actors, musicians, scientists, accountants, busmen, taxi-drivers, commercial travellers, architects, teachers, journalists, engineers, railwaymen, medical students and sixth formers. The *Daily Worker* commented on a large

Club Rally in 1938 that '[r]oughly speaking, one would class the gathering as a middle-class one'.[11] John Lewis estimated that 75 per cent of the membership were white collar workers, black-coated professionals and left-wing intellectuals.[12] A high proportion of its members were young and new to active politics.

One of the functions of local Groups was to be 'centres of active and energetic work for a "Popular Front" in their localities',[13] and to persuade local Labour and Liberal politicians to appear on the same platform as Communists. This brought some angry clashes. In May 1938 the Birmingham Borough Labour Party was persuaded to form a Council of Action upon which Club groups, the Birmingham Council of Labour, the Communist Party and other bodies were represented. The Birmingham Trades Council objected, however, and complained to the NEC.[14]

LBC AND THE BRIDGWATER BY-ELECTION

At Bridgwater – where Vernon Bartlett won a famous 'Popular Front' by-election victory in November 1938 – Left Book Club activities may have been a crucial factor. Gollancz maintained afterwards that 'had there been no Left Book Club there would have been no Bridgwater',[15] and it is very likely that Bartlett gained the backing of the constituency Labour Party (against fierce Transport House opposition) because of Left Book Club activities.

Richard Acland, Liberal MP for the neighbouring North Devon constituency and the Club's most prominent and active Liberal supporter, had taken part in a number of Club meetings in the Bridgwater constituency in the summer of 1938, before the seat became vacant. One of these, at Minehead, was announced by a poster which read 'Why not pull together, Liberal, Labour and Progressive Conservative for Peace, Democracy and Security.'[16] In September (when the imminence of a vacancy was still unsuspected) the Club's monthly journal, *Left News* reported that Minehead had no Labour Party but 'the LBC Group decided to take the necessary steps to bring one into existence...the LBC will give the new organisation the fullest assistance of its organisation and propaganda departments. The Club Secretary has agreed to become temporary Organising Secretary of the about-to-be-formed Party.' Later, Club members set up a local party in nearby Watchet, where Labour organisation was also dead.[17]

When it was announced on 10 October that the sitting Tory MP had been appointed a High Court judge, the news came as a complete surprise to local politicians.[18] Vernon Bartlett, a journalist without previous political affiliations, was suggested as an 'Independent Progressive' candidate by a local vicar who was an Acland supporter.[19] Local Liberals endorsed the candidacy without fuss. Labour opinion was split. According to Gollancz, 'the drive for the idea [of Bartlett's candidacy] came from the Minehead Left Book Club'.[20] A Transport House memorandum confirms that this was so: 'It is interesting to note that the "Minehead Local Labour Party" has been the chief advocate in the Bridgwater Division that the DLP should support the "Independent Progressive" candidature at the pending by-election.'[21] The constituency party was in a state of decay and insolvency, and so its general committee may have been easy to influence. Bartlett gained its backing. In the campaign, Club members from groups in Bath, Taunton, Glastonbury, Cleveden and North Somerset helped to canvas.[22]

Bartlett won the seat, overturning a ten and a half thousand Tory majority. The Government was embarrassed, and Popular Front supporters were jubilant. But the Left Book Club received no thanks from Transport House. A long document on the Club's nefarious activities – which included some twenty instances of 'interference' with local Labour Party activity – was instead presented to the NEC.[23] In December Morrison warned the Club that if such behaviour continued, 'those responsible for it will also be responsible for the further disciplinary action on the part of the Labour Party which will inevitably follow'.[24]

GOLLANCZ, KING ST AND THE LABOUR PARTY

The reason for Transport House's hostility was not just that the Left Book Club encouraged local parties to defy it, or that the Club had achieved an embarrassing popularity. It was also because of an accurate assessment that, for all practical purposes, the Left Book Club was a front for the British Communist Party.

This was true for at least two and a half years. From the middle of 1938 Strachey began to show an increasing interest in Keynesianism and Gollancz developed doubts about some aspects of the relationship with King Street. The Nazi–Soviet pact and the War broke the link and destroyed the Club's *raison d'etre*. But until the end of 1938, if not later, the Club pursued Communist aims with a diligence which made the absence of formal control unimportant.

The Club always claimed that it was merely the vehicle for a wide range of left-wing ideas, and that its intention in pressing for a Popular Front was to bring progressives together for mutual benefit and reinforcement. Even a cursory examination of Left Book Club literature shows that this was disingenuous. The private correspondence of Gollancz and Strachey indicates the extent of the Communist connection.[25]

Strachey was a fully committed Communist who found it convenient not to carry a card. Laski – a member of the Labour Party Executive from 1937 – made it clear that 'so long as the objectives that Harry Pollitt serves are my objectives, that so long as the ends that he seeks are the ends that protect the great ideals we have in common, National Executive or no National Executive I stand by his side'.[26] Early in 1937, Gollancz agreed with Strachey and Emile Burns (the chief propagandist of the Communist Party) that ideally 'there should be one or two good [Communist] Party members in all those [Left Book Club] groups in which there was none at present'.[27] About the same time Gollancz announced a scheme whereby there would be a special Left Book Club edition of every book published by Lawrence and Wishart, the Communist publishers.[28]

A Labour Party analysis of books issued by the Club in its first twelve months showed that 15 out of 27 were by Communists.[29] Gollancz maintained that this was not his wish. 'At present Communists . . . *offer* us books,' he wrote, 'we have to rack our brains to invent books for Liberals, Trade Unionists and Labour Party people to write – and then we have to find people to write them.'[30] But when the Club did commission books by prominent non-Communists, this was only to provide camouflage. 'The matter is a purely tactical one: our whole aim must be to win the maximum number of members and frighten the minimum', Gollancz wrote to Strachey in July 1936. 'In this connection, Laski has suggested that we might get Attlee to do a general book on Labour policy. I am inclined to think that as a tactical move . . . [this] might be very useful.'[31]

The Club's professed tolerance of all points of view was by no means open-ended. It did not extend to 'Trotskyists' – a category which, at this time, was defined by Communists to include a wide range of left-wing socialists who disagreed with the Soviet line. When the ILP paper *Forward* published a letter suggesting the possibility of the Club getting as book selectors 'broad-minded people of the left who are not open to the suspicion of merely being the latest gramophone record of Mr Joseph Stalin',[32] and presenting a list of possible names that included some from the ILP, Gollancz sneered: 'A miscellaneous lot! I was surprised in so varied a list not to find the name of Trotsky included.'[33] Gollancz refused to publish Orwell's *Homage to Catalonia* before a word of it had been written because he suspected, rightly, that it would support the POUM position against the Communists in Spain. Laski argued that Trotskyite attacks on the Soviet Union 'must be held to be strong allies of Nazi Germany in her militarist plans'.[34] No criticism of the Moscow Trials was permitted. 'I believe that no one who had not unalterably fixed his mind on the contrary opinion could read the verbatim reports of the trials without being wholly convinced of the authenticity of the confessions', Strachey wrote in July 1938. 'I can only say that no man can advance his political education more than by studying this supreme historical document of our time.'[35]

Like the CP itself, the Club combined a vigorous campaign against the Labour Party leadership with repeated overtures to Transport House suggesting cooperation – responding in tones of injured innocence when these were rejected. In the early days Labour leaders treated the Club with caution rather than outright hostility. Attlee (always the most sympathetic of the 'respectable' leadership to the campaigns of the extreme left) sent a message to the Club's first Albert Hall rally in February 1937, which the Club was later to treasure: 'Socialism cannot be built on ignorance, and the transformation of Great Britain into a Socialist State will need the active co-operation of a large body of well-informed men and women. For this reason I consider the success of the Left Book Club to be a most encouraging sign.'[36]

This attitude soon changed, however. In the autumn of 1937, stung into action by the Unity Campaign, the NEC announced a national campaign of its own. Gollancz offered to back this campaign with two bumper issues of *Left News* – to be filled as the Labour Party saw fit – and promised to galvanise the 600 Club groups into action to distribute them. 'I don't think I am claiming too much,' wrote Laski, 'when I say that a circulation would have been obtained previously unknown in the history of the country.'[37] At first Dalton, currently Party chairman, showed interest. For the Labour Party the proposition had some attractions. But Dalton was an old campaigner. 'The cost of publishing and pushing these two issues would, I fancy, have been a good investment for the Club in terms of new membership. But for us, to monopolise two issues, and then to finish, leaving this influx of new members to the one-sided propaganda of the Left News as hitherto conducted, was less attractive.'[38]

Dalton therefore came back with a set of conditions: first, regular contributions to *Left News* expressing official Labour policy; second, a better balance in future Club publications, with a better representation of official Labour views; third, 'the establishment of a better balance in the governing body of the Club itself, to correct its present pronounced pro-Communist tilt.'[39] Gollancz and Laski were prepared to accept the first condition, offering to devote half of *Left News* space to expressions of NEC policy; on the second they hedged; the third they found quite unacceptable, because 'it was plain from the whole character of the discussion on this proposal that Dr Dalton had in view the giving to the Club a kind of semi-official character'.[40] There the matter ended.

Dalton's offer, if accepted, might have provided an important bridge between Labour and the Communists – of precisely the kind the CP had long been seeking in other spheres. It would, however, have threatened Gollancz's personal control. This was the crunch: the prospect of any interference which involved distributing power in his new private empire was intolerable. Any suggestion that the Club might be democratised was dismissed out of hand. 'I want to make clear,' he wrote in July 1937. 'that the only article in the "Left News" which expresses *Club Policy* is this monthly article of mine, headed "Editorial" . . . *This monthly article is designedly headed*

"Editorial" precisely because it, and it alone, is to be taken as an expression of Club Policy.'[41] The Club was an integral part of Victor Gollancz Ltd; as such – as a piece of personal property, a commercial venture (though all profits were ploughed back) and part of a family business – it was guarded with a patriarchal jealousy.

The Left Book Club put into circulation over a million and a half anti-fascist, anti-war, socialist and communist books in the first three years by means of the first 35 monthly 'choices' alone. Millions of leaflets were distributed. Tens of thousands of discussion meetings, lectures, demonstrations, rallies, plays and film shows were organised. Members were recruited for the CP and the Labour Party. Bridgwater was won. Small sums of money were collected for Spain.

But the Club failed in its objectives. More than any other organisation of the Left, its aim was immediate, unpostponable changes in policy. Not only did it not produce a Popular Front: it almost certainly reduced the possibility of a progressive alliance being achieved by others. Gollancz hoped that the Club's stupendous expansion would force Labour leaders to take notice. Yet it was entirely fanciful to suppose that local Club groups could take over the Labour Party, or do anything other than create animosity among orthodox Labour activists. Gollancz's infatuation with Communism owed more to his belief in Moscow's policy of collective security than to a real conversion to revolutionary marxism. But its effect was to negate any positive influence of the Club's Popular Front propaganda, and it encouraged Transport House to treat the Club 'as though it were a dangerous type of vermin'.[42] Strachey later claimed that 'what the Left Book Club actually did do was to play a considerable part in making possible the Labour victory in 1945, through the influence of its publications.'[43] In the short run, however, as Robert Graves and Alan Hodge observed in 1940, the Club's existence served to embitter the controversy between Labour and the extreme left,[44] and identify the Popular Front even more clearly as a trap for innocents, a Communist device which hard-headed politicians would disregard.

17
Parliamentary Alliance?

That left-wing and Communist inspired campaigns for a Popular Front were not so much irrelevant as counter-productive, was demonstrated in the autumn of 1938. The Left Book Club was at a peak of popularity and enthusiasm. Yet when, for a few months, a parliamentary alliance between Tory rebels and Labour seemed a possibility, this had nothing to do with the campaigns of the extreme left, which served only as an irritant and distraction.

For a brief period after the Munich crisis, Conservative opponents of appeasement were so appalled by what Chamberlain had done that a number of them again considered very seriously the possibility of a tactical alliance with Labour. Secret and unofficial discussions were initiated to see what arrangements might be made in the Commons and in the constituencies. Labour leaders gave this initiative a cautious encouragement, and then made their own tentative approach. But nothing happened. Talks never went beyond the preliminary stages.

Responsibility for this was shared. The Tory rebels were divided and uncertain. But Conservative doubts were heavily reinforced by the hesitations and evident reluctance of the PLP leaders with whom they had to deal, and on whom their political lives might depend. The Labour leaders held back until the opportunity had passed, inhibited by memories of 1931, and by trade union and rank and file opinion which had been conditioned by several years of intra-party warfare to regard all 'fronts' and alliances as dangerous and disruptive.

MUNICH, LABOUR AND THE REBELS

During the summer of 1938 the Czech crisis worsened. On 13 September, with Hitler apparently poised to invade Czechoslovakia, the French Cabinet asked Chamberlain to negotiate for the best obtainable settlement. On 15 September Chamberlain flew to Berchtesgaden. Three days later he persuaded Daladier and Bonnet to agree to the destruction of Czechoslovakia, not so much giving in to Hitler's demands as anticipating them.[1] Hitler now raised the stakes, demanding the immediate occupation of the

162

areas to be ceded to Germany. On 24 September Daladier ordered a partial mobilisation; next day the British Cabinet rejected the German demands. By the night of the 27th, 'almost everyone in Great Britain expected that the country would be at war next day, or at least by the week-end.'[2] The Prime Minister, however, was determined that war should be avoided – at any cost. He offered to go again to Germany, and make further concessions. On 29 September he flew to Munich. He returned next day, having given Hitler everything he wanted and destroyed the structure of European defence against Germany.[3]

During the crisis, Labour sent delegations to the Prime Minister, urging a firm stand. On 21 September Attlee told Chamberlain: 'You have abandoned these people completely. You have made an absolute surrender. All Eastern Europe will now fall under Hitler's sway. We are full of the most profound disgust. This is one of the biggest disasters in British history.'[4] Protest meetings were held throughout the country. The party was more united than for years. In Parliament, there was closer agreement with Churchill, Amery, Eden and the Liberals on foreign policy than at any previous time.

Yet Labour leaders were inclined to keep their distance from these groups. On 20 September, Churchill, having seen a statement on the crisis issued by the National Council of Labour, rang Attlee and told him: 'Your declaration does honour to the British nation.' Attlee replied coolly: 'I am glad you think so.' Attlee told Dalton of this. Later in the day Dalton learned that it had been meant as 'an overture for some form of concerted action' and that Churchill was 'huffed that Attlee did not make a warmer response'. Some Labour leaders were sympathetic; Alexander, in particular, had been 'itching for more contacts with other critics of the Government', and approached Dalton about his feelings. Dalton was opposed. 'It would not strengthen any appeal of ours if it were associated with Winston or Eden or the Liberals, even if they would join, and I doubt whether it would strengthen any appeal of theirs for us to be associated with it.' Moreover 'we might upset a large number of our own Party and destroy our credit in our home market'. Yet he did not rule out an alliance altogether: 'it is possible to be too cautious, as well as too rash, towards any suggestion of conversations'.[5]

It was the shock of the capitulation, the realisation that the disunity of the Government's opponents had given the Prime Minister a free hand, which created a new willingness – on both sides – to come together. 'Thus, for a fleeting moment, it seemed possible that a large-scale Tory revolt against Chamberlain might change the whole scene.'[6]

Dalton was approached by Macmillan on 3 October after the first day of the Munich debate. Macmillan suggested that Dalton and Attlee might meet Churchill and some of his group to discuss the terms of Labour's amendment to the Government motion approving the Munich agreement. Dalton refused, but agreed to go back that night to Brendan Bracken's house in North Street, where he found Churchill, Eden, J. P. L. Thomas, Bracken and some others. This group was anxious to organise the maximum Tory abstention – and they urged that, to help achieve this, Labour's amendment should not be too patently a vote of censure. One draft pressed on Dalton spoke of 'national unity and strength'. Dalton said to Churchill: 'That is not our jargon.' Churchill replied: 'It is a jargon that we may all have to learn.' Dalton said that he thought an express vote of censure could be avoided, but that some Labour people 'were very anxious to be brave and uncompromising'. Churchill replied: 'It is not enough to be brave. We must also be victorious.'[7]

The Tory rebels now moved to a crucial question. Labour's reluctance to pursue an alliance arose, in the words of the Executive the previous May, from the fear that it 'would create more controversy in our ranks than it would remove. It would take the heart out of large numbers of our most loyal supporters.'[8] The Tories, however, needed an alliance precisely because of the controversy they had already created within their own ranks, and the consequent threat of stern disciplinary measures against them. Macmillan had told Dalton of rumours that the vote on the Government's motion would be treated as a test of loyalty: 'It would be like the Maurice debate during the First World War. Only those who voted for the Government would get the coupon. Those who abstained this week, as well as any who voted against the Government, would be marked down for destruction and official Tory candidates run against them.'[9] Dalton was now told of the rebels' fear that twenty or thirty of them might be victimised by the Whips – and he was asked what the chance was of some agreement for mutual support in the constituencies.[10]

Dalton's own account suggests that his reply was very cautious. 'I said that it was difficult to discuss anything of this kind at present; it was all much too hypothetical, but, if things went that way, we could speak of it again later.'[11] Macmillan, however, recalled a more encouraging response: 'Dalton was not unsympathetic. He pointed out that there were obvious obstacles to be overcome, but that if anything like a coupon election were tried and the dissident Conservatives, led by Churchill, fought as Independents, there should not be great difficulty in seeing that they were given a clear run by the Socialists, at any rate in most places.'[12]

The Tory dissidents had the assurance they wanted. Next day Labour tabled an amendment which substantially accorded with their requests, and on 6 October thirty or forty Tories abstained on the amendment and the Government's motion – twenty-two by sitting ostentatiously in their seats as the vote was taken. The ground had, apparently, been laid for more contacts between Labour leaders and Tory rebels.

A '1931 IN REVERSE'?

It was Cripps who pressed for the next step to be taken. On 6 October, the day of the vote, he approached Dalton with a plan.

> He thought we could agree on a programme to preserve our demo-
> cratic liberties, to rebuild collective security, and for national control
> of our economic life. He would put Socialism aside for the present. He
> thought that Attlee, Morrison and I – no more – should meet three or
> four of them, certainly Churchill, probably Amery, perhaps Eden, and
> it might, he thought, be wise to add Sinclair. From this there might
> come some new national appeal, signed by a small group of leaders
> who were prepared to take their political lives in their hands. He was
> sure that the response now would be tremendous. I asked whether he
> contemplated by-passing all our Executive bodies. He said no. We must
> try to persuade them. He thought we could. Only if we failed, should
> we break out on our own. This, he said, was a new and desperate
> situation. The Labour Party alone would never win. He regarded the
> old Popular Front idea as dead, but this move had much bigger pos-
> sibilities. On this last point I agreed with him. To split the Tory Party
> would be real big politics.[13]

Cripps' attitude had changed dramatically since the previous autumn. Then he had been a firm advocate of working-class unity against all capit-alist parties. In the early months of 1938 he had been an inactive supporter of the Popular Front – appearing infrequently in public because of ill-health. At the time of the Munich crisis he was returning by sea from a long convalescence in the West Indies. On 28 September he wrote in his diary that war was probable next day, and that Labour would presumably sup-port the Government in the policy of standing by Czechoslovakia. 'I agree that sooner or later it was necessary to stop the aggression of the Fascist powers,' he wrote. 'The question is whether it is better now to allow the present Government to try to call that halt by waging war, or whether it is necessary to continue to point out to the workers the acute danger, and, indeed, the uselessness, of allowing such a Government at the present to wage any war.'[14]

The outcome of the crisis determined Cripps' attitude. 'I would be prepared to see this country armed', he told a Bristol audience. 'If you are going to try to get collective security especially in a world where there are gangsters, then you have got to have armed forces to keep the peace. The vital thing is that those armed forces should be under the control of the common people, and not under the control of those people who ideologic-ally can sympathise with Hitler and Mussolini.'[15]

Hitler must be checked. But precisely because the Chamberlain govern-ment could not be trusted with arms, it was urgent that it should be re-moved – even if this meant a short-term political compromise.

For the moment Dalton shared Cripps' conclusion if not his premise, and proceeded to act on it. He approached Attlee, who said eagerly, 'Yes, I think it would be very useful.' Morrison was less enthusiastic though he agreed that 'it might be quite interesting'.[16] The odd thing, granted these reactions, is that Dalton waited until Cripps, nor normally regarded by him as a source of practical suggestions, prodded him. The explanation may be that Cripps' approach cleared up any uncertainty about the attitude of the Labour Left, and so made Dalton's position less vulnerable. Dalton's situation was certainly a delicate one. More than any other prominent leader, he had spoken out against united fronts and popular fronts; and he had played a major part in framing NEC decrees proscribing unauthorised involvements with other parties. For Dalton now to assume the role of broker for a new parliamentary alliance invited accusations of hypocrisy and contempt for the Party and its procedures.

Dalton, never a reluctant conspirator, was aware of the possibility of a sharp reaction from orthodox Party and trade union opinion. When Macmillan had suggested a meeting with Churchill on the morning of 4 October, just before the 11 a.m. PLP Executive, Dalton 'thought, but did not say, that it might make an embarassing time-table'.[17] To Cripps, Dalton stressed that it would 'be impossible...for us to go against the general opinion of the Trade Union leaders'.[18] Nevertheless, he was prepared to take some risks.

Dalton saw Macmillan and suggested a meeting between himself, Attlee and Morrison and three or four of the Tory group. But now the Tory rebels held back. The Prime Minister had ruled out an early punitive election, thereby quieting their immediate fears. At the same time, partly as a result of pressure from Conservative Central Office, many were in trouble with their constituency associations.[19] More important, with the crisis and the debate over, the rebels were no longer united. 'Eden and some others were very moderate and wanted "national unity" with everybody, while Churchill and Duff Cooper were out for Chamberlain's blood and inclined to join with anyone else to get it.'[20] The talks were therefore postponed.

Dalton saw Macmillan again on 12 October. The Tory dissidents were still divided on tactics. Macmillan gave the impression that he and Duff Cooper were the keenest of the rebels on an alliance. Eden seemed to be holding back, while Churchill was 'in danger of relapsing into a complacent Cassandra'.[21] Macmillan favoured a '1931 in reverse' – a union of Labour and Liberals with Tory rebels to form a new National Government. Dalton felt that this was still very remote, and told Macmillan that the Tories must vote against the Government instead of just abstaining. It was decided to hold a small private meeting if possible, consisting of Attlee, Morrison and Dalton with Churchill, Cooper and Macmillan to discuss 'how we could make our attacks and criticism of the Government from both sides of the House converge'.[22] Macmillan suggested four lines of attack: exposure of the humbug of the Munich settlement, foreign policy for the future, deficiencies in arms and ARP, and loss of trade to Germany in Eastern Europe.

But little came of all this. Dalton blamed the Tories. Cooper would not come to the meeting without Eden, and Eden would not come at all. 'Churchill was quite willing to come, but in view of the refusal of the others, we on our side thought it best to call a halt. Clearly the big Tory breakaway was off for the time being. And with Churchill himself, either alone or accompanied by Macmillan, it would always be easy to conspire.'[23]

Yet whatever the attitude of Eden or Cooper, it is clear that there were a significant number of Tories eager to maintain contact. Dalton's diary contains a passage – excluded from his memoirs – which reveals that Duncan Sandys spent an hour with him on 18 October. 'He tackled me…on possibilities of co-operation between anti-Chamberlain Conservatives and our Party. Could propaganda based on a common platform be started? He left a rough note on the lines on which this might be done.' Sandys recalls the meeting: 'Dalton was friendly, encouraging but evasive –wanting to maintain contact, but not wanting to do anything formal.'[24]

Contacts and rumours of contacts continued into the New Year. But the immediate opportunity seemed to have passed. Meanwhile two by-elections served to confuse the situation and hinder discreet diplomacy.

On 27 October the young Quintin Hogg, son of the Lord Chancellor, won Oxford against the Master of Balliol, A. D. Lindsay, who stood as an independent with the support of both the local Liberal and Labour Parties. Lindsay fought as an anti-Munich candidate, and was backed by leading Liberal, Tory and Labour supporters of the Popular Front, including Macmillan and Sinclair; thirty-nine Labour MPs (a quarter of the PLP) signed a letter of support.

The contest provoked a predictable row with the NEC, which instructed the prospective Labour candidate, Patrick Gordon-Walker, not to withdraw. Only after a fierce battle, and when it was clear that the Oxford Party would support Lindsay come what may, did the NEC finally relent, barely a fortnight before polling day. Even so, Frank Pakenham[25] and Richard Crossman, who led the campaign for Lindsay, were to have their knuckles sternly rapped by Transport House for their efforts.[26]

Oxford was a famous battle, closely followed in the press, and highly embarassing for the NEC despite (or because of) its capitulation in face of local pressure. Yet it was a clear defeat for the Popular Front. The second by-election – at Bridgwater on 17 November – was a triumph for Popular Fronters and an humiliation for the Party leadership.[27] Fought largely by local people (and with local groups of the Left Book Club apparently making the running), Bridgwater seemed to show that a Popular Front alliance could be a recipe for electoral success.

Yet this was anything but helpful to right-wing Labour supporters of secret negotiations with Tories in Parliament. Bridgwater was a great victory for the Left. To appear to give way under left-wing pressure would, in the Executive's view, be to open the flood-gates: it would undermine the authority of the NEC, strengthen the advocates of Communist affiliation, and antagonise the trade union leadership. 'We of the National Executive did not shift our ground', wrote Dalton: 'Only a big Tory breakaway would invalidate the argument we had published in May, and it would not be useful to say this publicly now.'[28]

The Tories stood to lose most if an alliance was tried and collapsed. They risked most by taking part in secret talks (which could never be kept secret for long). For the Eden group of 'moderates' – regarded as responsible leaders and with close contacts within the Government and Cabinet – a degree of aloofness from intrigue was essential. The Tories needed to be sure that a major revolt would not leave them isolated and vulnerable.

A generation later, Attlee was asked by Francis Williams why he had not pursued the Popular Front. He replied that the Communists were unreliable and the Liberals were weak. 'And then you could never get the revolting Tories up to scratch. There was the root of the trouble. You couldn't get them to vote against the Government.'[29] But in order to get the revolting Tories up to scratch it was necessary for Labour leaders to show clearly their willingness and determination to cooperate and compromise – and this they never were prepared to do.

An important factor was the attitude of the trade unions – suspicious of Communist pressure on the one hand, and of moves which might lead to another 1931 on the other. On 16 November *The Week* reported that feelers had been put out within the past few days to two Labour leaders to see if they were prepared to accept 'a spectacular but somewhat humble role' in an imagined coalition based on the Eden–Churchill group. It claimed that 'there had been a fairly close but invariably "unofficial" contact between the Labour Party and the Edenites during the past week' and there had been similar discussions for a number of weeks exploring the possibility of an alliance against the Government. 'On every occasion they have either broken down or ended in hot air because not unnaturally the persons approached have wanted to know just how "official" the approach is: in other words they want to know whether, if they jump out of association with this Government, there is another Government ready and waiting.'

Whatever the accuracy of this report, it caused a top level row. The union dominated National Council of Labour met on 22 November, sore after the Bridgwater by-election defeat on the 17th. A 'trade unionist as well as a politician' on the Council angrily drew attention to the report and wanted to know if there was any truth in it, and if so, who had authorised the attendance of Labour leaders, who had attended, and who had been responsible for leakages to the Press. He was told that the reports were untrue, but many members were not satisfied with the denial.[30]

It seems likely that contacts continued none the less. A month later *The Week* claimed that 'negotiations between the leaders of the Labour Party, Sir Archibald Sinclair for the Liberals, Lord Baldwin and Mr Eden and Mr Churchill have gone a long way'.[31] Dalton made no further reference to contacts with Tories in 1938 after the Parliamentary recess. Macmillan, however, commented that despite the abortion of these earlier contacts 'towards the end of the year some of the Labour leaders were beginning to look more favourably on the possibility of co-operating with the Liberals and the dissident Conservatives'. Those most in sympathy were Greenwood, Dalton, Morrison, Alexander and Citrine.[32]

But the situation in the Labour Party soon changed in a dramatic way. These leaders, identified with the Party and union establishment, were suddenly and unexpectedly pushed back into a traditional stance of resistance to left-wing 'disruptionism'. Cripps, recovered in health, with attitudes redefined, and determined on a new course of lonely messianism, presented the NEC with a new Popular Front demand in a way which was designed to create a maximum of controversy and publicity. Any chance of achieving an alliance was swiftly annihilated.

18

Cripps and the Petition Campaign

On 9 January 1939 Cripps wrote to Middleton, the Party Secretary, demanding a special meeting of the NEC to consider a number of proposals which he wished to put to it. These proposals, which became known as the 'Cripps Memorandum', set out familiar arguments for a Popular Front: Labour standing on its own was unlikely to win a majority in any election held within the next eighteen months; it was therefore necessary to join forces with other opposition groups on the basis of a programme of limited reforms, with constituency arrangement wherever possible. The situation was urgent 'in terms of days and not weeks'. 'I certainly should not desire to encourage the Party to any combination with other non-socialist elements in normal political times. I have in the past always strenuously opposed such an idea. But the present times are not normal, indeed they are absolutely unprecedented in their seriousness for democratic and working-class institutions of every kind.'

This combination was to include Liberals, Communists, and the ILP – but not the Churchill group of Tory dissidents:

> Winston Churchill has made an attempt through Sandys and the 100 000 movement to capture the Youth for reactionary imperialism and was much closer to success than many people imagine.[1] That movement is certainly checked and is, I hope, defeated. But the danger remains that some other such political group will make an attempt to take command of this very considerable force of young opinion to fashion it into the nucleus for a rapidly expanding centre party or democratic front. If this were to happen, and there are already steps on foot from another quarter which may possibly succeed, it would be a first-class political tragedy for the Labour Party and for the country for it would make even more difficult the defeat of Chamberlain by the forces under Labour leadership.

Cripps had moved a long way since October. Then he had urged other leaders to seek an immediate Parliamentary arrangement with Churchill.

Now, in his eyes, Churchill had become a warmonger, a threat to the peace which a Popular Front was intended to preserve. Cripps' attitude to appeasement was different from that of other opponents of the Government. The Tory dissidents, the Liberals, and most Labour MPs were opposed to further concessions to Hitler and wanted rapid rearmament. Cripps disliked concessions to Hitler but feared that the alternative under a right-wing Government was a battle between rival imperialisms. Resistance to Hitler was necessary, but it must be the right kind of resistance by the right kind of government for the right kind of ends.

> It is not at all unlikely that within the next few days or weeks Chamberlain will announce a reversal of his foreign policy upon the basis that he has tried appeasement and it has failed and that he must call on the Nation to fight fascism in what will be a purely imperialistic war. When that moment comes, if public opinion is allowed to remain in its uncrystallised state it will swing behind him, with results as disastrous as those of 1914–18 for the common people of this country and Europe.

To combat this danger, Cripps called for 'a nation-wide campaign' and 'an immediate and special appeal to the Youth movement as a whole upon the basis of combined Youth activities and a special Youth programme'. Whereas Cripps' post-Munich initiative had been aimed at a united opposition in the current Parliament, now the object was a vote-winning combination for the next election 'to provide an effective counter-blast to the "National" camouflage which will be used by the Government and also to convince people of all kinds that it is representative of the different interests and classes whom it is desired to attract within the Opposition'. It was to be a return to the heady days of the Unity Campaign, broadened to include non-socialists, but aimed not at MPs or the Government but at a mass public.

This was the plan presented in Cripps' memorandum, and formally addressed to the NEC for consideration. It is clear, however, that Cripps knew and intended that the Executive would reject the proposals; and that his real audience was not the Party leadership, but the rank and file. Indeed, Cripps' document was in reality a manifesto, designed to produce a confrontation. A key paragraph stated:

> In order that there may be no misunderstanding I desire to put on record that in the event of such a [NEC] meeting not seeing their way to accept the principles of this memorandum or to take any definite action in the direction indicated I shall claim the right to circulate it with the exception of those parts which might embarrass the Party, with the object of gaining support within the movement for the views therein expressed.

The Executive held a special meeting, as requested, on 13 January. Early in the proceedings, Clynes referred to this paragraph, and asked what Cripps had in mind.[2] According to Dalton, Cripps 'did not tell us that he had everything prepared',[3] and Pritt recalled later that '[i]t had not occurred to me at the meeting that Cripps had any plans for further action'.[4] After a two hour debate in which he was strongly opposed, especially by Attlee, Morrison and Walker, Cripps proposed and Pritt seconded the adoption of the memorandum. This was defeated by 17 votes to 3. Apart from Cripps and Pritt, the only supporter of the memorandum was Ellen Wilkinson; Laski was absent.[5]

Cripps' next move had been well planned. Yet he had apparently said nothing even to Pritt, who had backed him. According to Pritt, it was only after the meeting that Cripps told him 'I shall take this to the Party... I shall circulate all the Divisional and Borough Labour Parties, and other Party organisations.' Cripps then produced a letter which Pritt took to be a draft. Pritt said that he should think the matter over carefully, and modify the letter. Cripps replied: 'I *have* thought over it, and I shall move at once,' adding, 'I must not delay', and then, 'As a matter of fact all the documents are ready. I want everyone in the local organisations to be able to consider them before the weekend is over. The documents are in envelopes ready addressed, and my people are waiting to hear from me. I shall telephone them and they will post them at once.'[6] Sir Trevor Evans, then a *Daily Express* reporter, recalls Cripps rushing out of Transport House, and asking him for change for the telephone. Evans had two pennies, but no change for sixpence. 'Just now your tuppence is worth more than my sixpence', said Cripps, disappearing into a telephone kiosk.[7]

Letters asking for support went out that night to all Labour MPs, candidates and secretaries of affiliated organisations; a copy of the memorandum and a printed, stamped and self-addressed post-card was included in each envelope.

Next day the NEC issued a statement, broadcast by the BBC in the evening, stating that Cripps' appeal 'could only bring confusion and division within the Party'.[8] Cripps can scarcely have been surprised by this reaction. However, he wrote angrily to Middleton, complaining that this had given world-wide publicity to differences in the Labour Party over the Popular Front question, 'and is of course intended to be, as it is, an attack upon myself. As the National Executive have chosen to make this matter one of public discussion and have taken it out of the field of domestic difficulties within the Party, they will not of course, object to my following their example.'[9]

Middleton replied next day, sending Cripps a copy of the NEC statement, and informing him of another special NEC meeting to be held on the 18th. According to Dalton, the time of this meeting – 4.15 p.m. – was specially fixed to enable Cripps to attend after the Courts had risen.[10] Cripps, however, had no intention of submitting to an Executive carpeting. He excused himself on the grounds that he had to attend an urgent consultation with the Midland Bank.[11] Before the NEC meeting, Dalton went to see him. The conversation was not friendly. 'I should have preferred a tête-à-tête,' Dalton recalled, 'but Lady Cripps remained knitting throughout our conversation, though she took no part in it. Her presence cramped my style and probably stiffened his. I met a front of uncompromising self-righteousness.'[12]

The NEC meeting on 18 January referred the matter to the Organisation Sub-Committee which submitted a report to the NEC a week later. The report made much of Cripps' 'deception' in not telling his colleagues at the meeting on the 13th that the Memorandum had already been printed ready for dispatch; it accused Cripps of 'a prepared and organised campaign to change Party direction and leadership'. It advised the NEC to require Cripps, on pain of expulsion, to reaffirm his allegiance to the Labour Party, and to withdraw the circularised Memorandum.[13]

The NEC met on 25 January to consider these recommendations. When they were put to him, Cripps asserted that 'he had no intention of re-affirming his allegiance to the Labour Party as he thought that the work he had done on behalf of the Movement during the last eight years made this unnecessary', and he declared that under no circumstances would he recall the Memorandum issued to the Movement.[14] The recommendations were endorsed by 18 votes to 1, only Ellen Wilkinson dissenting. Pritt was absent with gout; Laski was in America.[15] Cripps then left the meeting, and the Party. John Wilmot, runner up in the constituency section, was co-opted to fill the vacant place on the NEC.[16]

That night Cripps addressed a huge 'Arms for Spain' meeting in the Queen's Hall, where, among devoted followers, 'it was legitimate to dream that a political breakthrough in Britain might be possible'.[17] With Cripps on the platform was a mixed group of Popular Front supporters – members of the International Brigade, Ebby Edwards and Will Lawther of the Miners' Federation, J. B. Priestley, A. D. Lindsay, Vernon Bartlett, Victor Gollancz, Nye Bevan. 'If Sir Stafford Cripps is expelled,' Bevan told the assembly, 'for wanting to unite the forces of freedom and democracy, they can go on expelling others... They can expel me. His crime is my crime.'[18] Newspaper placards proclaimed CRIPPS OUT, and next morning the *Daily Express* announced: 'The Labour Party has blown its brains out.'[19]

After that, wrote Dalton, 'we were in a fight to a finish'.[20] It was to be the biggest row and rupture in the Labour Party since 1931. In 1937 the 'Unity' conflict had been straightforwardly between Left and Right. The Popular Front appealed to fellow travellers and to 'Lib-Lab' elements as well.

173

The miners apart, Cripps had little support from trade unionists. March-bank of the NUR summed up the views of many: 'Some of us are beginning to think a grave mistake was made by the trade unions affiliated to the Party in assenting to changes in the constitution at the Bournemouth Conference in 1937, which seem to have placed a premium upon indiscipline and disloyalty within our ranks.'[21]

In the constituency parties, on the other hand, Cripps had built up a large number of devoted admirers, especially among the young. It was reported at the beginning of 1939 that seven out of ten requests from DLPs for Labour speakers asked specifically for Cripps.[22] Cripps had a power to generate, through words and his own deep conviction, a sense of socialism as a faith to live by. Richard Crossman felt that he appealed to younger Party members who suspected that the NEC's socialist commitment meant 'the determination to wait until the millenium arrives according to pre-war rules'. Those who had grown up since the war could not accept this attitude. 'We know that we are not living in a world which is evolving towards Socialism, and in which there is time to wait. That is why many of us, who often disagreed with Sir Stafford's tactics and opinions, feel that he is fundamentally on our side. He knows the urgency of the situation and realises that Labour cannot jog along in the old traditional way.'[23]

The National Petition Campaign, launched at the end of January, was an attempt to bring together those who shared this sense of urgency.

'BLOOMSBURY REVOLUTIONARIES'

The National Petition Campaign was based on the policies which Cripps had presented to the NEC in his Memorandum on 13 January. Instead of the pledge cards of the Unity Campaign, sympathisers were given copies of a petition to sign. The Petition read:

> WE BRITISH CITIZENS, looking out on a world threatened as never before by War and Fascism, call upon the Parties of progress to act together and at once for the sake of peace and civilisation.
> We ask for a Government that will:
> 1. DEFEND DEMOCRACY, protect our democratic rights and liberties against attack at home and from abroad;
> 2. PLAN FOR PLENTY, multiply the wealth of the nation by employing the unemployed on useful work; increase old age pensions; ensure a higher standard of life, education and leisure for old and young;
> 3. SECURE OUR BRITAIN, organise a Peace Alliance with France and Russia, that will rally the support of the United States and every other peace-loving nation and end the shameful policy which made us accomplices in the betrayal of the Spanish and Chinese people to Fascist aggression;

4. PROTECT THE PEOPLE'S INTEREST, control armaments and the vital industries, agriculture, transport, mining and finance;

5. DEFEND THE PEOPLE, provide effective protection for the common people against air attack and starvation in the event of war;

6. BUILD FOR PEACE AND JUSTICE, end the exploitation of subject races and lay the foundation of a lasting peace through equality of opportunity for all nations.

In the face of the perils that confront us, we urge you to combine in every effort to drive the National Government from office and win for us the SIX POINTS in our petition. To a Government of your united forces we pledge our wholehearted support.[24]

Cripps gathered impressive allies. Among early 'petitioners' were Sir Charles Trevelyan, Will Lawther and Alfred Barnes (Chairman of the Co-operative Party).[25] 27 Parliamentary candidates signed. But although seven MPs (including Bevan, John Parker, S. O. Davies and Philips Price) added their names to a letter of protest at Cripps' expulsion, most of the 39 MPs who had signed a letter of support for Bartlett at the Bridgwater by-election did not now support Cripps. D. N. Pritt, who had fought for Cripps on the Executive, refused to sign his petition: 'what Cripps did was, of course, a most direct act of defiance... For myself I decided that I ought to obey Party discipline and not follow Cripps into exile.'[26] So did Ellen Wilkinson, who told the Press she had decided 'to remain a loyal member of the Labour Party',[27] and resigned from the editorial board of *Tribune*.

Some sympathy for Cripps was based on liberal horror at his expulsion rather than on agreement with his point of view. Lord Addison, Tawney, C. M. Lloyd, Leonard Woolf, J. A. Hobson and the Webbs signed a joint letter to the NEC suggesting a gentlemanly compromise. Addison, veteran of Coalition and Labour Cabinets, was certain that the memorandum 'would not endure a fortnight in a Cabinet of Labour and Liberal leaders... On the other hand, I cannot imagine a case for expulsion and heresy hunting in a Party that professes loyalty to freedom of speech and opinion.'[28] Philips Price considered the memorandum 'a poor affair, badly drafted and full of loose thinking', and regarded Cripps' behaviour as 'incredibly bad tactics'. However, 'the Executive have poured oil on the flames by expelling Cripps instead of, say, temporarily suspending him from the Executive'.[29]

Yet there were others, bitter opponents of Cripps in the past, who now accepted part at least of his argument. A. L. Rowse, maverick right-wing Labour candidate for Penryn and Falmouth, dismissed the Popular Front, but insisted that an electoral understanding with the Liberals would make an election victory virtually certain.[30] Ivor Thomas, candidate for Spen Valley, and usually a strong Dalton supporter, tried to arrange a compromise involving the ending of Cripps' campaign, a free run for sitting ILP and

Communist MPs, and electoral arrangements between Labour and Liberals in appropriate constituencies.[31]

Some of Cripps' strongest supporters were Liberals or non-party 'centre' people. Sir Archibald Sinclair, the leader of the Liberal Party, endorsed the memorandum on 24 January.[32] 'In the spring Mr Chamberlain presented to Signor Mussolini the head of Mr Eden on a charger,' he observed, 'and now that the troops are battering their way into Barcelona, the Labour Party has presented the head of Sir Stafford Cripps.'[33] Other Liberal MPs, including Sir Richard Acland, Wilfrid Roberts and Lloyd George, backed the campaign. So did Keynes. He wrote to Cripps, 'I am in full sympathy with what you are doing',[34] and to the Press,

> The attitude of the official Labour Party towards all this strikes me as one of the silliest things in the history of British politics. Why cannot they face the fact that they are not sectaries of an outworn creed mumbling moss-grown demi-semi Fabian Marxism, but the heirs of eternal liberalism, whose sincere convictions reflect and should inspire those of the great majority of their countrymen?... I am all for Sir Stafford Cripps, and I would join his movement if he is successful in getting it launched.[35]

Within the Labour Party, it was those without roots in the trade union movement who were most inclined to regard themselves as 'heirs of eternal liberalism' and side with Cripps. For those with a union background, Cripps' flagrant defiance of Party decisions seemed disloyal, insolent and egotistical – symptomatic of a middle and upper class individualism which was really a kind of snobbery. 'People are much too fond of talking with condescension about the Labour Party, usually in middle-class tones', George Ridley, a trade union member of the NEC, complained in the *New Statesman and Nation*, a prime offender. 'They are Bloomsbury revolutionaries.'[36] Middle-class intellectuals expected to lead; they did not accept easily the dictates of long established leaders whom they regarded as their intellectual inferiors. Trade union leaders had not forgotten Sir Oswald Mosley's meteoric course through the Labour Party, nor that most of the Labour ministers who had joined the National Government in 1931 had been middle-class: they were inclined to see a parallel in the Popular Front.

The Petition Campaign began with a nation-wide speaking tour. Cripps was supported by two MPs, Bevan and G. R. Strauss, and with two candidates, Robert Bruce and Lieutenant-Commander Edgar Young, working as organisers. The tour started with meetings at Newcastle, York and Birmingham. 'When Cripps appeared on the platform, and when he rose to speak, there was often cheering lasting for minutes. It was a political revivalist campaign.'[37] He told the Birmingham audience: 'I do not think it is any good saying at this stage that we must have Socialism, pure Socialism, nothing but Socialism...first let us make sure of our democracy and freedom so that we may win our Socialism.'[38]

As a theme, it was easy to attack. Attlee commented drily:

> The swing over by a man of great ability in a few months from the
> advocacy of a rigid and exclusive unity of the working-classes to a
> demand for an alliance with the capitalists, and, from insistence on the
> need for a Government carrying out a Socialist policy to an appeal to
> put Socialism into cold storage for the duration of the international
> crisis is a remarkable phenomenon...Such instability gives me little
> trust in his judgement. In a few months he may ask us all to change
> again.[39]

Nevertheless, Transport House was seriously embarrassed. A general election could be called at any time. Cripps' suggestion that Labour could not take on the National Government single-handed appealed to Tory newspaper editors. 'Sir Stafford may easily prove to be the biggest figure thrown up by the Labour movement in the past twenty years', commented the *Daily Mail* which until recently had regarded him as only marginally less dangerous than Stalin. 'The Labour leaders call him an amateur, but all the time they know that they are working under his shadow. He towers above most of them in ability, conviction, sincerity, and determination.'[40]

The Executive had also to worry about the divisive effect of Cripps' activities in the constituencies. By late February, Transport House had received 221 resolutions from local organisations protesting against Cripps' expulsion, and only 32 supporting the NEC's action; of 153 Borough and Divisional Labour Parties sending resolutions, 94 were protests and 59 gave support.[41] Fearful that the situation would get out of control, the NEC decided to make support for Cripps a punishable offence.[42] At the beginning of March, the seven most prominently involved – Bruce, Young, Bevan, Strauss, Sir Charles Trevelyan, Will Lawther (Acting President of the MFGB) and a third Labour MP, C. C. Poole – received letters warning them that their participation in Cripps' campaign was inconsistent with Labour Party membership. They were also asked for a written recantation, indicating their intention to sever their connection with campaigns for a Popular Front, and their determination to behave better in future.[43]

Poole and Lawther promptly withdrew from the campaign, and gave the requisite assurances.[44] All the others reacted defiantly. Trevelyan declared that he would preside at Cripps' next big meeting, Bevan rejected the NEC's behaviour as 'intolerable', and Strauss announced that 'such bludgeoning tactics' would have no effect but to devitalise the whole movement.[45] On 15 March – the day that Nazi troops entered Prague – Bevan, Strauss, Young and Bruce wrote jointly to the NEC asking for advice 'as to the manner in which our views as well as its own can be placed before the Party', and giving no assurances about their future behaviour.[46]

Meanwhile the campaign was providing excitements for some of its younger supporters. '[W]e rallied, we campaigned', recalls Ted (now Lord) Willis, then chairman of the (Crippsite) League of Youth, 'and our activities reached a climax in February 1939, when we organised a great Youth Pilgrimage to London. It succeeded beyond our expectations: thousands of young people from all over Britain, travelling by train, bus, bicycles and on foot, descended on London.'[47] At a National Council of Labour rally in Trafalgar Square, Morrison and other speakers were jostled and shouted down with rhythmic cries of 'We want Cripps' while young *Tribune* sellers climbed on to the plinth and 'conducted a Crippsian chorus in the crowd'.[48]

But the tide of constituency opinion soon began to run against the rebels. A majority of resolutions received by the NEC in March supported its actions, and by 21 March the tally of DLP resolutions was 134 for the Executive and 134 against.[49] Cripps seemed to get a better response, moreover, where Labour's electoral support was weakest, 'where the hopelessness of a socialist victory has inclined the standard-bearers to look for allies even at the cost of exchanging thorough-going Socialism for social reform',[50] and consequently where there were no Labour MPs to be pressurised by rank and file opinion. Thus Cripps was backed by a large majority of DLPs in the Southern and Home Counties Area (25 against and 12 for the NEC position) where Labour had no seats, but by barely a third of DLPs in the working-class and Labour voting North East and North West (30 against, 58 for).[51]

The NEC reviewed the situation on 22 March. The division between disciplinarians and moderates produced an unusual alignment. It was Morrison who proposed an amendment (which Attlee seconded) calling for the matter to be held over until Conference.[52] Clynes was a strong supporter of moderation; so, surprisingly, was George Ridley. Dalton pressed for firmness: 'At this stage I could see no gain from hesitation.'[53] Voting was close. 10 backed the amendment, 13 opposed it. It was then decided to send an ultimatum to the rebels – giving them seven days to recant, withdraw from the Campaign and reaffirm their allegiance to the Party.[54] But the rebels refused, and were expelled on 30 March. Trevelyan wrote to Attlee with aristocratic disdain: 'If you are a big enough man, you will stop the destruction of the soul of the Party.'[55]

OUT OF THE PARTY

A purge of lesser people followed. No action was taken against 30 prospective candidates who had written to the NEC declaring their intention of continuing their activities on behalf of the Campaign;[56] Bristol East DLP, which stood firmly behind Cripps, was threatened but not disaffiliated; when Brailsford asked the NEC to expel him too because 'I have committed all the offences with which the last batch of criminals is charged...may I assure you that I shall repeat my offences?' – this was ignored.[57] But others were treated less indulgently. Within a few days of the expulsion of the well-known rebels, Dennis Gordon, candidate for Kingston, G. H. Loman, secretary of the Surrey Labour Federation, the president, vice-president and nine other members of the Bury Labour Party were all expelled for associating with the Cripps campaign.[58]

The policy of extreme severity was effective. As in 1932 after the disaffiliation of the ILP, and in 1937 after the proscription of the Socialist League, very few councillors or party officers were prepared to risk their political careers for a cause which had become hopeless.

Moreover, the international situation had entered a new phase. Hitler had moved into Prague on 15 March, in contemptuous defiance of the Munich settlement. The British Government at last faced the necessity of confronting Hitler from a position of strength; appeasement was replaced by a policy of making guarantees to Germany's weaker neighbours, combined with rapid rearmament.

These developments had less impact on the Left, however, than events in Spain, where the civil war ended bloodily during the last two weeks in March. Franco's victory, long expected, was a bitter and stunning blow when it came. This 'more than any edicts from Transport House, had broken the spirit of the Left'.[59] For many, consciously or unconsciously, the Petition Campaign was a final throw to save Spain; when it failed there seemed little worth fighting for.

The only question at the Whitsun Party Conference was whether the Executive's victory over Cripps would be overwhelming. By the time delegates had assembled at Southport, this seemed likely. At Easter the Co-operative Party (which a year earlier had been one of the first bodies to back Sydney Elliott's United Peace Alliance) rejected the Popular Front decisively. The only major national union backing Cripps fully was NUDAW, rejecting the advice of its political secretary, W. A. Robinson MP, who had moved the expulsion of Cripps on the NEC. Support also came from the National Union of Clerks and the South Wales Miners, always faithful to the causes of the Left, and now standing solidly behind Nye Bevan. Elsewhere there was little sympathy for the rebels. The mood varied from exasperation to an ugly anti-intellectualism. 'Away with all those cranks who cumber the policy of the Labour Party with all the damned -isms under the sun', shouted a delegate at the NUPE conference, 'Away with those senseless females and those ladylike young gentlemen who waste their time advocating everything from the establishment of nudist colonies to pensions for indigent cats.'[60]

Cripps had asked for the right to state his case at Conference in person. Since he was no longer a Party member, he was not constitutionally entitled to do this; the NEC, however, resolved to let Conference decide whether to give him a hearing. By a narrow majority (1 227 000 to 1 083 000) it agreed to do so.

Cripps was heard after lunch on the first day. As delegates returned, 'Cripps was standing by the orchestra pit, slim, aloof, and dignified, his notes in his hand waiting to be called.'[61] As he mounted the rostrum 'the entire Conference, including the public gallery... broke into a storm of cheers and boos'.[62]

This issue before Conference was Cripps' expulsion, not the Popular Front. Nevertheless, it was an opportunity for Cripps to indict the leadership, to call for unity against fascism, and to seek to rouse the Movement to the urgency of the crisis. This was what delegates expected. They were disappointed. Cripps read a lawyer's brief, page by page and point by point, arguing that in circulating his Memorandum he had broken no law in the Party's Constitution; it was the speech of a defence counsel appealing against the decision of a lower court.

Labour Party Conference is not a forum of debate in the normal sense. Delegates are not moved by cold analysis. They expect to be enthused, aroused, outraged, stirred. They are won by appeals to their noblest aspirations, by reaffirmations of hallowed principles. The spectacle of a rich and clever lawyer pleading a detailed case on his own behalf evoked no response. The impression created was that the Petition Campaign had been concerned less with a Popular Front than the issue of Cripps' expulsion.

'The harshness of the comments upon Cripps were terrible for those of us who knew his complete sincerity and devotion', wrote Richard Crossman. 'But as it was, he played the part not of the victim beside the block, but of a pale ghost returning from Hades and arguing that he was still alive.'[63]

Dalton replied for the Executive. '[I]f we had not taken that act [the expulsions], disintegration and demoralisation would have spread throughout the Labour Movement. Little people would have grumbled that big people were getting off while little people were being disciplined, and demoralisation would have spread. Decent, loyal people would have packed up and got out.'[64] Decent, loyal delegates nodded their agreement. But the star of the debate was an unknown delegate from St Albans. It was the first day of George Brown's first Conference. Cripps' speech angered him. When he was called to speak 'I nearly fell off the rostrum with fright. But I knew what I wanted to say.'[65] He made a bombastic speech of a kind delegates had been waiting all day to hear: voicing their irritation with Cripps and appealing unashamedly to class resentment against the rebels:

> The fact is that we have wasted nine blasted months in a pre-election year just doing nothing but argue the toss about Cripps... I think we

ought to remind Sir Stafford Cripps, Mr Bevan, and my old boss, Lieutenant-Commander Young, who probably remembers ordering me around the show-rooms in Oxford Street – we ought to remind these people that the part is not greater than the whole, and while we are members of the Party and the Executive may be a pack of idiots, once we have decided we are, we may as well go forward.[66]

When the vote was taken, the humiliation of the Crippsites was complete. Cripps' expulsion was approved by 2 100 000 to 402 000. Two days later the Popular Front received the support of a derisory 248 000. Cripps had not even rallied the constituency vote; more than three fifths of DLPs apparently voted against him on the expulsion issue, and fewer than one DLP in six backed the Popular Front – despite Dalton's private suspicions of 'a pro-Cripps block vote among the DLPs'.[67]

Five of the rebels – Cripps, Bevan, Strauss, Young and Bruce (but not Trevelyan) – applied for readmission to the Party immediately after the endorsement of the expulsions. The NEC was in no hurry. In October it offered readmission – on condition that the rebels not only promised to mend their ways, but also expressed regret at their past misdeeds. All refused. Bevan, however, was readmitted on slightly moderated terms in December following pressure from his union, and Strauss was accepted back on the same basis the following February. Cripps spent the war as an Independent MP, not returning to the Party until March 1945.

The Whitsun Conference killed the Petition Campaign and the Popular Front as well. Any serious chance of an effective alliance in Parliament had been destroyed.

Cripps' supporters later claimed an educative effect for the Petition Campaign. '[W]hen the chips were down,' argues Lord Willis, 'the youth who made up our fighting services were not entirely unaware of the enemy or of the issues at stake.'[68] At the time, however, its most important effect was to limit the political manoeuvrability of the PLP leadership. The position of the NEC and Parliamentary Executive would have been insupportable if it had been discovered that while rank and file Popular Front supporters were being sharply disciplined and even expelled, 'big people' at Westminster were secretly plotting with capitalists.

According to Michael Foot, '[Cripps'] manoeuvre in circularizing the local parties was regarded almost as a piece of sharp practice and was made to figure prominently in the controversies of the next few weeks. While the nation debated the political issues at stake and while Barcelona was falling, several Executive members chiefly complained of Cripps' outrage against constitutional propriety.'[69]

Yet it is impossible to interpret Cripps' behaviour as other than deliberately provocative. Cripps' secretiveness, his refusal to consult his colleagues on the Executive (even Pritt, a political ally) about his plans, makes it clear that he envisaged a highly personal confrontation right from the start, and. that he relished the disruption his behaviour would cause.

No doubt, for Cripps, the matter was one of high principle: 'The right which I then asserted, and still assert, is the right of any member of the Party to communicate in any way that he or she wishes, and at any time that he or she considers necessary, any suggestion or argument in favour of changing the policy or tactics of the Party.'[70]

But at such a time of national crisis it was an indulgence to split the Party over this. Cripps' extraordinary conscience drove him to pursue a particular solution once he had decided that it was the right one, regardless of consequences. Yet careful negotiation and delicate diplomacy, not a highly personalised populism, were required if, in the circumstances of 1939, an effective combination against Chamberlain were to be achieved.

19

Labour and the War 1939–40

The War gave Labour an opportunity for influence greater than it had had since 1931 – and one which it now used with striking effectiveness. The collapse of the Chamberlain Government in May 1940 was brought about partly because of a growing disaffection on the Tory backbenches – but also as a result of a collective Labour determination not to be bought off. In all parties, a broad 'national' coalition was regarded as desirable, if not essential. By indicating their willingness to serve in such a government, but only if Chamberlain was not at the head of it, Labour leaders were able to exert a crucial pressure. Meanwhile the Nazi–Soviet pact removed, at a stroke, one factor which had hitherto stood in the way of Parliamentary alliances. Soviet 'benevolent neutrality' towards Germany after August 1939 shattered the far left in Britain, and the Popular Front ceased to exist as a symbolic and divisive issue.

After the publication of Cripps' 'Memorandum', there were no further serious attempts by Labour leaders to coordinate activities with other opponents of the Government before War was declared. One reason was the Petition Campaign. Another was Labour's uncertainty about military service. Early in 1939, the Churchill and Eden groups increased pressure on the Government to accept conscription. Labour remained opposed to any form of compulsory military service. At the end of March, Churchill, Eden, Cooper and other Tories signed a motion calling for a National Government 'on the widest possible basis', and linked this to military and industrial conscription. At the end of April, the Government introduced a limited form of compulsory National Service. The PLP and most Liberals opposed.

Once this decision had been taken, however, Labour quickly accepted it, and it soon ceased to be contentious. A resolution at the Whitsun Labour Party Conference calling for non-cooperation in defence measures was defeated by a huge majority – 1 670 000 to 286 000. Tory rebels and the PLP maintained their distance. But on foreign and defence policy they continued to find themselves fighting on the same side – opposing any further concessions to Hitler, insisting that the Polish guarantee must be honoured, and pressing for a serious attempt at an alliance with Russia.

THE INVASION OF POLAND

All through the summer months, the Labour leaders pressed the Government to take a strong line against Hitler, and to create an effective alliance for this purpose. But the Government, having set aside appeasement, showed no urgency about finding an alternative and the Russians, suspicious of Britain's intentions, decided to make separate arrangements. On 23 August Ribbentrop and Molotov concluded a non-aggression pact between their two countries, freeing Hitler to attack Poland, and removing any serious hope that a major European war could be averted.

Next day, Parliament voted the Government special powers, and all three parties gave their support, with Chamberlain, Greenwood, Eden and Sinclair making it clear that there could be no repetition of Munich. The National Council of Labour (designated 'the authority of the Labour Movement' in the event of war)[1] issued a *Message to the German People* indicating that Labour stood fully behind the Government's guarantee to Poland. Next day the Anglo-Polish treaty of alliance was signed reaffirming the agreement between the two countries.

Early on 1 September German troops entered Poland. A British message demanding the cessation of German aggression and a withdrawal was not delivered until the evening. It contained no time limit. Next day there was a further delay: Mussolini had offered to mediate. When Parliament met on the evening of the 2nd, there were rumours of another British sell out. Chamberlain made a vacillating speech which seemed to confirm these fears. Greenwood (leading the Opposition in place of Attlee, absent through illness) rose to reply. There was a cry from the Tory backbenches: 'Speak for England!'[2] Greenwood spoke simply:

> Every minute's delay now means the loss of life, imperilling our
> national interests (Mr Boothby: 'Honour') – let me finish my sentence. I
> was about to say imperilling the very foundations of our national
> honour, and I hope, therefore, that to-morrow morning, however hard
> it may be to the Rt Hon. Gentleman – and no one would care to be in
> his shoes to-night – we shall know the mind of the British Government,
> and that there shall be no more devices for dragging out what has been
> dragged out too long.'[3]

Greenwood was cheered loudly. One Tory critic of Chamberlain considered this speech 'certain to be the greatest of his life; a speech that would illuminate a career and justify a whole existence.'[4] Later that night, Greenwood went to Chamberlain and told him that unless war was declared in the morning, it would be impossible to hold the House.[5]

The attitude of the Commons was probably decisive in bringing an immediate declaration of war. The same night, the Prime Minister told Halifax that his statement

had infuriated the House and that he did not believe, unless we could
clear the position, that the Government would be able to maintain itself
when it met Parliament the next day... Then followed an hour of
frantic telephoning to the French Government, Daladier and Bonnet,
and to our Ambassador in Paris, Sir Eric Phipps, with the object of
getting an agreement to give the Germans as short a time-limit as
possible.[6]

The Cabinet met from 11.30 p.m. to 1.30 a.m. When it was over, Halifax
returned to the Foreign Office. As he went in, he met Dalton. Dalton said,
'Foreign Secretary, can you give me any hope?' Halifax replied, 'If you
mean hope of a war I think I can promise you a certainty for to-morrow.'
Dalton replied, 'Thank God'.[7]

Two days earlier Chamberlain had suggested to Greenwood that Labour
leaders might accept office in a possible War Ministry. The PLP Executive
rejected the offer unanimously. The Labour leadership had already anticipated this move, and the answer had been prepared. The question had been
discussed by the PLP Executive on 24 August. The fear was that the Prime
Minister would make selective pickings among Labour leaders to give his
government a more 'National' appearance, as MacDonald had done in
1931. It was agreed that nobody should commit himself without authority,
and a joint meeting next day with the General Council and the NEC endorsed this conclusion.[8] A move to publish a resolution declaring that if
Labour was asked it should refuse was not taken up after H. B. Lees-Smith
had argued that this would be good propaganda for the Germans, and
Citrine that it would make Labour look ridiculous.[9]

Labour also feared tying its hands and losing all influence through the
acceptance of minor posts. Dalton pointed out to R. A. Butler, Halifax's
number two at the Foreign Office, that

> if, for instance, members of the Labour Party were given, say, one
> seat in the Inner Cabinet, plus the Postmaster General and the
> Secretaryship of State for Latrines, we should not only be uninfluential
> within, but we should lose most of our power to exercise influence
> from without... Further, we should lose much of our own credit
> amongst our own people, who would be filled with suspicions at our
> official participation.[10]

Labour's refusal prevented Chamberlain from presenting the country
and the Commons with a genuinely 'National' Government. It may also
have persuaded him of the distasteful necessity of including in the war
administration Churchill and Eden, the two most influential Tory critics of
his pre-war Government. According to Churchill the Prime Minister
'mentioned that the Labour Party were not, he understood, willing to
share in a national coalition. He still had hopes that the Liberals would

join him. He invited me to become a member of the War Cabinet. I agreed to his proposal without comment.'[11]

Churchill urged the Prime Minister to press the Liberals to come in, giving Labour's refusal as a reason, and to bring in Eden. The Liberals refused. Eden became Dominions Secretary.[12]

LABOUR AND THE PHONEY WAR

For the next eight months Labour pursued a policy of limited cooperation with the Government. It declared its full support for the war effort, while retaining the right to criticise. It agreed to an electoral truce, subject to the right to terminate it at any time. It agreed to allow members to assist the Government in an administrative capacity, locally and nationally. It cooperated in evacuation plans and in National Service and Ministry of Information local committees. It decided to maintain a special liaison with leading Ministers – Greenwood keeping in touch with the Prime Minister and Foreign Secretary, Alexander with the First Lord of the Admiralty, Lees-Smith with the Secretary of State for War, Pethick-Lawrence with the Chancellor of the Exchequer, and Dalton with the Air Minister and Minister of Economic Warfare. The War Cabinet refused to give these 'patriotic gadflies to ministers'[13] information as of right, but did not object to informal contacts.[14]

Officially the electoral truce did not mean a political truce. But the subtleties of Labour's notional position of 'candid friend' of the Government[15] were confusing to the rank and file. Urged to support local information committees often sponsored jointly by Conservative and Labour agents, many members were perplexed. Opposition to the truce grew, and came from all sections. In December, the NEC decided to maintain the truce – but only by a small majority.[16] The following month, Labour leaders faced a barrage of criticism at political rallies.[17] When the agenda for the Labour Party's Annual Conference was published in March, it contained a mass of resolutions attacking the truce – and adding to the discomfiture of the leaders. A sense of frustration among the rank and file may have contributed to a rapid decline in Party membership – from 409 000 in 1939 to 304 000 in 1940 according to official figures, which almost certainly masked a greater decline.[18]

Though Party leaders were sure that they could not serve under Chamberlain, they did not try to get rid of him. The general view was that the Government could only be changed if there was a serious breakdown among Chamberlain's supporters, 'and if, as someone says to me [Dalton] privately, "Winston is ready to strike". Not clear that we are here yet.'[19] This meant, in effect, that Labour's attitude towards shifting Chamberlain had not substantially changed since 1938. It also left Labour leaders as unclear as the government about objectives. Labour statements of war aims in November and February were not helpful – and indicated that, at heart, Labour was as committed to the 'phoney war' as the Cabinet. Thus the February statement declared: 'Victory for democracy must be achieved, either by arms or economic pressure or – better still – by a victory of the German people over the Hitler regime, resulting in the birth of a new Germany.'[20]

Chamberlainite Tories clung to the hope of a German economic collapse. Many on the Left indulged a no less dangerous, or absurd, fantasy – that the German people would miraculously come to their senses. 'To have begun the war by dropping leaflets instead of bombs on the towns of Germany is a right and imaginative stroke', commented the *New Statesman and Nation*, whose record for repeatedly underestimating Hitler was unrivalled in the English press, 'to enlighten the German people about the behaviour of their rulers is the most important of the tasks before us.'[21]

Labour's small pacifist wing meanwhile pressed for talks with Hitler. In November 1939, twenty Labour MPs signed a 'Memorandum on Peace Aims' calling for an immediate conference to end the war and secure 'a negotiated peace at as early a date as possible'. Signatories included Lansbury, Sorensen, Sidney Silverman and James Barr, and former ILP Clydesiders: George Buchanan, Neil Maclean and David Kirkwood.[22] The views of this group were shared by Trevelyan, still out of the Party. 'It is not so impossible as in the last war to discuss terms,' he wrote privately in October: 'I have a deep-seated feeling that none of the people want to fight and that the war will collapse.'[23]

The Executive took no action against pacifist opponents of the war; its purge of Communist sympathisers, however, was not quite over. When Stalin attacked Finland at the end of November, Labour backed the British Government's offer of help to the Finns. Luckily Finland capitulated before the British Government could carry through its apparent intention of fighting wars against the Soviet Union and Germany at the same time. But feelings of sympathy for the heroic resistance of the Finns were running high.

For some Communists and fellow travellers the invasion of Finland was the cause of a final break with the Communist Party. For others it was no harder to accept than the Russo-German pact. D.N. Pritt, the most consistent supporter of Comintern policies on the Labour NEC, responded to this new development with two books: *Must the War Spread?* and *Light on Moscow* which sought to justify Soviet policy. In March 1940 he was expelled from the Labour Party, and a number of local parties which showed Communist leanings were reorganised by Transport House. Meanwhile, events were moving towards an end of the 'phoney war', which for the Opposition, as for the Government, had been a period of unease and uncertainty.

LABOUR AND THE TORY REBELS

In the new year, the Tory critics' attitude stiffened, and new attempts were made to create a bridge between them and the official Opposition; An All Party Action Group was formed by Eleanor Rathbone (an Independent) with Boothby and T. L. Horabin as secretaries, and Clement Davies, a Liberal, as Chairman.[24] The 'Eden Group' (which no longer contained Eden) had continued to meet regularly under Amery's leadership. Rumours that appeasers in the War Cabinet were working out a deal with the German General Staff to make peace in return for the elimination of Hitler now roused its members to fury. Lord Cranborne, a leading figure in the group, suggested a small committee of 'very respectable Conservatives' to exercise pressure on the Cabinet. Harold Nicolson noted in his diary:

> We all agree that such pressure would only be possible if it could be indicated that in the event of reluctance on the part of the Government, we should tell them quite frankly that we will go to the leaders of the Opposition and promise them that if they insist on a Secret Session we shall go to the point not only of supporting them at that session but of voting against the Government if necessary.[25]

This 'Watching Committee', formed early in April, and led by Cranborne's father, Lord Salisbury, made very tentative contacts with Labour – at first through the mediacy of Clement Davies. A series of confidential meetings with Attlee took place in which Attlee apparently tried to find out whether the Tories would carry their increasing dissatisfaction with the conduct of the war to a vote in the Commons.[26] No agreement was reached, and discussions were still continuing when the crisis which was to bring the Government down occurred.

The German invasion of Norway early in April brought the first major British attack of the war. British troop landings at two Norwegian fishing ports, Namsos and Andalsnes, were beaten back in the face of German air power, and both forces were evacuated on 1 and 3 May. Another force sent on Churchill's advice to capture Narvik was eventually withdrawn on 8 June. By then the repercussions of this humiliating episode had transformed the political situation at home in a way which was to determine the course of the war.

Under pressure from the Opposition, the Government agreed to a debate on the Norwegian campaign, to be held on 7 and 8 May. Both Opposition and Tory critics now viewed Chamberlain's departure as a matter of urgency. To get rid of Chamberlain, it was essential that official and 'unofficial' opposition should work together. But despite Attlee's contacts with the Watching Committee, there was apparently no attempt at coordination until the last day or two. Both groups acted separately, not knowing how or whether the other would move, basing actions on rumour and hearsay, and with a near-fatal tendency to caution.

On 2 May a meeting of the All Party Action Group decided that the debate on 7 and 8 May should be used for a showdown.[27] There was talk of persuading Attlee to put down a vote of no confidence. Nothing came of this. But the first day of the debate made it clear to Labour that the moment for a serious attack had arrived. Yet nobody knew if there would even be a division. The motion before the House was for an adjournment for the Whitsun recess; division on an adjournment motion was highly unusual. Much depended on the Opposition, and whether it decided to divide the House.

That night Dalton told Macmillan that the PLP Executive would decide next morning what to recommend. Macmillan reported this to the Watching Committee, which also met in the morning. Salisbury's view at this stage was that the Tory rebels should abstain in the event of a vote.[28] The PLP Executive met at 10.30 a.m. Morrison, Attlee and Lees-Smith supported a division; Dalton, Tom Williams, Pethick-Lawrence and Wedgwood Benn were opposed. Dalton argued that 'a vote at this stage was likely to consolidate the Government majority and that Chamberlain and Margesson [the Conservative Chief Whip] would like us to have one'.[29] Eventually it was decided that there should be a division, and a full PLP meeting immediately afterwards endorsed this decision.

When the House divided, many thought the Government would be brought down. Bitterness was intense. For the Tory rebels, 'it was no pleasure to note the curious and gleeful glances of Socialists and Liberals as unused to the company of Conservatives in their lobby as we were to seeing them in ours'.[30] 'Quislings', jeered the Chamberlain supporters, 'Rats', 'Yes-men', replied the rebels.[31] Then the figures were announced: 281 to 200. The Government had won, but 41 Government supporters had voted with the Opposition, and 65 were absent unpaired. There was uproar; Josiah Wedgwood and Harold Macmillan broke into a tuneless rendering of 'Rule Britannia'; this was drowned in shouts of 'Go, go, go, go'.[32]

The rebels did not anticipate that Chamberlain's departure would be immediate, nor did they know who should succeed him. Early in the afternoon, Amery chaired a meeting of Conservatives who had voted against the Government and persuaded them to agree to support any Prime Minister 'who would form a truly National Government with a real War Cabinet based on personal merit and not just a Whips' coalition'.[33] It was decided not to publish this for the moment.[34] Boothby immediately told Dalton and James Walker, who were talking together at Annie's Bar in the House of Commons, and asked them whether, in view of the imminence of the Labour Party Conference (due to start four days later), it would be helpful if he passed on the rebels' verdict to the press. Receiving an affirmative answer, Boothby duly leaked to hovering journalists.[35]

RESIGNATION

There were only two possible successors to Chamberlain – Halifax and Churchill. The Prime Minister favoured Halifax; so, probably, did a majority of Tory backbenchers. It was widely believed, and probably accurately, that most Labour MPs shared this preference.[36] But it was Halifax himself who decided the issue – by refusing to serve. Labour thus had little influence over the choice of the new Prime Minister. But in determining Chamberlain's decision to resign, and in overcoming his hesitations and procrastinations, the firmness of the Labour leaders appears to have been a crucial factor.

On the afternoon of 9 May, the Prime Minister held a consultation at No. 10 with Churchill, Halifax, Attlee and Greenwood. According to Attlee:

> [The Prime Minister] appeared calm. He had Winston and Halifax with him. He told us he believed there was now a paramount need for a National Government and asked us if we would join it and serve under him. Then Winston joined in and urged us to come under Chamberlain... I said: 'Mr Prime Minister, the fact is our party won't come in under you. Our party won't have you either'... In order that there could be no doubt I said I would put to [the Executive] two questions 1) Are you prepared to serve under Chamberlain? 2) Are you prepared to serve under someone else? and would wire or telephone back. On that we parted politely.[37]

Attlee's cold statement did not, however, settle the issue. When news came through in the early hours that Hitler had invaded Holland and Belgium, Chamberlain's reaction to this new factor was to feel that, if possible, he should stay on. He telephoned Attlee, possibly to make this suggestion. Sinclair, the Liberal leader, was prepared to back the Prime Minister. He saw Attlee and pressed that it might, after all, be desirable for Chamberlain to remain for a time. Attlee disagreed. Responding to a request from Chamberlain for a message saying that Labour supported the Government in the crisis, he and Greenwood issued a carefully worded statement:

> The Labour Party, in view of the latest series of abominable aggressions by Hitler, while firmly convinced that a drastic reconstruction of the Government is vital and urgent in order to win the war, reaffirms its

determination to do its utmost to achieve victory. It calls on all its members to devote all their energies to his end.[38]

At what point did Chamberlain finally make up his mind to go? According to Churchill, when he and Halifax met the Prime Minister at 11 a.m. on the morning of 10 May Chamberlain 'told us that he was satisfied that it was beyond his power to form a National Government. The response he had received from the Labour leaders left him in no doubt of this. The question therefore was whom he should advise the King to send for after his own resignation had been accepted.' Halifax then said that he was not willing to be Prime Minister.[39]

A difficulty about this is that the Labour NEC – assembling in Bournemouth, where the Party Conference was to be held – had not yet discussed its attitude. Attlee and the other leaders had, however, indicated that its decision was a foregone conclusion. Chamberlain may have decided after talking earlier to Attlee that further delay was pointless.

Another obstacle (or excuse) for delay may also have been removed. A letter written by Chamberlain next day suggests that a reason for the Prime Minister's hesitations was a belief that the Labour Party shared his preference for Halifax. Before Chamberlain resigned, however, the situation had apparently changed: 'Later I heard that the Labour Party were veering towards Winston and I agreed with him and Halifax that I would put Winston's name to the King.'[40] That the Prime Minister's perception was correct is confirmed by Dalton: 'Since that morning, with the new sharp twist in Hitler's offensive, all of us had felt, and most had said to one another, that now it *must* be Churchill not Halifax.'[41] Hitherto Chamberlain may have been holding out in the hope that Halifax might change his mind, or (if he would not) that Labour would baulk at the prospect of a Churchill premiership. Now any such illusions had been removed.

The NEC met at the Highcliffe Hotel in Bournemouth at 3.30 p.m. It resolved unanimously 'That the National Executive Committee of the Labour Party is prepared to take its share of responsibility as a full partner in a new Government under a new Prime Minister which would command the confidence of the nation.'[42] As the meeting broke up, the Prime Minister's Private Secretary rang through to ask the answer to the two questions Attlee had promised Chamberlain the previous night to put to the Executive. Attlee replied: 'The answer to the first question is, no. To the second, yes.'[43]

When the War Cabinet met at 4.30 p.m., the Prime Minister read out the Labour Executive's resolution, and said that 'in the light of this answer, he had reached the conclusion that the right course was that he should at once tender his resignation to the King'.[44] He did so forthwith. Churchill kissed hands at six o'clock.

Alliance

A Parliamentary combination had at last, in a moment of acute crisis, and with the minimum of cross-bench cooperation, brought about a critically important change in national leadership. The alliance and united challenge which had eluded Government opponents in peace time had been achieved in one crucial Commons division. Above all, the persistent refusal of Labour to join any government under Chamberlain's leadership had determined the Prime Minister's fate.

LABOUR AND THE COALITION

Churchill's Coalition was established over the next few days. The possibility that Chamberlain might be made Chancellor of the Exchequer or Leader of the House was successfully resisted by Attlee and Greenwood;[45] the former Prime Minister became Lord President instead. Discussions on 11 May between Greenwood, Attlee and Churchill about the structure of the new government were reported to the Labour NEC as they took place: Attlee spoke to Dalton on the telephone, who relayed messages back and forth. After Churchill had given the assurance that 'he was very anxious that several of the Industrial Leaders not now in Parliament should be given office', the NEC accepted, by 17 votes to 1, the outlines of a proposed government, including a recommendation that Attlee and Greenwood should be members of a five-man War Cabinet.[46] The National Council of Labour then met and endorsed this decision.

Conference, which met on 13 May, created no difficulty. There was some suspicion of the new Prime Minister. 'The first time I heard of Winston Churchill,' recalled one delegate, 'was in 1910 when he sent soldiers to South Wales not to fight Hitlerism but to fight the miners, and ever since then Churchill's attitude has been one of sheer naked honest reaction.'[47] But a pacifist motion received no support. 'You cannot dither in a crisis', said Attlee: 'You have to take your decision. You cannot leave these things over for days',[48] and almost everybody agreed that the decision was the right one. The Movement was, at last, united. A NEC resolution backing the decision to join the government was carried out by 241 300 to 170 000.[49]

When Churchill completed his government a few days later, there were fifteen Labour members – six more than in the first 'National' Government of 1931. In the War Cabinet, Attlee became Lord Privy Seal and Deputy Prime Minister, and Greenwood became Minister without Portfolio. Alexander was given the Admiralty, Dalton the Ministry of Economic Warfare, Bevin the Ministry of Labour, Morrison the Ministry of Supply. Junior ministers included Tom Williams, Chuter Ede, Dai Grenfell and Ellen Wilkinson. Almost all had a wide following in the Movement, and there were few whose status seemed to entitle them to a place who were left out.[50] 'I have formed the most broad-based Government that Britain has ever known', boasted Churchill: 'It extends from Lord Lloyd of Dolobran to Miss Ellen Wilkinson.'[51] The contrast with 1931 could not have been greater.

20

Conclusion

Might the Labour Party in the 1930s have been used as an instrument for aiding the unemployed at home, restraining fascism abroad, or making a significant step towards the achievement of socialism? The answer of this book is that opportunities existed but were wasted – partly because of left-wing pressures which, so far from encouraging brave initiatives, inhibited the Party leadership and restricted its room for manoeuvre. Such a view is opposed to the argument of marxist historians that Labour's failure reflected the 'tentative and doctrinaire' nature of Labour socialism, 'an overriding commitment at all levels of the Party to Parliamentary politics' and a consequent failure 'to politicise a depressed and potentially militant working-class in more than the requirements and ethics of electoral politics'.[1]

For those whose approach is revolutionary (in the sense of a belief that the pursuit of a fundamental transformation of society should normally take precedence over other aims) a case can be made for the second indictment. It can be pointed out that Transport House rejected any strategy aimed at creating in the workers a realisation of their own power; that the TUC followed the Mondist doctrine of cooperation with Government and employers, preferring local unemployed associations to hunger marches, recreational facilities for the out of work to industrial action; and that it was left to the Communists to organise the unemployed, and (through the Communist-inspired Left Book Club) to discover and cater for a mass demand for socialist political education.

Yet Labour has never been a revolutionary party, and revolutionary socialists among its members have never been more than a tiny minority. The Labour Party as a whole has always seen itself as a party of the present as much as of the future. Capitalist institutions and organisations have been regarded suspiciously, but there have been few members, even on the Labour Left, who have consistently argued that no use should be made of capitalist structures in the pursuit of immediate remedies for existing problems. The Labour Party is, indeed, a reformist party, claiming to be a reformist party, and it has been on its reformism, rather than its long-run socialist aspiration, that its appeal to the electors has been based.

194

It is possible, of course, to argue that such an attitude is misconceived – that a party which compromises with capitalism cannot win any significant gains for the working-class. Whatever view may be taken of this as a general proposition, it is especially hard to justify when applied to Britain in the Depression. Mass unemployment was a tragedy not just because of the misery it caused – but because it was unnecessary. The steps which needed to be taken to reduce it drastically were comparatively simple, and involved no great threat to vested interests; they were also accepted by many politicians, administrators and intellectuals of different political persuasions.[2] Nor were the events which led to the Second World War inevitable: a Government which Hitler had been forced to respect might have averted catastrophe. In both foreign and domestic spheres, the kind of policy employed by a British Government of the 1930s, whether that Government were Labour, Conservative or Coalition, was of crucial importance to the British working-class.

Labour in power, with the right policies, could have changed the situation on both fronts in a fundamental way. Out of power, its possibilities were greatly reduced. Nevertheless they existed, and might have been exploited; that they were not, that Labour's influence on events in the 1930s was minimal, had little to do with attributes ascribed to Labour by the marxists. Indeed the marxist interpretation suffers from two central weaknesses.

First, the view that Labour failed because it did not try to radicalise the working-class rests on the assumption that the working-class in the 1930s was 'potentially militant' – that it might have been roused to a greater level of political effectiveness. There is little to suggest that this was so. Certainly, the working-class showed few signs of *actual* militancy after the General Strike and until post-war full employment had created a new sense of security and strength. Membership of extreme left bodies remained minimal. The Communist Party grew slowly, and the (largely middle-class) Left Book Club flourished after 1936; but the (largely working-class) ILP disintegrated and died after 1932 – and the Socialist League never captured its following. It is true that the Communist-led NUWM attracted widespread support, and the hunger marches and rallies of the unemployed assembled large numbers of people in some impressive demonstrations. Yet these appeared as a bearing of witness to the despair and anger caused by the miseries of the Depression rather than as a display of mass power. Later in the decade political rallies in support of a united or popular front, or against fascism in Spain, served to maintain enthusiasm and a degree of public interest; but they were on no greater scale, and had no greater significance in terms of creating a 'militant' or 'radical' working-class, than the nuclear disarmament or Vietnam demonstrations of the 1950s and 1960s.

The argument that this picture of working-class 'moderation' was a consequence of conditioning by a moderate or faint-hearted trade union movement and Labour Party ignores the constraints of the time: the effect of a depressed labour market in undermining those in work as well as out of it, and in making the defence of existing employment and wage levels the primary requirement of trade unionism. Indeed the experience of other countries gives no ground for believing that the British working-class lost a great opportunity for self-assertion in the 1930s – rather it would lead one to doubt whether 'depressed' and 'militant' are character-istics which a working-class as a whole can simultaneously maintain for any length of time. In those non-fascist countries where expansionist policies were successfully used to tackle unemployment – the United States, Sweden, New Zealand – this was because of the electoral victories of re-formist parties and politicians, not as a consequence of mass action.

The second weakness of the marxist case, and a more basic one, is to regard 'radicalising the working-class' as one of the objectives or purposes of the British Labour Party. For those who regard this activity as crucial to the achievement of any significant change, it is logical to dismiss the Labour Party because it does not do it. It makes no sense, however, to blame the Labour Party for not doing what it never set out to do. For the reality is not that Labour is bad or dilatory or half-hearted about radicalising the working-class, or has not lived up to the high hopes once placed in it, or any similar formulation. It is simply that this never was a function the Labour Party intended to perform.[3] The Labour Party has never been a mass movement, still less a revolutionary vanguard. It was founded as, and remains, an electoral machine.

It has frequently been pointed out, by defenders as well as detractors, that Labour's socialist conversion was late and superficial. 'In 1918 the Labour Party finally declared itself to be a Socialist Party', wrote Tawney fourteen years afterwards. 'It supposed and supposes, that it thereby became one. It is mistaken. It recorded a wish, that is all; the wish has not been fulfilled.'[4] In its internationalism, in its economics, and in no small measure in its personnel as well, Labour long remained true to its Liberal origins. Yet the 'Lib–Labism' of Labour's outlook, in contrast to the social-ism of its rhetoric, has not been the crucial factor in determining its relationship with the masses.

Far more important has been Labour's Parliamentarism. This has not been merely an orientation or predilection; it has been the very reason for its existence. When the trade unions set up a political committee to arrange for their representation in Parliament, representation was what they had in mind: policy was secondary. Since 1918 Labour Party Con-ferences have consistently announced their belief in socialism and their support for socialist policy. But the purpose of the Labour Party has not been to create a socialist (or a liberal) Britain, still less to create a 'mighty force of Socialist faith' which, as Miliband points out,[5] it declared as its aim in the heady autumn of 1932, and from time to time reaffirms. Though a majority of individuals and bodies within the Labour Party may be, in some sense, socialist, the national organisation which calls itself the Labour Party is everywhere geared to a purpose which has no connection with governmental policy. The purpose of the Labour Party has always been to win seats: to gain the election, at local and national levels, of men and women who are the representatives of the working-class.

The Labour Representation Committee had been set up in 1900 to pursue this simple objective, and from 1900 the aim of the Labour Party and its local organisations was 'to organise and maintain a Parliamentary Labour Party with its own Whips and policy' and to secure the election of candidates for this purpose.[6] From 1918, Labour's fortunes improved dramatically. This was not a consequence of the Party's new socialist pretensions – though its broad-ranging appeal, inaugurating a new 'Christmas tree'[7] approach to politics, with gifts for everybody, may have helped. Far more important was Henderson's transformation of Party organisation from a loose coalition of electoral allies into a body of tightly-knit local branches, rigorously based on electoral boundaries – constituencies, boroughs and wards – and subordinating all other considerations to the electoral aim. This new structure, firmly resting on trade union money, power and repute, and relegating the socialist ILP to a subservient role, was able to exploit the disarray of the Liberals and dragoon newly enfranchised working-class voters to the polls. The aim was not to raise the level of working-class consciousness – but to gain the election of Labour MPs to the House of Commons.

Those who have criticised Labour for not doing what it never sought to do – that is, for not creating a militant working-class – have taken little notice of its extraordinary success in creating the machinery necessary for carrying out its aim. Tawney accused it of having 'mistaken luck for merit'[8] in its electoral success. Yet the mushroom growth of local party organisation was not luck. It was one of the most remarkable political achievements of the twentieth century. Individual Labour Party membership barely existed in 1918. By 1928 there were 215000 members. The expansion continued steadily, despite the humiliations of 1931, and by 1936 this figure had doubled to 431000 – at a time when the three left-wing bodies which sought to mobilise the working-class could barely muster 15000 between them.

A consequence of this expansion was that by the mid 1930s the individual membership had become a powerful collectivity in its own right, able to insist on direct representation to the National Executive. What is significant is that the Constituency Parties Movement (which unlike the Socialist League, really could speak for the grass roots) succeeded in its demands because of its view of the role of the rank and file: not as the educators of the masses nor as the vanguard of the proletariat, but as people who selected candidates, raised money for elections, knocked on doors, licked envelopes, and got voters to the polls.

The lesson of 1924 and 1929–31 was not that Labour should use its growing rank and file in order to educate the masses in the requirements of socialism. Rather, it was that incoming Governments of limited experience stood no chance of introducing new policies, or carrying out significant changes, if their only weapons against a highly skilled conservative bureaucracy with a monopoly of information were good intentions and uplifting slogans. The trouble with Labour's 1928 document *Labour and the Nation*, and with *Labour and the New Social Order* ten years earlier, was not that they did not measure up as blue-prints for socialism. It was that they were not blue-prints at all. Labour's false start in the 1920s did not arise because Labour was committed to gradualism; still less because it refused to contemplate a political approach which by-passed constitutional procedures; it was because, in Tawney's words, it 'drugged itself with the illusion that, by adding one to one, it would achieve the millenium, without the painful necessity of clarifying its mind, disciplining its appetites, and training for a tough wrestle with established power and property'.[9]

Put another way, it was because Labour leaders – with wide experience of political organisation and propaganda, and in some cases, of Parliament as well – had little perception of, or preparation for, the highly complex technical problems which major changes in the political and economic system involved. They had some idea about what they wanted. They had very little idea about how to achieve it.

Some of those who emerged to lead the Party after 1931 saw this clearly, and set about remedying it. Dalton and Morrison, both of whom had seen the processes of Government at close quarters, were involved in setting up and operating the NEC Policy Committee, and in developing new plans for industry and finance during the 1930s, based on practicalities as they had seen them. The Labour Left, however, perceived the situation differently – and in consequence lost a unique opportunity to influence the development of Labour socialism at a time when many people in the Labour Party were rethinking their ideas, and were especially prepared to consider left-wing solutions.

It was not inevitable that the Labour Left should play little part in the process of detailed policy-making. It had been G. D. H. Cole – a man of left-wing (indeed, syndicalist) attitudes – who had revived the Fabian tradition of providing the nuts and bolts of socialist policy with the formation, in 1931, of NFRB and SSIP. Both of these bodies initially included dominating elements of left-wing intellectuals. After 1932, however, the two moved in different directions. SSIP merged into the new Socialist League, and rapidly forgot about research. NFRB soon became the natural home for planners and economists who found Dalton and Morrison more constructive as leaders than Cripps. Whereas in the 1920s it had been the left-wing ILP which had produced the most interesting and advanced ideas in the Labour Party, in the 1930s the most seminal work came from men associated with the highly 'gradualist' New Fabians. The literary output of the far left – within and outside the Labour Party – was prodigious, and much of it of lasting interest: Strachey's marxist critiques, for example, or exposés of the worst aspects of the Depression by Orwell, Wilkinson and Hannington. But nothing was ever produced to provide the Labour Left with the left-wing equivalents of Dalton's *Practical Socialism For Britain* and Jay's *The Socialist Case*.

The Labour Left refused to reject Parliamentary democracy, but at the same time maintained a profound reluctance to accept the possibility of achieving much by means of it. This was the consequence of a strange congruence of contradictory traditions: a strong pacifist tendency, opposed to revolutionary violence, and a liberal constitutionalism, highlighted by the row over the expulsion of Party rebels in 1939, accompanied by, and conflicting with, a desire for revolutionary change and an often uncritical admiration for Soviet communism.

Cripps, and the Socialist League, tried to reconcile constitutionalism with revolution by stressing the need for a Labour Government to take Emergency Powers immediately on assuming office, in order to anticipate the likelihood that capitalists would close ranks, as in 1931, and frustrate socialist measures by all possible means. In this way capitalism could be destroyed and socialism brought about without bloodshed, while democratic liberties were preserved. This was based on the assumption that all that stood in the way of a Labour Government and the inauguration of socialism were a few dangerous and reactionary individuals – provided, of course, that Labour was led by men of genuine socialist conviction and had the wholehearted backing of the people.

The moral was that Labour should 'make socialists' – a view which owed more to the Christian socialism of Lansbury, Cripps or Gollancz than to marxism–leninism. For the Socialist League, as later for the Left Book Club (one of whose platform favourites was the theatrical 'Red Dean', Hewlett Johnson), the rhetoric and imagery were as often theological as political. The struggle was a crusade, the object was to win converts to a socialist faith. 'If we cannot within the framework of our party get together a body of men and women, especially young men, who will see the cause of Socialism as a religion,' Lansbury wrote to Cripps, who shared his beliefs, in 1932, 'to be served as St Francis, Savonarola, and Tolstoy served their faiths, all our work is hopeless.'[10]

One consequence was the emphasis on symbolic campaigns, seen as having a value independent of the issues, based on meetings with all the trappings of revivalism – for example, the mass signing of 'pledge cards' or of Cripps' Petition. Another consequence, far more dangerous, was a belief that the widespread expression of a sentiment constituted a major step towards its achievement. Thus in 1932 the Labour Left hailed as a great victory Trevelyan's Conference resolution committing Labour to the immediate promulgation of 'definite socialist legislation' upon attaining office. It would have been as useful for the Party to have bravely announced that it favoured virtue, and intended, upon winning an election, to do good.

Scarcely more significant was the paper victory for the Labour Left of a commitment to nationalise the joint stock banks. If this had been part of a comprehensive financial plan for the next Labour Government, it might have formed the basis for an alternative Labour strategy. Without such a background, and manifestly advanced by people who (with a few exceptions) had little understanding of banking, it was easy for opponents (such as Dalton) to bury the proposal long before Labour came to power.

In this respect, the death at the end of 1933 of Frank Wise, by far the most financially sophisticated of left-wing leaders, was a specially serious blow to the Labour Left. Wise combined a deep commitment to the need for socialist change with a unique experience of the governmental machinery which had to be operated in order to carry it out. As Chairman of the Socialist League, he might (in contrast to Cripps and Mellor) have persuaded its highly talented members to construct a cohesive left-wing plan, based on serious research and study. His death removed this possibility – and also removed a lingering chance that the Labour Left might appropriate new Keynesian economics and make it central to a left-wing attack on unemployment.

In the 1920s Wise had been one of a number of outstanding ILP intellectuals, including Mosley and Strachey, who had tried to inject Hobsonian and Keynesian economic ideas into the Labour Party. During the 1931 crisis Mosley and Wise had been almost alone in the House of Commons in attacking the sterility of orthodox financial policy, so stalwartly defended by both front benches. It was the next two years which made sure that the seed of economic radicalism planted in the Labour Left (and never widely understood) should not bear fruit. The Labour Left was already suspicious of ideas which seemed to involve compromise with the forces of capitalism. The espousal of fascism by Mosley, the man who so strongly championed them, reinforced this prejudice, while Strachey, disenchanted with Mosley, rejected Keynes for an uncritical acceptance of the marxist dialectic, using his great skills and influence on the Left to cultivate the view that Keynes was a threat to socialism. Wise's death destroyed a remaining chance that the progressive expansionism of the ILP in the 1920s might be developed into the basis of a powerful campaign for a British New Deal as a frontal assault on mass unemployment, perhaps seeking to enlist non-Labour Keynesians and planners. A left-oriented Next Five Years Group could have provided a convincing alternative to the economic retrenchment of the National Government. Instead the Socialist League was taken over by Mellor's marxism and Cripps' political rootlessness and economic immaturity. On the Labour Left Keynes' eloquent appeal to socialists in 1932 to take up policies which were 'economically sound'[11] on the basis of their own principles went unheeded.

Rejected by the Left, Keynes entered Labour policy by way of the Right: introduced by dons and professional economists who had learnt their socialism in university common rooms and who saw Keynes' demonstration that in the world of the 1930s 'the growth of wealth, so far from being dependent on the abstinence of the rich, as is commonly supposed, is more likely to be impeded by it',[12] as the essential link uniting socialist principle with the requirements of economic efficiency. The proponents of the new approach – men like Jay, Clark, Gaitskell, Durbin, friends and protégés of Dalton – combined a distaste for what they regarded as the self-indulgent expressivism of the Labour Left with an intellectual scorn for demands for wholesale nationalisation and workers' control which seemed to them naive and irrelevant to the main job of abolishing poverty. For this among other reasons, there was resistance to Jay's pragmatism ('The case for socialism is mainly economic, and rests on fact'[13]) from those who cared as much about the location of power as the maximisation of wealth. Keynesian ideas were taken up only hesitantly by Labour in the 1930s, and the Party's conversion remained incomplete. More important, Keynes, who might have been used by the Labour Left (as Mosley had used him) for an all out attack on the existing distribution of wealth, became identified with the caution and 'revisionism' of the Labour Right.

Nevertheless, it was this revisionism which eventually became dominant in Labour Party thinking. Working through the NEC Policy sub-committees, the industrious and prolific New Fabians, and other groups such as the City-based XYZ Club, embryonic 'Gaitskellites' established a tradition of reformist economic management which Labour's 1945 document *Let Us Face the Future* plainly reflects, and which soon became the basis of post-war British socialism. Not until after the failures of 1964–70 was the idea that socialism comprised a superior understanding of the working of the economy generally questioned by the Party as a whole.

If Keynesianism, which originally made its appearance on the Left of the Labour Party, became identified with the Right, inter-party alliances, pioneered and discredited by the Right, with even greater irony, came to be identified with the Left. Coalitions gained a bad reputation in the Labour Party because of 1931. Until 1935 support for a progressive alliance was regarded as a sign of weakness, proof of Lib–Labism. It was the change of line at the 7th Congress of the Comintern in 1935 which paved the way for the conversion of the far left to the Popular Front. Yet, as with the other campaigns of the Labour Left, the united front and Popular Front campaigns were more symbolic than real, vehicles for the frustration and alarms which the international situation, and above all the struggle in Spain, had created. The Left Book Club in particular was able to use the demands for a socialist alliance or a broad progressive coalition as the basis for its mission to win converts to socialism and create an awareness of the dangers of fascism.

That the united front was entirely a fantasy was rapidly demonstrated by the Unity Campaign. The Popular Front might have had more substance; yet, based as it was on the extreme left, and aimed at masses not at leaders, it was rightly perceived as having far more to do with a struggle for support within the Labour Movement than with the realities of Whitehall and Westminster. A progressive alliance was not an impossibility. Genuine attempts were being made by responsible and influential political leaders to see what might be achieved. 'People were feeling their way from different directions', comments a leading Tory rebel of the time: 'None of us felt we had a completely right answer.'[14] There were difficulties on the Tory side, and there would probably have been resistance in the trade unions. There were also major areas of disagreement – Labour held back from a full acceptance of the conscription and rearmament demands which were central to the Tory rebels' argument. But what, in the end, prevented a more thorough exploration of possibilities was undoubtedly the identification of the Popular Front as a 'trap for innocents', a tactic for the extension of left-wing influence, or, at the very least, part of the hackneyed jargon of the marxist left which serious politicians became tired of denouncing. That this was so was certainly not to the credit of the Labour leadership, which in accepting this stereotype displayed the closed mindedness which the Labour Left, understandably, found frustrating. Equally, it reflected the lack of subtlety of left-wing tactics – or, possibly, its lack of ultimate commitment to the idea it found it convenient to support. At any rate, if the idea of a progressive alliance had not been identified as the 'Popular Front' and a central aim of the Communist Party, the chances that it might have been achieved would have been far greater.

Thus, the Labour Party might have played an important part in the events which preceded the Second World War. That its role was minor was not because of its excessive moderation, or its Parliamentarism, or because it did not try to politicise the working-class. Rather, it was due to an inability to try new approaches, and to show flexibility at a critical time, because of the political strait-jacket which its own internal conflicts had imposed. Labour might have been in the vanguard of the Keynesian revolution, working with others who could contribute positive remedies to the central problem of mass unemployment. Later, Labour had a chance to lead a broad united opposition against the inadequacies of Chamberlain's foreign policy. Instead it chose to maintain a debilitating exclusiveness, resisting staunchly (if ultimately unsuccessfully) new economic ideas, and permitting the divisions among critics of Government foreign and defence policy to continue almost until it was too late.

Appendix

TABLE I   *General Election Results, 1929–35*

	Total votes	MPs elected	Candidates	Unopposed returns	% share of total vote
1929 Thursday, 30 May					
Conservative	8 656 473	260	590	4	38.2
Liberal	5 308 510	59	513	–	23.4
Labour	8 389 512	288	571	–	37.1
Communist	50 614	–	25	–	0.3
Others	243 266	8	31	3	1.0
Electorate 28 850 870	22 648 375	615	1730	7	100.0
Turnout 76.1%					
1931 Tuesday, 27 October					
Conservative	11 978 745	473	523	56	55.2
National Labour	341 370	13	20	–	1.6
Liberal National	809 302	35	41	–	3.7
Liberal	1 403 102	33	112	5	6.5
(National	(14 532 519)	(554)	(696)	(61)	(67.0)
Government)					
Independent	106 106	4	7	–	0.5
Liberal					
Labour	6 649 630	52	515	6	30.6
Communist	74 824	–	26	–	0.3
New Party	36 377	–	24	–	0.2
Others	256 917	5	24	–	1.2
Electorate 29 960 071	21 656 373	615	1292	67	100.0
Turnout 76.3%					
1935 Thursday, 14 November					
Conservative	11 810 158	432	585	26	53.7
Liberal	1 422 116	21	161	–	6.4
Labour	8 325 491	154	552	13	37.9

	Total votes	MPs elected	Candi-dates	Unop-posed returns	% share of total vote
Independent Labour Party	139 577	4	17	—	0.7
Communist	27 117	1	2	—	0.1
Others	272 595	4	31	1	1.2
Electorate 31 379 050	21 997 054	615	1348	40	100.0
Turnout 71.2%					

Source: Butler and Freeman, *British Political Facts*, pp. 142–3.

TABLE II   *Labour Party Conferences 1929–40*

Year	Place of conference	Chairman	No. of delegates	Nationally affiliated membership
1929	Brighton	Herbert Morrison	967	2 077 199
1930	Llandudno	Susan Lawrence	727	2 102 948
1931	Scarborough	Stanley Hirst	716	2 069 697
1932	Leicester	George Lathan	621	2 061 063
1933	Hastings	Joseph Compton	669	2 000 180
1934	Southport	Walter R. Smith	686	1 939 017
1935	Brighton	W. A. Robinson	664	1 897 231
1936	Edinburgh	Jennie L. Adamson	664	1 958 904
1937	Bournemouth	Hugh Dalton	705	2 013 663
1939	Southport	George Dallas	775	2 642 618
1940	Bournemouth	Barbara A. Gould	743	2 663 067

Source: LPACR.

TABLE III *The Labour Party National Executive 1929–40*

Division 1 *Trade Unions' Section*

	1929	1930	1931	1932	1933	1934	1935	1936	1937	1939	1940
Brothers, M. (United Textile Factory Workers' Association)											
Bradley, S. (AEU)	2	12	6	10	7	9	5	5	3	5	3
Clynes, J. (NUGMW)		1	2	1	4	1	1	1	1	7	
Compton, J. (National Union of Vehicle Builders)	5	6	4	9	2	2	7	8			
Dennison, R. (British Iron, Steel and Kindred Trades' Ass.)	4	8	7								
Dobbie, W. (NUR)				2	3	6					
Dobbs, A. (National Union of Boot and Shoe Operatives)								9	9	10	7
Gooch, E. (National Union of Agricultural Workers)							11				
Henderson, J. (NUR)							3	3	2	1	
Hewitson, M. (NUGMW)										2	
Hirst, S. (TGWU)	7	7	1	5	5	5	2	2	6	4	1
Hutchinson, W. (AEU)	8										
Jarman, C. (National Union of Seamen)										9	9
Jones, J. (MFGB)	10	4									
Jowett, F. W. (ILP)	11										
Kaylor, J. (AEU)					11	8	12	7	10		
Lathan, G. (Railway Clerks' Association)	6	9	8	3							
Prain, R. (Electrical Trade Union)		2	3	8	1	7	4		12		
Ridley, G. (Railway Clerks' Association)								6	7	3	
Roberts, F. (Typographical Association)	1	5	5	11	9	3	10	12	8		5
Robinson, W. (NUDAW)	9	10	11	6	12	11	6			8	
Smith, W. (National Union of Boot and Shoe Operatives)	13	3	9	7	6	4		4	11		11
Snell, H. (Fabian Society)			10	4	8	12	8	11			
Swan, J. (MFGB)	12								4		2
Thomas, J. H. (NUR)	3										
Thompson, J. (Amalgamated Society of Woodworkers)											10
Turner, B. (National Union of Textile Workers)		11	12								
Walker, J. (British Iron, Steel and Kindred Trades' Ass.)				12	10	10	9	10	5	6	6
Wall, A. (London Society of Compositors)										11	12
Whitworth, J. (United Textile Factory Workers' Ass.)										12	8
Williamson, T. (NUGMW)											4

Division II *Socialist, Co-operative and Professional Organisations*

	1929	1930	1931	1932	1933	1934	1935	1936	1937	1939	1940
Green, W. H. (Royal Arsenal Co-operative Soc.)							1	1	unopposed	1	unopposed
Jowett, F. W. (ILP)		1									
Williams, T. E. (Royal Arsenal Co-operative Soc.)			1	1	1	1					

Division III *Constituency and Central Labour Parties*

	1929	1930	1931	1932	1933	1934	1935	1936	1937	1939	1940
Atlee, C.						3	3				
Cripps, Sir S.						5					
Dallas, G.	5	5	4	4	2	4	4	3	5	6	5
Dalton, H.	3	3	3	2	1	2	1	2	2	4	4
Griffiths, J.										7	
Jenkins, A.			5					4			
Jones, Morgan	4										
Lansbury, G.	1	1	1								
Laski, H.									3	1	1
Morrison, H.	2	2	2	3	3	1	2	1	1	3	2
Mosley, Sir O.		4									
Noel-Baker, P.									4	2	3
Pritt, D. N.									7	5	
Shinwell, E.											6
Toole, J.				5	4		5	5			
Trevelyan, Sir C.					5						
Wilmot, J.											7

Division IV Women

	1929	1930	1931	1932	1933	1934	1935	1936	1937	1939	1940
Adamson, Mrs J. (Local Party)	1	4	3	3	1	2	2	1	1	1	unopp.
Bentham, Dr E. (Local Party)	4	2									
Carlin, Miss M. (TGWU)			5	4	3	3	3	3			
Dollan, Mrs A. (Scottish Socialist Party)							5	4	5		
Gould, Mrs B. A. (Local Party)	3	3	2	2	5	5	4	5	3	5	unopp.
Lawrence, Miss S. (Fabian Society)	2	1	1	1	2	1	1	2	2	2	unopp.
Manning, Miss L. (Labour Teachers)			4							4	
Smith, Lady M. (Local Party)		5		5	4	4					
Stewart, Miss E. (TGWU)											unopp.
Wilkinson, Miss E. (Local Party)									4	3	unopp.

Treasurer

	1929	1930	1931	1932	1933	1934	1935	1936	1937	1939	1940
Henderson, A.		unopp.	unopp.	unopp.	unopp.	unopp.	unopp.				
Lathan, G.								1	unopp.	unopp.	unopp.
MacDonald, G.R.	unopp.										

The Party Leader was a member of the NEC ex-officio.

Before 1930, Division I was called the National Societies' Section, and included the nominees of socialist societies and other non-union nationally affiliated organisations.

In 1937, Division III was expanded from 5 to 7 members, and members were elected by local party delegates alone.

There was no Conference in 1938, and the NEC elected in October 1937 held office until May 1939.

Figures indicate the position of successful candidates in the ballot for each section.

TABLE IV Elected members of the executive of the Parliamentary Labour Party 1931–9

	1931	1932	1933	1934	1935	1936	1937	1938	1939
Cripps, Sir S.	1	1	2	1					
Grenfell, D. R.	2	2	1	2	5	4	4	4	4
Hicks, G.	4	3	3	5					
Jones, Morgan	7	7	4	7	10	8	11	12	
Lunn, W.	5	4	6	4	11				
Maclean, N.	6	6	7	6	12				
Williams, T.	3	5	5	3	7	7	6	7	3
Alexander, A. V.					6	5	2	2	1
Benn, W. Wedgewood						6	7	5	2
Clynes, J.					1				
Dalton, H.					2	3	5	3	10
Hall, G.									7
Johnston, T.					3	2	3	6	
Lawson, J.									12
Lees-Smith, H. B.					9	11	8	8	5
Morrison, H.					4	1	1	1	8
Noel-Baker, P.						10	12	10	11
Pethick-Lawrence, F.					8	9	9	9	6
Pritt, D. N.						12			
Shinwell, E.							10	11	9

Figures indicate the position of successful candidates in the annual ballot. The Executive was reduced in size to 7 members in 1931, but was restored to its former strength of 12 after the 1935 general election. Executive elections took place in November.
Source: LPACR 1931–9.

Notes

ABBREVIATIONS USED

Dalton, *FY*	Hugh Dalton, *Fateful Years, Memoirs 1931–1945* (London, Muller, 1957).
DH	*Daily Herald.*
HC Deb.	House of Commons Debates.
LPACR	Labour Party Annual Conference Report.
MG	*Manchester Guardian.*
NS & N	*New Statesman and Nation.*

NOTES FOR CHAPTER 1

1 Ralph Miliband, *Parliamentary Socialism* (London, Merlin Press, 1961), pp. 193f.

2 North country cotton workers struck in 1932, London busmen in 1937. The textile workers were fighting a cut in pay; the busmen were demanding shorter hours. Both disputes ended in defeat on essentials for the strikers. Otherwise there were no stoppages involving a loss of more than half a million working days. D. Butler and J. Freeman, *British Political Facts 1900–1967*, 2nd edn (London, Macmillan, 1968), p. 218.

3 The second Labour Government contained two prominent ministers who had been Conservative MPs – Lord Parmoor (Lord President) and Sir Oswald Mosley (Chancellor of the Duchy of Lancaster). Christopher Addison (Minister of Agriculture) had served as a Coalition Liberal until 1921 in Lloyd George's Tory dominated post-war Government. For an examination of the factors influencing such changes of allegiance, see C. A. Cline, *Recruits to Labour – The British Labour Party 1914–1931* (New York, Syracuse University Press, 1963).

4 Formerly Clifford Allen, a central figure in the ILP until the mid 1920s. In the 1931 crisis he supported MacDonald.

5 *The Next Five Years – An Essay in Political Agreement* (London, Macmillan, 1935), p. 313.

6 See J. F. Naylor, *Labour's International Policy – the Labour Party in the 1930s* (London, Weidenfeld & Nicolson, 1969), Chapter 7.

7 Dalton, *FY*, p. 200.
8 And many of whom were selected as candidates in the late thirties, in anticipation of a 1939 or 1940 election.

NOTES FOR CHAPTER 2

1 C. L. Mowat, *Britain Between the Wars* (London, Methuen, 1955). pp. 274f; G. D. H. Cole, *British Trade and Industry* (London, Macmillan, 1932), p. 215; G. P. Jones and A. G. Pool, *A Hundred Years of Economic Development in Great Britain (1840–1940)* (London, Duckworth, 1940), p. 298.
2 Government public works schemes gave employment to an estimated 226 500 men by March 1931. About ten times that number were out of work. Robert Skidelsky, *Politicians and the Slump – The Labour Government of 1929–31* (London, Macmillan, 1967), p. 305.
3 Cabinet Conclusions, 23 August 1931.
4 ibid., 24 August.
5 Arthur Henderson had joined Asquith's Coalition Government in 1915, and Lloyd George's War Cabinet in 1916. John Hodge, George Barnes and a number of other Labour MPs had also accepted ministerial posts – with the blessing of the Parliamentary Labour Party and the Party Executive.
6 e.g. 'What Happened in 1931: A Record', *Political Quarterly* Vol. 3, No. 1, January–March 1932. Ed. M. Cole, *Beatrice Webb's Diaries 1924–32* (London, Longmans, Green & Co., 1956), p. 282. Hugh Dalton, *Call Back Yesterday – Memoirs 1887–1931* (London, Frederick Muller, 1953), p. 271.
7 Dalton, *FY*, p. 274.
8 R. Bassett, *Nineteen Thirty-One, Political Crisis* (London, Macmillan, 1958), pp. 195f.
9 Unpublished diary.
10 Earl Attlee, *As It Happened* (London, Heinemann, 1954), pp. 73f.
11 It appears that unsuccessful approaches were made to E. Shinwell, C. L'Estrange Malone, F. W. Pethick-Lawrence, L. MacNeill Weir, Tom Shaw, Sir Stafford Cripps, Lord Snell, Sir Norman Angell, Leah Manning, George Isaacs and (possibly) Herbert Morrison. (E. Shinwell, *Conflict Without Malice* (London, Odhams, 1955), p. 110; Dalton's unpublished diary and *Daily Herald* 7 September 1931; F. W. Pethick-Lawrence, *Fate Has Been Kind* (London, Hutchinson, 1943), p. 165; L. MacNeill Weir, *The Tragedy of Ramsay MacDonald* (London, Secker & Warburg, 1938), p. 395; Bassett, op. cit., p. 178; E. Estorick, *Stafford Cripps* (London, Heinemann, 1949), p. 88; Lord Snell, *Men, Movements and Myself* (London, J. M. Dent, 1936), p. 253; Sir Norman Angell, *After All* (London, Hamish Hamilton, 1951), pp. 256–8; G. W. Jones and B. Donoughue, *Herbert Morrison – Portrait of a Politician* (London, Weidenfeld & Nicolson, 1973), pp. 162–8 and author's interview with Dame Leah Manning.)

12 Only 14 Labour MPs were supporting MacDonald by the time of the dissolution in September, and only 9 posts in the first National Government were filled by ministers who had previously supported the Labour Party. These were thoroughly unrepresentative. 4 of the 9 were law officers, and only one, Thomas, was a trade unionist.

13 NEC minutes.

14 Five or six others who opposed approval of the Joint Meeting resolution were left-wing ILP rebels. They were voting against Henderson, not for MacDonald.

15 HC Deb., vol. 256 col. 314 (10 September 1931).

16 ibid. col. 52–3 (8 September).

17 ibid. col. 332–41 (10 September).

18 ibid. col. 79 (8 September).

19 *NS & N* 26 September 1931.

20 *TUC Ann. Report* 1931, p. 83.

21 ed. M. Cole, *Beatrice Webb's Diaries 1924–32* (10 October 1931), p. 291.

22 HC Deb., vol. 256 col. 1333 (21 September).

23 *NS & N*, 3 October 1931.

24 *New Clarion*, November 1931.

25 K. Martin, *Harold Laski 1893–1950 – A Biographical Memoir* (London, Gollancz, 1953).

26 *MG*, 2 November 1931.

27 Butler and Freeman, *British Political Facts*, p. 142. The total Labour poll fell from 8 389 512 in 1929 to 6 649 630 in 1931. Labour's 1931 vote would have been greater, but its proportion of the total vote smaller, if it had contested 61 seats returned for Government supporters unopposed. Only 6 Labour candidates were unopposed in 1931. In 1929 all Labour candidates were opposed, and only 4 Conservatives were unopposed.

28 *MG*, 13 November, 1931.

29 Yet a crucial question remains. What happened to the Liberal vote in over 300 contested seats where Liberals stood in 1929 but not in 1931? In a climate of opinion favourable to the Government, and with most Liberal leaders supporting MacDonald, it is likely that the majority voted Conservative. But some anti-Conservative Liberals, with nowhere else to go, must have voted Labour. Thus Labour's total vote must be presumed to have been *higher* than if there had been a larger Liberal intervention – and Labour's performance in retaining its 1929 support must be regarded as worse than a crude comparison of total votes suggests. The accretion of Liberal votes was, however, almost certainly a permanent gain, as the number of Liberal candidatures did not increase in 1935.

30 The PLP meeting of 28 August had already pushed them into the background. Henderson, the new leader, and the two deputy leaders, J. R. Clynes and Graham, had been in the Cabinet minority, against the cuts in unemployment benefit. Five of the remaining six 'minority'

ministers were among the top seven in the PLP Executive election which followed the election of officers: Johnston, Lansbury, Arthur Greenwood, Addison and A. V. Alexander, in that order. W. Adamson, who had also voted against Snowden over the cuts, did not stand. The only 'majority' ex-minister to stand was H. B. Lees-Smith, who was elected in eleventh place out of thirteen elected members in all. Of the 'majority' ex-ministers remaining with Labour, only Herbert Morrison was to play an important part in Labour politics during the 1931 and 1935 Parliaments (though W. Wedgwood Benn, as Lord Stansgate, was to serve in the 1945 Government).

31 Henderson returned to Parliament in 1932, Clynes (a member of the NEC) in 1935.

32 See R. T. McKenzie, *British Political Parties* (London, Heinemann, 1955), p. 422.

33 The other was D. R. Grenfell.

34 McKenzie, op. cit., p. 422.

35 1 was sponsored by the Co-operative Party, and the remaining 13 by Divisional Labour Parties. G. D. H. Cole, *A History of the Labour Party from 1914* (London, Routledge & Kegan Paul, 1948), p. 265.

36 *NS & N*, 7 November 1931.

37 NEC Minutes. The original initiative for this move came before the election. On 30 September, the General Council adopted the recommendation of its own special Committee to Select Committees 'that the National Joint Council should be the authoritative body for consultation on all matters concerning the Labour Party, the Parliamentary Labour Party, and the General Council'. The Special Committee had been set up on 11 September with Bevin as by far the most prominent and powerful of its five members. (TUC General Council Minutes).

38 LPACR, 1932, p. 67.

39 Henry Pelling, *A Short History of the Labour Party* (London, Macmillan, 1961), p. 71.

40 See below, pp. 191–2. At the Joint Meeting of the TUC General Council, Labour Party NEC, and PLP Executive on 25 August 1939, which determined the war-time status of the National Council of Labour, it was nevertheless pointed out that the Council 'was not a policy-making body but a co-ordinating body'. (Minutes).

41 Lansbury to Bevin, 9 March 1933. (Lansbury papers)

NOTES FOR CHAPTER 3

1 Dalton, *FY*, p. 299. 'Severance from Philip Snowden was a wound too deep for Willie to discuss'. T. N. Graham, *Willie Graham. The Life of the Rt. Hon. W. Graham* (London, Hutchinson, 1948), p. 187.

2 ed. M. Cole, *Beatrice Webb Diaries, 1924–1932*, p. 288 (20 September 1931).

3 The NEC, as part of a policy of creating a more disciplined party

structure, was trying to integrate the Co-operative Party more closely with the Labour Party in Parliament and in the constituencies.

4 Dalton, *FY*, p. 20.

5 Unpublished diary.

6 Lansbury's popularity in the PLP is indicated by his achievement of second place in the Parliamentary Executive election, just before the dissolution. He also emerged easily top in the Constituency Parties' Section in the 1931 NEC election.

7 See R. Jenkins, *Mr Attlee. An Interim Biography* (London, Heinemann, 1948), pp. 148f.

8 Lansbury to Trevelyan 5 January 1932. Trevelyan papers.

9 R. Postgate, *The Life of George Lansbury* (London, Longmans, 1951), p. 283.

10 See James Johnston, *A Hundred Commoners* (London, Herbert Joseph, 1931), p. 163. Johnston was lobby correspondent for the *Yorkshire Post*.

11 Jenkins, *Attlee*, p. 145.

12 Attlee, *As It Happened* (London, Heinemann, 1954), p. 75.

13 Johnston's *A Hundred Commoners*, published early in 1931 and containing pen portraits of prominent MPs, did not include a sketch of Attlee. Yet Tom Williams, John Lawson, W. Lunn and Aneurin Bevan, all of whom later held their seats, were included.

14 Attlee, op. cit., p. 20.

15 R. Jenkins in ed. H. Tracey, *The British Labour Party*, vol. 3 (London, The Caxton Publishing Co., 1948), p. 5.

16 Attlee, op. cit., p. 30. Hugh Dalton was also in for the job. He had academic qualifications, but lacked the practical experience.

17 As Attlee's record shows, it was not pure chance that he should have sat for a safer seat than other middle-class leaders. Yet his 1931 victory cannot be regarded as a personal triumph. The swing in Limehouse away from Labour was greater than in the neighbouring Stepney constituency of Whitechapel.

18 Francis Williams, *Nothing So Strange* (London, Cassell, 1970), p. 135. MacDonald, by contrast, would seek to impress those he met with wordy expositions of their own fields of expertise.

19 Beatrice Webb's unpublished diary, 16 September 1935.

20 ibid., 2 September 1935.

21 Williams, op. cit., p. 135.

22 Attlee, *The Granada Historical Records Interview* (London, Panther Record, 1967), p. 12.

23 Jenkins, *Attlee*, p. 149.

24 *Observer*, 24 April 1932.

25 In 1938 Greenwood was relieved of the daily direction of the Research Department because it was felt that he was unable to provide 'that continuous scrutiny which we think is essential in its present proportions'. *Report of Special Sub-Committee of Inquiry into the Research Department* (NEC minutes, 1938).

26 John Strachey, 'The Education of a Communist', *Left Review*, No. 3,

December 1934, pp. 63–9, quoted in N. Wood, *Communism and British Intellectuals*, (London, Gollancz, 1959) p. 113.

27 Dalton, *Call Back Yesterday*, p. 34.

28 ibid., p. 36.

29 ed. M. Cole, op. cit., 20 June 1927, pp. 144f.

30 Dalton, *FY*, p. 20.

31 R. Jenkins, *Pursuit of Progress* (London, Heinemann, 1953), p. 60.

32 H. Dalton, *Practical Socialism for Britain* (London, Routledge, 1935), p. 15.

33 Attlee, *The Granada Historical Records Interview*, p. 53.

34 ed. M. Cole, op. cit., p. 144.

35 Mary Agnes Hamilton, *Remembering My Good Friends* (London, Cape, 1944), p. 187.

36 H. Morrison, *Socialisation of Transport* (London, Constable & Co., 1933), pp. 235f.

37 Maurice Webb MP in ed. H. Tracey, *The British Labour Party*, vol. 3, p. 31.

38 Beatrice Webb's unpublished diary, 17 January 1932.

39 P. Strauss, *Cripps – Advocate and Rebel* (London, Gollancz, 1943), p. 37.

40 Herbert Morrison, *An Autobiography by Lord Morrison of Lambeth* (London, Odhams Press, 1960), p. 114.

41 Leah Manning, *A Life for Education* (London, Gollancz 1970), p. 81. Leah Manning subsequently won East Islington at a by-election in February 1931, only to lose it again in October. She returned to Parliament as MP for Epping in 1945, but lost the seat in 1950. She was a member of the NEC 1931–2, and 1939–40.

42 E. Estorick, *Stafford Cripps. A Biography* (London, Heinemann, 1949), p. 82.

43 ibid.

44 P. Strauss, *Cripps – Advocate and Rebel*, p. 43.

45 Estorick, op. cit., p. 88.

46 C. A. Cooke, *The Life of Richard Stafford Cripps* (London, Hodder & Stoughton, 1957), p. 126.

47 Beatrice Webb's unpublished diary, 23 January 1932.

48 Cooke, op. cit., p. 127.

49 LPACR 1931, p. 205.

50 Dalton, *FY*, p. 24.

51 Beatrice Webb's unpublished diary, 4 October 1932.

52 *Daily Express*, 29 May 1934.

53 P. Strauss, *Cripps – Advocate and Rebel*, p. 103.

54 *DH*, 2 July 1932.

55 Dalton's unpublished diary, 23 January 1934.

56 ed. M. Cole, op. cit., 7 March 1932, p. 304.

57 Morrison, *Autobiography*, p. 159.

NOTES FOR CHAPTER 4

1 Dalton, *FY*, p. 23.

2 M. Cole, *The Life of G. D. H. Cole* (London, Macmillan, 1971), p. 175.

3 For the relationship between NFRB and SSIP see below p. 44.
4 *NFRB Quarterly.*
5 By 1936 members included Lord Addison, C. A. Attlee, Sir Norman Angell, Philip Noel-Baker, H. N. Brailsford, Harold Clay, Sir Stafford Cripps, Hugh Dalton, Hugh Gaitskell, George Lathan, Harold Laski, G. R. Mitchison, D. N. Pritt, Sir Arthur Pugh, R. H. Tawney, Beatrice Webb, Francis Williams, Leonard Woolf, Evan Durbin and Colin Clark.
6 Later Sir Vaughan Berry.
7 E. F. Williams, *Nothing So Strange* (London, Cassell, 1970), p. 112.
8 ibid.
9 Dalton, *FY*, p. 23.
10 Williams, op. cit., pp. 112f.
11 cf. ed. S. Pollard, *The Gold Standard and Employment Policies Between the Wars* (London, Methuen, 1970), p. 161.
12 *Labour and the Nation* had proposed the control of the Bank of England by a public corporation, including representatives of the Treasury, the Board of Trade, Industry, Labour and the Co-operative Movement.
13 ibid., p. 33.
14 R. Jenkins, *The Pursuit of Progress* (London, Heinemann, 1953), p. 68.
15 *NS & N*, 20 November 1937.
16 R. Jenkins, op. cit., pp. 62ff.
17 *NFRB Quarterly*, Summer 1938.
18 R. Harrod, *The Life of John Maynard Keynes* (London, Macmillan, 1951), p. 439.
19 E. F. Williams, op. cit., p. 110.

NOTES FOR CHAPTER 5

1 Lansbury to Sir Charles Trevelyan, 5 January 1932 (Trevelyan papers).
2 *NS & N*, 14 November 1931.
3 Unpublished diary, 19 March 1932.
4 'The Choice Before the Labour Party'. *Political Quarterly*, Summer 1932, reprinted in ed. W. A. Robson, *Political Quarterly in the 1930s* (London, Penguin, 1971), p. 109.
5 ibid. p. 103ff.
6 A. J. P. Taylor, *English History 1914–45* (Oxford, Clarendon Press, 1965), p. 349.
7 See below, p. 113.
8 See below, p. 61.
9 R. E. Dowse, *Left in the Centre. The Independent Labour Party 1893–1940* (London, Longmans, 1966), p. 177.
10 ibid.
11 *MG*, 25 and 26 February, 1932.
12 Frank Wise, quoted in *New Leader*, 5 August 1932.
13 M. Cole, *Growing Up Into Revolution* (London, Longmans, Green & Co., 1949), pp. 148f.

14 Ernest Bevin was Chairman; D. N. Pritt, Cole, Arthur Pugh and (until his death in January 1932) W. R. Blair were vice-chairmen. H. L. Beales and Margaret Cole were joint Hon. Secretaries, and E. A. Radice was Secretary. The original committee included Colin Clark, C. M. Lloyd, Frank Horrabin, and Raymond Postgate. At the first, and only, annual meeting of SSIP in May 1932, Sir Stafford Cripps, Major Attlee, and William Mellor were also elected to the Executive Committee. Mitchison and Pritt and, later, Cripps (all of whom became prominent Socialist Leaguers) were SSIP's 'chief financial supporters' according to Margaret Cole (op. cit., p. 145).

15 By September 1932 there were SSIP branches in Birmingham, Bristol, Cambridge, Cornwall, Cupar, Glasgow, Leeds, Liverpool, Manchester, North Staffordshire, Preston, Selsden, Sheffield and Southampton (*SSIP News*).

16 M. Cole, quoted in A. Bullock, *The Life and Times of Ernest Bevin*, vol. 1, *The Trade Union Leader 1881–1940* (London, Heinemann, 1960), p. 501.

17 23 May 1931, quoted in Bullock, op. cit., p. 501.

18 *DH*, 16 June 1931.

19 3 September 1932. Trevelyan Papers.

20 Cole to Cripps, 19 September 1932. Cole papers.

21 Cole, *History of the Labour Party Since 1914* (London, Routledge & Kegan Paul, 1948), p. 284.

22 Bevin to Cole, 24 September 1932. Cole papers.

23 See B. Pimlott, 'The Socialist League – Intellectuals and the Labour Left in the 1930s'. *Journal of Contemporary History*, 1971, Vol. 6, No. 3, pp. 12–39.

24 ibid.

25 Pugh and Kirkwood. Both left the Council within a few months.

26 K. Martin, *Editor: A Second Volume of Autobiography 1931–45* (London, Hutchinson, 1968), p. 49.

27 This included Hugh Gaitskell, Evan Durbin, Colin Clark, Lieut.-Col. L'Estrange Malone and George Dallas.

28 3 October 1932. Five weeks later SSIP held a special meeting to ratify the decision. It was a disaster. A motion in support of the decision failed to get the two thirds majority required by the society's constitution. Instead SSIP decided to dissolve itself. Hence, the Socialist League was in the end not an amalgamation, as the SSIP never formally accepted the agreement to merge. (*MG*, 7 November 1932.)

29 *New Clarion*, 8 October 1932.

30 F. Henderson to Cole, 10 August 1932; 20 September 1932. Cole papers.

31 ibid. This was Fred Henderson's interpretation of Horrabin's views.

32 *The Socialist Leaguer*, 15 December 1934.

33 *New Clarion*, 17 December 1932.

34 ibid., 14 January 1933.

35 1 April 1933.

36 Cole, *History of the Labour Party from 1914*, p. 284.

37 This was issued as a pamphlet in September 1933, under the name of Cole and the National Council.
38 Wise died of a stroke in November.
39 The two central figures in the League after Wise's death were Cripps and Mellor, both from SSIP. The other three who probably had most influence within the League were Mitchison (from SSIP), Horrabin (who had a foot in both camps, and who edited the League's journals, the *Socialist Leaguer* and the *Socialist*), and the ex-communist J. T. Murphy, general secretary of the League 1934–6.
40 What Wise actually wrote was 'Free speech, a so-called Free Press, are no more part of the eternal verities than is Free Trade'. His point was that the entire popular daily press except the *Daily Herald* opposed the Labour Party. (*New Clarion*, 13 May 1933.)
41 *The Times*, 6 June 1933.
42 *New Clarion*, 24 June 1933.
43 *New Leader*, 9 June 1933.
44 *Socialist Leaguer*, 15 October 1934. *Report of the First Annual Conference of the Socialist League*, 1933.
45 *Adelphi*, July 1933.
46 Quoted in C. A. Cooke, *The Life of Richard Stafford Cripps* (London, Hodder & Stoughton, 1957), p. 159.
47 ibid.
48 Dalton's unpublished diary, 17 January 1934.
49 *New Clarion*, 19 March 1934.
50 *Socialist Leaguer*, August–September 1934.
51 ibid.
52 LPACR, 1934, pp. 158f.
53 ibid., p. 160.
54 *Socialist Leaguer*, October–November 1934.
55 ibid.
56 Storm Jameson in *Socialist Leaguer*, 15 October 1934.
57 *Socialist Leaguer*, October–November 1934.
58 ibid., November–December 1934.
59 *English History*, p. 349.
60 *Report of the Annual Aggregate Meeting of the Socialist League, London Area*, 18 July 1936.
61 *Socialist*, November 1935.
62 *New Clarion*, 25 March 1933; *Report of the Annual Aggregate Meeting of the Socialist League, London Area*, 18 July 1936.
63 This was Cripps' own branch at Bristol. (*Socialist Leaguer*, July–August 1935.)
64 Reginald Groves, Area Secretary for London 1935–6, and Regional Member of the National Council for London 1936–7; author's interview.
65 Unlike the ILP and CP, the SL did not have Scottish members. In Scotland its role was assumed by the Scottish Socialist Party.
66 Nat. Council Report to Annual Conference of Socialist League 1936 and 1937.

67 Annual Conference Report of Socialist League, 1933.

68 Ruth Dodds, regional member for the North East from 1933, national member from 1935.

69 R. E. Dowse, *Left In The Centre*, p. 185. The exception was Dr Alfred Salter's branch at Bermondsey. Significantly it continued to call itself the Bermondsey ILP although it was a branch of the Socialist League. In 1935 it was no longer functioning.

70 ibid., p. 193, n. 3.

NOTES FOR CHAPTER 6

1 J. Strachey, *Revolution by Reason* (London, Leonard Parsons, 1925), p. 5.

2 R. Skidelsky, *Politicians and the Slump*, pp. 169–82, *et passim*, which, with a lecture on 'Sir Oswald Mosley' given by Dr Skidelsky at St Antony's College, Oxford, in October 1968, influenced the ideas developed in this chapter. See also R. Skidelsky, *Oswald Mosley* (London, Macmillan, 1975), chs. 7–11.

3 And in a different form, of the economic thinking of the Lloyd George Liberals and the Macmillan group of Tory planners.

4 Sir Oswald Mosley, *My Life* (London, Nelson, 1968), pp. 180f.

5 ibid.

6 *The Living Wage* (London, The ILP Publication Department 1926.) Also cf. Skidelsky, *Politicians and the Slump*, pp. 47f.

7 November 1933.

8 *Forward to Socialism*, 1934.

9 1933 Report, op. cit.

10 M. Foot, *Aneurin Bevan. A Biography*, Vol. 1, 1897–1945 (London, MacGibbon & Kee, 1962), p. 131.

11 While still a member of the Labour Government, Mosley was very closely associated with another future Socialist Leaguer, Sir Charles Trevelyan. Of the latter Mosley writes 'With him I formed a much closer friendship [than with the Buxtons] and he was my chief, certainly my most intelligent supporter in the Cabinet when it came to the crunch.' (op. cit., p. 217)

12 ibid., p. 186.

13 Foot, op. cit., p. 131.

14 Hugh Thomas, *John Strachey* (London, Eyre Methuen, 1973), p. 175.

15 G. R. Mitchison, 'Corporate State – or Socialist Plan' in *Socialist Leaguer*, November–December 1934.

16 *New Clarion*, 25 November 1933.

17 Mitchison, op. cit.

18 *Socialist Leaguer*, October–November 1934.

19 *Fascism: The Socialist Answer* (London, The Socialist League, 1935.)

20 ibid.

21 W. Mellor, *The Claim of the Unemployed* (London, The Socialist League, 1933.)

22 e.g. *The Socialist Control of Industry* (London, The Socialist League, 1934.)

23 Frank Horrabin's political involvements were diffuse. Having moved from Guild Socialism to Communism, he left the CP for the ILP in 1925, where he remained until disaffiliation. He was also in the unique position of having been a member of Mosley's group (and a 'Manifesto' signatory), and on the Executive of both SSIP and of the affiliationists' committee.

24 On the National Council (as a regional member) 1933–5.

25 Bullock, *Bevin*, p. 514.

26 ibid., p. 529.

27 Labour Party Conference Report 1932, p. 216.

28 Mitchison, op. cit.

NOTES FOR CHAPTER 7

1 'But he had practically to be pushed out!... Clynes and two or three more were deputed to see him... they found that, in spite of his health, and a solemn doctor's report, he wanted to drag on till the General Election, devolving some of the work. They had to insist, in the interest both of his health and the Party, that the changeover should come at the end of the year. He was very sore at this.' (Dalton, unpublished diary, end of 1934.)

   Beatrice Webb referred to 'his practical dismissal by the NEC from the General Secretaryship of the Labour Party – the Executive declaring that they could not meet another conference with the general secretary "an habitual absentee"!' (unpublished diary, 19 August 1934).

2 Lord Citrine, *Men and Work* (London, Hutchinson, 1964), p. 351.

3 R. Postgate, *The Life of George Lansbury* (London, Longmans, 1951), p. 300.

4 ibid.

5 *British Political Parties*, p. 378.

6 NEC minutes. Lansbury had withdrawn, and Cripps had already resigned.

7 Unpublished diary, 20 September 1935.

8 Postgate, op. cit., p. 302.

9 LPACR 1935, p. 177.

10 ibid., p. 178.

11 F. Williams, *Ernest Bevin* (London, Hutchinson, 1952), p. 196.

12 A. Bullock, *Bevin*, p. 569.

13 Dalton, *FY*, p. 69.

14 *MG*, 8 October 1935.

15 *Morning Post*, 8 October 1935.

16 ibid.

17 ibid.

18 *News Chronicle*, 9 October 1935.

19 ibid., 11 October 1935.

20 ibid., 9 October 1935.

21 The main sources for this story were, however, friendly to Morrison (e.g. Dalton, *FY*, p. 82).

22 E. F. Williams, *Nothing So Strange* (London, Cassell, 1970), p. 135. Dalton saw Clynes on 18 November and tried (unsuccessfully) to persuade him to move Morrison at the PLP meeting. 'He says I am the first to speak to him about this', Dalton noted: 'I say to myself that all the others have been bloody slow.' (Unpublished diary.)

23 Dalton, *FY*, p. 81.

24 The last point, however, applied also to Greenwood.

25 Beatrice Webb's unpublished diary, 27 November 1935.

26 'A change in the leadership is, I understand, to take place at the end of the forthcoming Parliamentary session', the *Morning Post* reported confidently on 9 September 1936: '[Mr Attlee] is understood...to have expressed the desire to be relieved of his office before another General Election.'

27 See B. Donoughue and G. W. Jones, *Herbert Morrison – Portrait of A Politician*, pp. 234–43 for additional material on the 1935 leadership contest.

28 Clem Attlee, *The Granada Historical Records Interview* (London, Panther Record, 1967), p. 13.

NOTES FOR CHAPTER 8

1 The Manifesto was signed by William Mellor, Sir Stafford Cripps and G. R. Mitchison on behalf of the Socialist League; James Maxton, William Jowett and Fenner Brockway for the ILP; and Harry Pollitt, William Gallacher and Palme Dutt for the Communists. Other signatories, apart from other leaders of these groups, included Aneurin Bevan, Arthur Horner, Harold Laski, Tom Mann, John Strachey, G. R. Strauss and Jack Tanner.

2 *New Leader*, 22 January 1937.

3 M. Foot, *Aneurin Bevan*, (London, MacGibbon & Kee, 1962), p. 243.

4 Author's interview.

5 See below p. 79.

6 R. Palme Dutt, *Labour Monthly*, August 1932 (cited in R. E. Dowse, *Left in the Centre*, London, Longmans, 1966, p. 186).

7 F. Brockway, *Inside The Left* (London, Allen & Unwin, 1942), p. 248.

8 R. E. Dowse, op. cit. p. 193, n. 5. In 1932 there were 635 branches. By 1935 there were 284, of which about 50 were merely nominal.

9 H. Pelling, *The British Communist Party. An Historical Profile* (London, A & C. Black, 1958), p. 77, n. 1.

10 The few intellectual recruits to the ILP included Middleton Murry, who joined in 1932, but left in 1934 because of the ILP's cooperation with Communists. He took with him most of the ILP in Lancashire and scattered members from other parts of the country. These combined to form the Independent Socialist Party. Murry's friend and protégé

George Orwell joined the ILP after serving with the ILP
contingent in Spain. Orwell's membership derived mainly from a
characteristic sympathy for the underdog: 'the ILP is not backed by
any money or interest, and is systematically libelled from several
quarters. Obviously it needs all the help it can get, including any help
I can give it myself.' *New Leader*, 24 June 1938. Reprinted in *The Collected
Essays, Journalism and Letters of George Orwell*, Vol. 1, ed. Sonia Orwell
and Ian Angus, (London, Secker & Warburg, 1968) p. 338.

11 A group of Trotskyists joined the ILP in 1934, and took control of six
London branches; they left the Party in November 1936. (Dowse, op.
cit., p. 192.) Brockway himself had some sympathy for Trotskyism,
though he deplored the attempt to establish a Fourth International. 'I
frequently concurred with Trotsky's analysis of events, but I saw little
difference between Mexico and Moscow.' (Brockway, op. cit., p.
263.)

12 In preparing this section, extensive use has been made of H. Pelling, *The
British Communist Party. An Historical Profile*. (London, A. & C. Black, 1958).

13 'Lenin on Britain', cited in H. Pelling, op. cit., p. 8.

14 ibid., cited in ibid., p. 10.

15 A legacy of the National Left Wing Movement was a paranoid suspicion
at Transport House of the Constituency Parties' Association, founded in
1936, which had no connection with the Communists. (See Part III,
below)

16 Butler and Freeman, *British Political Facts* (London, Macmillan, 1968),
p. 142. In 1935 the Communists only put up two candidates. Comparison
with 1922 and 1923 is impossible because some Communists stood on the
Labour Party ticket.

17 'Stalinist' General Secretary of the CPGB, appointed in 1929.

18 *The Times*, 25 May 1933.

19 NEC minutes, 27 February 1934.

20 *The Times*, 3 March 1934.

21 *Daily Worker*, 7 March 1934.

22 ibid.

23 NEC minutes, 16 May 1934.

24 ibid.

25 *Daily Worker*, 26 May 1934.

26 ibid. 15 August 1934.

27 ibid., 18 October 1934.

28 ibid., 9 August 1934.

29 ibid., 10 November 1934.

30 ibid., 10 November 1934.

31 ibid., 21 November 1934.

32 28 November 1934.

33 *Daily Worker*, 5 December 1934.

34 *Daily Telegraph*, 7 August 1935.

35 *DH*, 7 August 1935.

36 Communist results in 1935 were as follows (1931 figures in brackets)

W. Fife	W. Gallacher	(Comm.)	13462	(6829)
	Rt Hon. W. Adamson	(Lab.)	12869	(11063)
	C. Milne	(Con.)	9667	(12977)
	Turnout 77.8% (71.4%)			
Rhondda E.	W. H. Mainwaring	(Lab.)	22088	(D. W. Morgan 22086)
	H. Pollitt	(Comm.)	13655	(A. L. Horner 10359)
	Turnout 80.8% (73.7%)			

(*The Times House of Commons*, London, The Times Office, 1935)
37 *Daily Worker*, 26 October 1935.
38 *MG*, 30 November 1935.
39 *Daily Worker*, 6 December 1935.
40 *MG*, 30 January 1936.
41 *DH*, 5 August 1936.
42 *Foreward*, 27 June 1936.
43 Cited in *MG*, 16 July 1936.
44 *Daily Worker*, 8 August 1936.
45 24 July 1936.
46 28 July 1936.
47 *NS & N*, 8 August 1936.
48 *I Search For Truth in Russia*, (London, Routledge & Kegan Paul, 1936).
49 Cited in *NS & N*, 29 August 1936.
50 *Daily Worker*, 2 November 1936. Dalton, however, believed that all 400000 miners' votes were cast in favour (*NS & N*, 24 October 1936).
51 ibid.

NOTES FOR CHAPTER 9

1 *New Leader*, 28 April 1933.
2 Report of 1933 Conference of the Socialist League (cited in James Jupp, *The Left in Britain 1931–41*, unpublished thesis, London M.Sc.Econ., 1956).
3 *New Leader*, 14 June 1935, cited in Jupp, op. cit.
4 R. W. Barnes in the *Socialist Leaguer*, March–April 1935.
5 *Socialist Leaguer*, July–August 1935.
6 ibid.
7 Sir Charles Trevelyan, *Mass Resistance to War* (London, The Socialist League, 1934, pp. 8f.).
8 Cripps in the *Socialist*, December 1935.
9 *Socialist*, January 1936.
10 ibid.
11 Cripps in the *Socialist*, March 1936.
12 ibid.

13 ibid.
14 *News Chronicle*, 14 September 1936.
15 *Socialist*, November 1936.
16 ibid.
17 F. Brockway, *Inside The Left* (London, Allen & Unwin, 1942), p. 264.
18 ibid.
19 ibid., p. 265.
20 ibid.
21 ibid.
22 D. N. Pritt, *From Right to Left* (London, Lawrence & Wishart, 1965) 1965, p. 98.
23 In J. T. Murphy's view 'William Mellor was the most dominating figure in the Socialist League and exercised more influence on Stafford Cripps than any other member', *New Horizons* (London, John Lane 1940), p. 312.
24 National Council Report to the Socialist League Conference, 1937, Appendix.
25 Author's interview with Lord Brockway.
26 The ILP over-ruled Maxton on this issue. It used the growth of the Constituency Parties Movement as an excuse for its change of tack. See *Nottingham Guardian*, 21 December 1936.
27 Brockway, op. cit., p. 270.
28 *Tribune*, 1 January 1937.
29 *Reynolds' News*, 24 January 1937.
30 *Tribune*, 22 January 1937.
31 *NS & N*, 22 May 1937.
32 9 January 1937.
33 *DH*, 18 January 1937.
34 *Morning Post*, 19 January 1937, *NS & N*, 30 January 1937.
35 According to the Socialist League Rules: 'Each branch shall be entitled to send to [Conference] not more than one delegate for every 25 members or part thereof.' Thus the 56 delegates who supported participation could in theory have represented a maximum of 1400 members, if every branch contained an exact multiple of 25 and was fully represented. But most branches contained less than 25, some which sent delegates were little more than nominal, and many were not represented at all. The Manchester branch, for example, which was one of the largest with 125 members, firmly opposed the Campaign but had no delegate at this Conference. *NS & N*, 30 January 1937.
36 M. S. Davidson, letter in *NS & N*, 30 January 1937.
37 18 January 1937.

NOTES FOR CHAPTER 10

1 *DH*, 15 January 1937.
2 25 January 1937.
3 *MG*, 25 January 1937.

4 NEC minutes, 27 January 1937.

5 Ted Willis, *Whatever Happened to Tom Mix?* (London, Eyre & Spottiswoode, 1970), pp. 150f.

6 M. Foot, *Aneurin Bevan* (London, MacGibbon & Kee, 1962), p. 262.
Michael Foot was a member of the London Area Committee of the
Socialist League 1936–7.

7 *Tribune*, 19 February 1937. This meant an average of 1500; and
the Committee would scarcely have made an under-estimate. Nor did
this increase. On 5 March, after 19 meetings, the total was 30000 – an
average of 1579. The number of *different* people attending each meeting
was probably much smaller than the aggregate figures suggest.

8 *News Chronicle*, 8 February 1937.

9 *MG*, 25 March 1937.

10 *DH*, 3 February 1937.

11 Brockway, *Inside The Left* (London, Allen & Unwin, 1942), p. 269.

12 cf. Hugh Thomas, *The Spanish Civil War*, (London, Eyre & Spottiswoode,
1961), pp. 452f.

13 Of whom George Orwell was one. He described his experience in
Homage to Catalonia (London, Secker & Warburg, 1938).

14 op. cit., p. 303.

15 *Editor*, p. 230.

16 op. cit., p. 268.

17 *Morning Post*, 22 August 1932.

18 *MG*, 23 March 1936.

19 *DH*, 28 December 1936.

20 *DH*, 1 February 1937.

21 *DH*, 12 March 1937.

22 *Morning Post*, 19 January 1937. He could not, however, push his case too
hard. Greenwood was President of the University Labour Federation,
a body affiliated to the Labour Party, which had never banned Communist members, and had been operating a 'united front' of a very
effective kind for over a year. In 1933 about 40% of the affiliated
membership in University Labour Clubs had broken away from the
Federation to form a separate Federation of Socialist Societies under
Communist leadership. In January 1936 the two Federations reunited,
and in the following twelve months membership rose from 1500 to
3017, and the number of branches rose from 16 to 28. Unity Campaign
supporters made much of this success – and Greenwood's continued
association with it.

23 *New Chronicle*, 25 January 1937.

24 *MG*, 16 November 1936.

25 *DH*, 1 December 1936; *Morning Post*, 3 December 1936.

26 *Tribune*, 19 February 1937.

27 *The Week*, 10 February 1937.
In March, after the LCC elections, Morrison sacked Strauss, his former
PPS, from the Chairmanship of the Highways Committee and Vice-
chairmanship of the Finance Committee. Strauss was a Unity Manifesto

signatory, and had accepted Communist help in his own LCC election campaign (*NS & N*, 20 March 1937).

28 K. Martin, *Harold Laski*, p. 100.

29 ibid., pp. 11f.

30 *Daily Express*, 20 February 1937.

31 *News Chronicle*, 22 February 1937.

32 *Daily Telegraph*, 25 February 1937.

33 *Extracts from Reports of the Organising Staff Respecting the Socialist League and the Unity Campaign*. Confidential NEC circular 24 March 1937.

34 The Constituency Parties Association. See Part III.

35 *The Unity Campaign* (NEC minutes 24 March 1937).

36 NEC minutes.

37 Brockway, op. cit., p. 268. According to Brockway the suggestion to dissolve came from Pollitt.

38 ibid.

39 G. D. H. Cole, *A History of the Labour Party from 1914*, p. 348.

40 *News Chronicle*, 17 May 1937. Cripps had told the 1936 League Conference that his contribution for the ensuing year would be limited to £800. He later denied having contributed as much as £1000. Some large sums must therefore have come from other sources – possibly Strauss and Mitchison. (*News Chronicle*, 12 April 1937)

41 *MG*, 12 April 1937.

42 *Tribune*, 16 April 1937.

43 17 April 1937.

44 *News Chronicle*, 17 May 1937. Afterwards a number of branches, including several in London, set up a Socialist Left Federation, led by Reginald Groves and Donald Barber. This linked up with Middleton Murry's Lancashire breakaway from the ILP, the Independent Socialist Party, before petering out (See Ch. 8 n. 10, p. 221–2).

45 21 May 1937.

46 *MG*, 7 June 1937. In six months only 36 000 people had signed the Campaign's 'pledge cards' in support of Unity. This compared with a total individual membership of the Labour Party of 447 000.

47 Brockway, op. cit., p. 269.

48 *Labour Party Conference Report*, October 1937, p. 163.

49 In the United Front vote, the minority included one large union, NUDAW (137 000), three smaller ones – the Shop Assistants (40 000), the Dyer, Bleachers and Textile Workers (39 000) and the Furnishing Trades Association (2000), and in addition, part of the Woodworkers' vote (21 000 approx.) – making a total union vote of some 234 000. The constituency party vote for Unity must therefore have been about 92 000 – a small proportion of the total local party Conference vote of 502 000. (*Labour Organiser*, October 1937)

50 Brockway, op. cit., pp. 269f. Cripps could, however, claim two minor victories. The Labour Party issued a Short Programme, a distillation of policy, a step long urged by the Socialist League; and the National Executive decided to launch a nationwide campaign of its own. Both

steps were largely stimulated by a desire to outflank the Campaign.

51 *DH*, 9 November 1936.
52 Cole, *A History of the Labour Party from 1914*, p. 341.
53 M. Foot, *Aneurin Bevan* (London, MacGibbon & Kee, 1962), p. 245. Gollancz was planning a paper on similar lines. Instead he joined the *Tribune* board, and *Tribune* undertook to devote space to Left Book Club news.
54 M. Foot, op. cit., p. 245.
55 Bevan was editor of *Tribune* 1942–5.
56 M. Foot, op. cit., p. 155.
57 M. Foot in W. De'Ath, *Barbara Castle – A Portrait from Life* (London, Clifton Books, 1970), pp. 34f.
58 M. Foot, op. cit., p. 245.
59 M. Foot, op. cit., p. 279n and p. 302.
60 P. Strauss, *Cripps – Advocate and Rebel* (London, Gallancz, 1943), p. 90.

NOTES FOR CHAPTER 11

1 For the role of the National Council of Labour in the 1930s, see Chapter 2, pp. 18–19 above.
2 Constituency parties, or Divisional Labour Parties (DLPs), were federal bodies based on a general committee made up of delegates from affiliated bodies. Since 1918, the latter had consisted of local or ward Labour Parties (which were composed of individual members living within an area usually defined by local government boundaries); trade union branches; and local branches of socialist societies. In practice, in the 1930s as now, the majority of politically active people in the constituencies were individual party members in local or ward parties (though these were often members of a trade union or socialist society as well). Central Labour Parties also existed in urban areas as federations of affiliated bodies from different constituencies within divided boroughs. The term 'local parties' was used to refer both to the small units of individual members affiliated to the general committee of a constituency, and more loosely to refer to local organisation in general. For convenience, in this chapter the terms 'local parties', 'constituency parties' and 'Divisional Labour Parties' are used interchangeably, except where indicated.
3 In 1922, 19 out of 142 MPs had been DLP sponsored; in 1929 the number had risen to 128 out of 288 (G. D. H. Cole, *A History of the Labour Party from 1914* London, Routledge & Kegan Paul, 1948, pp. 155 and 223).
4 R. T. McKenzie, *British Political Parties* (London, Heinemann, 1955), p. 460. The SDF was given one member, the ILP and the Fabian Society two each. In 1902 owing to the withdrawal of the SDF, the societies' representation was reduced to three – two for the ILP, one for the Fabians – on a thirteen man Executive.

5 R. E. Dowse, *Left In the Centre* (London, Longmans, 1966), p. 70. An official estimate put membership as high as 80 000.

6 McKenzie, op. cit., p. 472. For a careful analysis of this crucial stage in Labour's organisational development, see Ross McKibbin, *The Evolution of the Labour Party 1910–24* (Oxford, Oxford University Press, 1974).

7 McKenzie, op. cit., pp. 476 ff.

8 In 1929 a socialist society member was added, chosen in the same way as the Local Parties' member – i.e. elected by the whole Conference. The Party Leader was also made an *ex-officio* member of the Executive.

9 Morrison was elected to the NEC as a local party nominee by the same Conference. The amendment had been seconded by another local party delegate, G. R. Shepherd. Ironically, Shepherd became National Agent in 1928 and in the 1930s acted as chief hatchet man for the NEC against those who wanted to give the local parties more say.

10 The Amalgamated Engineering Union (AEU) was formed in 1920, the National Union of Distributive and Allied Workers (NUDAW) in 1921, the Transport and General Workers' Union (TGWU) in 1922 and the National Union of General and Municipal Workers (NUGMW) in 1924.

11 Realistic Labour Party membership figures are hard to estimate. Official totals are based not on paid up members, but on the payment of affiliation fees. Since constituencies have been required to pay for a minimum number of members, whether the latter were on their books or not, there has always been an element of distortion in published figures. This distortion is, however, far greater now than in the 1930s. Between 1929 and 1955, all constituency parties were required to affiliate for at least 240 members; since 1962 the minimum has been 1000. This makes comparison difficult. However, a comparison of the number of parties which have affiliated for more than 1000 in 1935 (125) and in 1973 (117) suggests that total individual membership, which reached a peak in 1952, is now down to the level of the mid-thirties.

12 H. Pelling, *The British Communist Party* (London, A. & C. Black, 1958), p. 40. These were individual members' sections, not constituency parties.

NOTES FOR CHAPTER 12

1 *The Labour Candidate*.

2 *The Times House of Commons, 1931* (London, The Times Office, 1931), p. 79.

3 Lord Garnsworthy. (Author's interview) In 1935 Greene was apparently reading for the Bar, and living on a private income.

4 Lord Garnsworthy. (Author's interview)

5 Malone was also something of a political eccentric. In the course of seven years in the House of Commons between 1918 and 1931 he had served successively as Lloyd George Liberal, Communist, Independent, and Labour PPS. Both Malone and Greene had been present at the inaugural meeting of the Socialist League – and both had opposed

the formation of the new body. Along with other SSIP dissidents Malone had formed the '1932 Club' which favoured an alliance with Liberals.

6 MP for Aberdeen North 1945–70. A founder of the Socialist Party of Ireland, 1918.

7 *The Times*, 28 July 1933.

8 NEC minutes, 27 July 1933.

9 *Memorandum on the Activities of Mr. Ben Greene compiled for the information of the Organisation Sub-Committee in considering his nomination for the parliamentary candidature for South West Hull*. NEC papers, 4 May 1937.

10 LPACR, 1933, p. 152.

11 LPACR, 1934, p. 26. The 1933 NEC Report had rejected this proposal in similar terms (LPACR, p. 33).

12 ibid., p. 225.

13 This was a good starting point. In 1933, after years of semi-official existence, County Federations had been given the recognition of national affiliation and representation at Conference.

14 13 December 1934 (Lord Garnsworthy papers; all other letters cited in Chapters 12 and 13 are from this collection, unless otherwise indicated).

15 NEC minutes 19 December 1934.

16 Simmons to Shepherd 14 January 1935. Transport House could scarcely treat Simmons as a hot-headed rebel. He had worked as a minor official at party headquarters since 1918.

17 Report to First Assembly of Home Counties Labour Association, 29 June 1935.

18 LPACR, p. 125.

19 Simmons to Shephard, 10 March 1935. Shepherd told the Executive on 26 February that only 40 divisional parties sent delegates, and that the Association was set up by 21 votes to 14 (NEC minutes).

20 28 February 1935.

21 Its full title was: 'The Southern and Home Counties Association of Labour Parties'.

22 G. J. Garnsworthy (1906–74), became Chairman of Reigate consti-tuency party in 1931. Member of Banstead UDC 1937–47, Surrey County Council 1952–74. Contested Reigate as Labour candidate six times – at every election between 1945 and 1964. Life peer 1967. February 1974 made a Government whip in the Lords.

23 LPACR, 1935, p. 60.

24 Provisional Executive Report to the First Annual General Assembly of HCLA.

25 LPACR, 1935, pp. 134f.

26 NEC, *Memorandum on Ben Greene*, op. cit.

27 ibid.

28 ibid.

29 Letter in *NS & N*, 28 August 1937.

30 *The Times*, 1 June 1936.

31 Report of the Provisional Committee of Constituency Labour Parties, October 1936.
32 ibid.
33 Born 1902. A London solicitor. Contested North Hackney 1929, 1931 and 1935, and a Preston by-election in 1936. MP for Nuneaton 1942–65. Life peer 1965.
34 1903–73. Newly appointed agent for Halifax; National Agent of the Labour Party 1962–9. Acting General Secretary of the Labour Party, 1968.
35 Bevan, however, took no part in the Committee's activities. (Author's interview with Lord Garnsworthy.)
36 ibid.
37 *The Times*, 30 November 1936.
38 The Railway Clerks' Association's Annual Conference had called for an inquiry into the question of constitutional changes.
39 LPACR 1936 p. 247.
40 Larrard had been elected to the local parties' Provisional Committee the previous evening.
41 *MG*, 10 October 1936. It is interesting to note that none of this exchange (after Dalton's speech) appears in the official Conference Report.

NOTES FOR CHAPTER 13

1 Report of the Provisional Committee of Constituency Labour Parties, October 1936.
2 *The Times*, 29 November 1936.
3 Report of the Executive Committee to the 2nd Annual General Assembly of HCLA. 21 November 1936.
4 HCLA also set up a 'Tribune Committee' to liaise with Greene on editorial policy.
5 December 1936 – January 1937.
6 Greene to Garnsworthy, 1 January 1937.
7 HCLA Executive minutes, 7 February 1937.
8 Report of Executive Committee to the Spring General Assembly of HCLA, 23 May 1937.
9 *The Times*, 28 December 1936.
10 *The Times*, 23 November 1936.
11 Cripps maintained a puzzling distance from his rank and file associates. After this meeting, Cripps, Greene and Garnsworthy took the same train back to London. Cripps closeted himself in a first class compartment and did not speak to the others for the whole of the journey. (Author's interview with Lord Garnsworthy)
12 MP for Newcastle East 1945—59, South Shields since 1964. Parliamentary Secretary, Ministry of Pensions 1946–49, Ministry of Health 1949–51.
13 Greene circular letter, 11 February 1937.
14 ibid.

15 NEC minutes 23 June 1937.

16 Dalton, *FY*, p. 116.

17 Greene to Dalton, 25 January 1937; Dalton to Greene 28 January 1937; Greene to Dalton 1 February 1937 (Dalton papers II 5/4).

18 NEC memorandum, 24 February 1937.

19 Memorandum on Ben Greene, op. cit. When an outraged local official sent Dalton an offending copy of *Revally*, Dalton replied 'I suppose that Mr Ben Greene is responsible for this paper . . . I think that such stuff will defeat its own end by disgusting others as it has disgusted you.' (Dalton to W. M. Kempster, 4 May 1937. Dalton papers II 5/4).

20 NEC Organisation Sub-Committee minutes.

21 James Walker, a member of the Sub-Committee.

22 2 June 1937.

23 Greene to Alexander Baird, 27 May 1937.

24 Greene to Garnsworthy, 2 June 1937.

25 NEC minutes, 3 June 1937.

26 Others present on 3 June were: Mrs J. L. Adamson, Mrs B. Ayrton Gould, M. Brothers, W. H. Green MP, S. Hirst, A. Jenkins MP, R. Prain, G. Ridley MP, and J. Walker MP. (NEC minutes)

27 Dalton *FY*, p. 116.

28 ibid.

29 ibid.

30 ibid.

31 *Left News*, September 1937.

32 *MG*, 21 September 1937.

33 *Tribune*, 24 September 1937.

34 *MG*, 25 September 1937.

35 2 October 1937.

36 4 October 1937.

NOTES FOR CHAPTER 14

1 *DH*, 4 October 1937.

2 4 October 1937.

3 According to the *Manchester Guardian* (5 October), the miners voted against the main proposal of direct election to the NEC, but both the *Daily Herald* and Dalton put the miners on the side of reform.

4 LPACR, 1937, pp. 141f.

5 Dalton *FY*, p. 143.

6 LPACR, 1937, p. 143.

7 ibid., p. 144.

8 ibid.

9 ibid., p. 145.

10 ibid., p. 146.

11 ibid., p. 145–60.

12 ibid., p. 151.

13 ibid., p. 153.
14 5 October 1937.
15 Dalton, *FY,* p. 144.
16 The minority consisted only of the TGWU, the AEU, the iron and steel workers and a few smaller unions. (*MG,* 5 October 1937).
17 Dalton, *FY,* p. 145.
18 'They had got their way and the executive had received a smack for its weakness in running away to please Mr. Bevin. The minority unions had got their blow in too. It was a good joke.' (*MG,* 5 October 1937.)
19 Voting in Division III for the 7 successful candidates and 6 leading runners-up was as follows:

H. Morrison	348 000	J. Wilmot	144 000
H. Dalton	306 000	D. R. Grenfell	124 000
H. Laski	276 000	Lord Addison	117 000
P. Noel-Baker	267 000	G. R. Strauss	107 000
Sir S. Cripps	260 000	B. Greene	84 000
G. Dallas	187 000	J. Toole	79 000
D. N. Pritt	155 000	(LPACR, 1937).	

20 George Dallas was, in fact, a native of Glasgow.
21 *MG,* 7 October 1937.
22 H. Pelling, *A Short History of the Labour Party,* p. 83.
23 Dalton, *FY,* p. 118.
24 A right-wing trade union journal commented in 1952: 'When, in 1937, the Party altered its constitution to permit the constituency parties not only to nominate but also to elect their representatives on the National Executive, the late Charles Dukes warned the Conference of the dangerous course it was embarking upon. It has taken us fifteen years to recognise how right he was.' *Men and Metal,* October 1952, quoted in M. Harrison, *Trade Unions and the Labour Party Since 1945* (London, Allen & Unwin, 1960), p. 307.
25 *The Times,* 6 October 1937.
26 Lord Garnsworthy. (Author's interview)
27 NEC Circular on regional organisation, July 1939.
28 Dalton allowed only that the reforms were intended 'to conciliate many of our most active workers'. Dalton *FY,* p. 116.
29 LPACR, p. 145.

NOTES FOR CHAPTER 15

1 *New English Review,* reprinted in ed. Sonia Orwell and Ian Angus *The Collected Essays, Journalism and Letters of George Orwell* (London, Secker & Warburg, 1968), Vol. 1, p. 305.
2 *NS & N,* 20 February 1932.
3 January 1932.
4 *Labour's Future at Stake,* cited in *NS & N,* 19 December 1931 and 23 January 1932.

5 19 January 1932.
6 T. Wilson, *The Downfall of the Liberal Party 1914–35* (London, Collins, 1966), p. 382.
7 *MG*, 2 November 1931.
8 Unpublished diary, 11 January 1932.
9 *MG*, 27 April 1932.
10 27 September 1932.
11 7 April 1934.
12 *The Next Five Years – An Essay in Political Agreement* (London, Macmillan, 1935), p. 313. A valuable account of the Next Five Years Group, and of other groups based on 'centre' opinion such as Political and Economic Planning (PEP), is given in A. Marwick, 'Middle Opinion in the Thirties: Planning, Progress and Political "Agreement"', *English Historical Review*, 1964, pp. 285–98. The Next Five Years group had its origins in a grouping known as the 'Liberty and Democratic Leadership' Group which published a manifesto in February 1934. Signatories included Dalton, Bevin, Noel-Baker and Lansbury. Under pressure from within the Labour leadership, however, all these withdrew, leaving Tom Johnston, John Bromley and Arthur Pugh as the most prominent Labour signatories of a second manifesto issued in May 1934 (ibid., p. 293).
13 ed. M. Gilbert, *Plough My Own Furrow: The Story of Lord Allen Told Through his Writings and Correspondence* (London, Longmans, 1965), p. 304.
14 *The Next Five Years*, op. cit., p. 1.
15 ibid., Part I.
16 ibid., cited in ed. M. Gilbert, op. cit., pp. 308f.
17 Signatories included Sir Norman Angell, Vernon Bartlett, Isaac Foot MP, Julian Huxley, Gilbert Murray, Sir Arthur Pugh, Eleanor Rathbone MP, B. Seebohm Rowntree, Allan Young, Ernest Barker, Gerald Barry, Lord Elton, H. A. L. Fisher, J. A. Hobson, C. E. M. Joad, Commander Stephen King-Hall, David Low, Lord Rutherford, Wickham Steed, H. G. Wells and the Archbishop of York. (*Next Five Years*. pp. v–x).
18 Sir Arthur Pugh and John Bromley.
19 H. Macmillan, *Winds of Change 1914–39* (London, Macmillan, 1966), pp. 347f.
20 *Next Five Years*, op. cit., p. 43.
21 ed. M. Gilbert, op. cit., p. 306.
22 ibid., p. 317.
23 Macmillan, op.cit., p. 487.
24 Cited in A. Sampson, *Macmillan – A Study in Ambiguity* (London, Penguin, 1967), p. 42.
25 Hugh Dalton, "The Popular Front', *Political Quarterly* (October–December 1936, Vol, VII, No. 4, p. 487).
26 *Forward*, 7 September 1935 (Laski).
27 *MG*, 24 August 1935.
28 Cf. F. W. S. Craig, *British Parliamentary Election Statistics 1919–68* (Glasgow, Political Reference Publications, 1968), p. 66.

29 *MG*, 2 September 1936.

30 *News Chronicle*, 14 September 1936.

31 H. Macmillan, *The Middle Way* (London, Macmillan, 1938).

32 H. Macmillan, *Winds of Change*, p. 489.

33 *DH*, 15 December 1936.

34 ibid.

35 LPACR, 1937, p. 4.

36 30 October 1937 (London, Panther Books, 1969. First published 1957).

37 A. J. P. Taylor, *The Troublemakers*, pp. 180f.

38 LPACR, 1937, p. 138 cited in J. F. Naylor, *Labour's International Policy – The Labour Party in the 1930s*, p. 200.

39 Aneurin Bevan, LPACR, 1937, pp. 208f., cited in Naylor op. cit., p. 202.

40 T. Jones, *Diary with Letters 1931–50* (Oxford, Oxford University Press, 1954), p. 123. (27 February 1934).

41 ibid., p. 280 (3 November 1936).

42 ed. N. Nicolson, *Harold Nicolson Diaries & Letters 1930–39* (London, William Collins, Fontana Books 1969. First published 1966), p. 325. Attlee later denied that such conversations ever took place.

43 23 March 1938. Tom Jones noted on the 20th that 'many would like a reconstruction of the Government on more national lines for this emergency, bringing in Bevin and Citrine'. (T. Jones, op. cit., p. 397).

44 Macmillan, op. cit., p. 543.

45 ed. R. Rhodes James *Chips: The Diaries of Sir Henry Channon*, (First published 1967). Edition cited: London, Penguin, p. 189.

46 Nicolson, op. cit., p. 325.

47 Dalton, *FY*, p. 162.

48 16 November 1938 and 22 February 1939.

49 Dalton's unpublished diaries. 'I report this talk,' noted Dalton, 'in which I let K. M. make nearly all the running, with no more comment of mine except that he is a most emotional, unstable person with little judgement.' Citrine had denied that any approaches had been made to Trade Union leaders 'except by quite irresponsible people in our own Party', and did not believe that Bevin had been willing to be Minister of Labour in a Coalition Government – though on grounds of health, not policy. (11 April 1938.)

50 19 April 1938.

51 *Reynolds' News*, 27 March 1938.

52 ibid.

53 21 April 1938.

54 *Political Quarterly*, October 1936.

55 21 March 1938. In this, of course, the *News Chronicle* was absolutely right.

56 *DH*, 18 April 1938.

57 Though *Tribune* – under the uncompromising Mellor – held back for a time.

58 28 April 1938. According to this account, Attlee and the TUC president H. H. Elvin, were strongly supporting the Popular Front.

59 29 April 1938.
60 28 April 1938.
61 *DH*, 14 April 1938.
62 Dalton, *FY*, p. 209.

NOTES FOR CHAPTER 16

1 John Lewis, *The Left Book Club – An Historical Record* (London, Gollancz, 1970,) p. 25.
2 The scheme was soon expanded to allow a choice of 'Additional Books'. Later there were Topical Books, Reprints from Classics, an Educational Series, and pamphlets.
3 J. Lewis, op. cit., 1970, p. 25.
4 *More for Timothy* (London, Gollancz, 1953), p. 357.
5 *News Chronicle*, 4 June 1937.
6 *Daily Worker*, 28 January 1938.
7 *Left News*, April 1939.
8 *Daily Worker*, 28 January 1938.
9 7 July 1939, cited in S. Samuels, 'The Left Book Club', *Journal of Contemporary History*, 1966, pp. 65–86.
10 These included Randall Swingler, John Lehmann, C. Day Lewis, Rex Warner, Jack Lindsay, Alick West, Arthur Calder-Marshall, Stephen Spender, Sylvia Townsend Warner and Montagu Slater. (*Left News*)
11 Cited in *News Chronicle*, 17 January 1938.
12 S. Samuels, op. cit., pp. 65ff.
13 *Left News*, October 1936.
14 NEC Memorandum.
15 *Left News*, December 1938.
16 ibid., June 1938.
17 ibid., December 1938.
18 I. McLean, 'Oxford and Bridgwater' in ed. C. Cook and J. Ramsden, *By-Elections in British Politics* (London, Macmillan, 1973), p. 149.
19 ibid.
20 *Left News*, December 1938.
21 NEC memorandum.
22 Lewis, op. cit., p. 94.
23 NEC memorandum.
24 *DH*, 31 December 1938.
25 cf. Hugh Thomas, *John Strachey* (London, Eyre Methuen, 1973), Chapter 10. As Samuel Hynes indicates (*The Auden Generation – Literature and Politics in England in the 1930s*. London: The Bodley Head. 1976. p. 211.) the Left Book Club was technically not a front organisation, if that term is taken to mean a body actually controlled from King St., or accepting its discipline.
26 *Left News*, March 1937. He was elected to the NEC in October.
27 cited in Hugh Thomas, op. cit., p. 161.

28 ibid., p. 163.
29 *Memorandum Concerning Activities of the Left Book Club.* NEC records, November 1938.
30 *Left News,* July 1937.
31 Thomas op. cit., p. 157. Attlee's *The Labour Party in Perspective* was published as the Club's 'choice' in August 1937.
32 *Forward,* 25 June 1938.
33 ibid., 9 July 1938.
34 *Left News,* August 1937.
35 *Left News.*
36 *News Chronicle,* 8 February 1937.
37 *Left News,* August 1937.
38 Dalton letter in *NS & N,* 28 August 1937.
39 ibid.
40 Laski letter in *NS & N,* 4 September 1937. Attlee had sought a similar status for SSIP in 1932.
41 Gollancz's italics. (*Left News*)
42 *NS & N,* April 1939.
43 J. Strachey, *The Strangled Cry* (London, Bodley Head, 1966) p. 220.
44 *The Long Weekend* (London, Four Square, edn 1961), p. 330. (First published 1940).

NOTES FOR CHAPTER 17

1 C. L. Mowat, *Britain Between the Wars 1918–1940* (London, Methuen, 1955), p. 615.
2 ibid.
3 cf. Mowat, op. cit., pp. 609ff.
4 Dalton, *FY,* p. 188.
5 Dalton's unpublished diary. 20 September 1938.
6 Dalton, *FY,* pp. 209f.
7 ibid., p. 199.
8 *Labour and the Popular Front.* (NEC document)
9 Dalton, *FY,* pp. 198f.
10 ibid. The same night Churchill and his group told Amery that they favoured the creation of their own distinctive group of Chamberlain decided to call an election. (cf. Neville Thompson, *The Anti-Appeasers – Conservative Opposition to Appeasement in the 1930s,* Oxford, Oxford University Press, 1971, p. 186.)
11 Dalton, *FY,* p. 199.
12 Macmillan, *Winds of Change* (London, Macmillan, 1966).
13 Dalton, *FY,* p. 200.
14 C. A. Cooke, *The Life of Richard Stafford Cripps* (London, Hodder & Stoughton, 1957), pp. 225f.
15 *MG,* 9 October 1938.
16 Dalton, *FY,* p. 201.
17 ibid., p. 199.

18 ibid., p. 201.

19 N. Thompson, op. cit., p. 192.

20 Dalton, *FY*, p. 201.

21 ibid., p. 202.

22 ibid.

23 ibid., p. 203.

24 Author's interview with Lord Duncan-Sandys.

25 Now the Earl of Longford.

26 NEC Organisation Sub-Committee minutes, 14 December 1938.

27 See above pp. 157–8.

28 Dalton, *FY*, p. 207.

29 E. F. Williams, *A Prime Minister Remembers* (London, Heinemann, 1961), p. 20. In 1962 Attlee gave another reason for having opposed the Popular Front: the danger of consorting with Communists. In a critical review of the first volume of Foot's biography of Bevan, he claimed that Labour leaders 'were very conscious of how many democratic socialist parties on the Continent had been given the kiss of death by the Communist Party…The refusal of the Labour Party to be beguiled into joining the Popular Front was fully justified when British Communists fell into line with the Russians in joining the Fascists in the Molotov – Ribbentrop Pact.' (*Observer* 21 October 1962).

30 *Daily Telegraph*, 23 November 1938.
    The minutes of the NCL contain a hint that there might indeed have been something in the accusation, and that *The Week*'s story, picked up and given wider currency by the *Manchester Guardian* and the *Yorkshire Post* on November 21st, may have sabotaged some kind of informal initiative. Dalton admitted to the Council that the NEC Policy Sub-Committee had 'recently considered the political implications of the Oxford By-Election', and he suggested that this discussion had been the basis of newspaper reports which were, however, 'inaccurate' (not, it should be noted, actually wrong). Dallas added that 'no decisions had been taken' and 'no such action as indicated in the newspaper reports had been contemplated either by the Policy Sub-Committee or by the National Executive Committee' (not that no related action had been considered at all); while Attlee stated that 'so far as conversations with leaders of the other Political Parties had been alleged he had not engaged in any such discussions' – as carefully guarded a denial, one might feel, as could be devised (NCL minutes, 22 November 1938).
    An historian who attaches less importance to such events than does the present writer considers, nevertheless, that a NEC decision on the Popular Front two days later might have been designed to leave open the possibility of an anti-government alliance at or after a general election (M. Cowling. *The Impact of Hitler. British Politics and British Policy 1933–1940*. Cambridge: Cambridge University Press, 1975, p. 218).

31 21 December 1938.

32 Macmillan, op. cit., p. 587. It appears, however, that Bevin was strongly opposed. (Cited in P. Addison, *The Road to 1945. British Politics and the Second World War*, London, Jonathan Cape, 1975. p. 76.)

NOTES FOR CHAPTER 18

1 The '100 000 movement' had been a scheme of Sandys to convince 100 000 people in key positions – in local government and the professions, for example – of the urgency of the international situation, so that they would press the Government for action. It was a complete failure. A premature press leak resulted in some unfavourable publicity, and the idea never got off the ground. (Author's interview with Lord Duncan-Sandys)
2 NEC minutes.
3 Dalton, *FY*, p. 210.
4 D. N. Pritt, *From Right to Left* (London, Lawrence & Wishart, 1965), p. 103.
5 NEC minutes. *DH*, 14 January 1939.
6 Pritt, op. cit., p. 103.
7 Sir Trevor Evans. (Author's interview.) According to Dalton, Cripps' secretary had rung Middleton asking to be warned when the meeting was about to end. (Dalton, *FY*, p. 210.)
8 P. Strauss, *Cripps – Advocate and Rebel* (London, Gollancz, 1943), p. 113.
9 NEC minutes.
10 Dalton, *FY*, p. 210.
11 ibid. and NEC minutes, 18 January 1939.
12 Dalton, *FY*, p. 212.
13 *Statement on the memorandum issued by Sir Stafford Cripps and on his attitude to the Party during recent years.* NEC minutes, 24 January 1939.
14 NEC minutes.
15 ibid. Dalton states, incorrectly, that Laski voted 'both against the Popular Front and in favour of expulsion' (Dalton, *FY*, p. 212). If he had been present, however, he might have done. Late in 1938 he wrote privately: 'I am more and more convinced that, with all its superficial attractions, the popular front business won't do'. (Cited in K. Martin, *Harold Laski*, London, Gollancz, 1953, p. 103.)
16 NEC minutes.
17 M. Foot, *Aneurin Bevan* (London, MacGibbon & Kee, 1962), vol. 1, p. 288.
18 ibid.
19 Cited in P. Strauss, op. cit., p. 114.
20 Dalton, *FY*, p. 213.
21 *DH*, 21 January 1939.
22 *News Chronicle*, 24 January 1939.
23 *NS & N*, 28 January 1939.

24 P. Strauss, op. cit., p. 115.

25 Foot, op. cit., p. 288; Shinwell, *Conflict Without Malice* (London, Odhams, 1955), p. 133. Foot refers, incorrectly, to George Barnes as Co-operative Party Chairman.

26 Pritt, op. cit., p. 103.

27 P. Strauss, op. cit., p. 116.

28 Letter in *NS & N*, 25 March 1939.

29 Trevelyan papers. Philips Price to Sir C. Trevelyan, 13 April 1939.

30 Letter in *MG*, 13 February 1939.

31 Letter in *MG*, 16 February 1939.

32 Foot, op. cit., p. 288.

33 Cited in P. Strauss, op. cit., p. 117.

34 Estorick, *Stafford Cripps* (London, Heinemann, 1949), p. 166.

35 P. Strauss, op. cit., p. 116. Bernard Shaw was another supporter: 'Sir Stafford Cripps proposes a Holy Alliance to get rid of the present Government as Napoleon was got rid of at Waterloo by a mixed force of British, Belgians, and Prussians under an Irish general. If a Labour member may not propose this, he may not propose anything.' (Cited in ibid., p. 117.)

36 *NS & N*, 25 June 1938.

37 P. Strauss, op. cit., p. 116.

38 ibid., pp. 117f.

39 *DH*, 22 February 1939.

40 Cited in P. Strauss, op. cit., p. 119.

41 NEC minutes 22 February 1939.

42 ibid.

43 Letter from National Agent, 2 March. NEC papers.

44 Brailsford suggested that this was because of union pressure. 'There were leading personalities in the movement, Mr Will Lawther for example, and several MPs whom I need not name, who in the first week, backed the Popular Front idea and afterwards withdrew. In some cases this withdrawal was brought about by financial pressure. The penalty for perseverance would have been the loss of the substantial grant paid towards election expenses by certain of the more powerful Trade Unions'. (*NS & N*, 10 June 1939)

45 *MG*, 6 March 1939.

46 NEC papers.

47 Ted Willis, *Whatever Happened to Tom Mix?* (London, Eyre & Spottiswoode, 1970), p. 172. The National Advisory Council of the League of Youth was suspended by the NEC in the summer of 1939; most of its leaders, including Willis, joined the Young Communist League.

48 *NS & N*, 4 March 1939.

49 NEC minutes, 22 March 1939.

50 *Times*, 12 April 1939.

51 NEC minutes, 22 March 1939.

52 When Beatrice Webb wrote to Morrison that people should not be expelled for expressing their opinion, Morrison replied that 'up to

a point I am not unmindful of the considerations you put to me'.
(16 March 1939. Passfield papers).

53 Dalton *FY*, p. 217.

54 Shepherd to Bevan, 23 March 1939 (NEC papers).

55 *DH*, 29 March 1939. Trevelyan's dedication to the Popular Front cause was a recent phenomenon. He had refused to back Bartlett at Bridgwater the previous autumn. (Correspondence with Sir Richard Acland, October 1938. Trevelyan papers).

56 NEC minutes, 22 March 1939.

57 P. Strauss, op. cit., p. 123.

58 *News Chronicle*, 4 April 1939.

59 M. Foot, op. cit., p. 295.

60 Cited in P. Strauss, op. cit., p. 129.

61 ibid., p. 130.

62 ibid.

63 *NS & N*, 3 June 1939.

64 LPACR, 1939.

65 G. Brown, *In My Way* (London, Penguin, 1972. First published 1971), p. 37.

66 LPACR, 1939, p. 235. Dalton and Laski were so impressed by this speech that they began to take a close interest in Brown's career, and six years later engineered his adoption as candidate at Belper. (Brown, op. cit., pp. 38f.)

67 Unpublished diary, 2 June 1939.

68 Willis, op. cit., p. 112.

69 M. Foot, op. cit., p. 210.

70 LPACR, 1939.

NOTES TO CHAPTER 19

1 NEC, 28 June 1939.

2 Amery claimed to have said it, and others who were there recalled that this famous intervention was made by him. Hansard records nothing. According to Harold Nicolson, it was Boothby who called out '*You* speak for Britain' – and Boothby confirmed this in 1965 (N. Nicolson ed., *Harold Nicolson Diaries*, London, Collins, Fontana Books, 1969, p. 412n). According to Dalton, Greenwood was greeted with Tory cries, led by Amery, of "Speak for England", and with supporting cries from our side of "Speak for Britain" and "Speak for the Workers".' (Dalton, *FY*, p. 265).

3 HC Deb. 2 September 1939, cols. 282–3.

4 Sir E. Spears, *Assignment to Catastrophe*, Vol. 1, *Prelude to Dunkirk* (London, Heinemann, 1954), p. 21.

5 L. Amery, *My Political Life*, Vol. 3, (London, Hutchinson, 1955), p. 324.

6 The Earl of Halifax, *The Fulness of Days* (London, Collins, 1957), p. 270.

7 ibid., p. 211. Dalton himself gives a slightly different version of this exchange (*FY*, p. 267).

8 Dalton, unpublished diary.
9 ibid.
10 ibid., 6 September 1939.
11 W. S. Churchill, *The Gathering Storm* (London, Cassell, 1948), p. 361.
12 ibid., p. 362.
13 Dalton, op. cit., p. 272.
14 War Cabinet Conclusions, 6 September 1939. An excellent account of politics during the 'phoney war' period is provided by Paul Addison, in *The Road to 1945*, pp. 57–91.
15 W. Ivor Jennings, 'Parliament in Wartime I', *Political Quarterly*, April–June 1940.
16 *NS & N*, 30 December 1939.
17 ibid., 27 January 1940.
　　Attlee himself regarded an election as a possibility. In the same month he told Middleton to correct the impression given in the draft of a circular that 'under no circumstances' could there be an appeal to the electorate until the end of the war. (Attlee to Middleton, 25 January 1940. Attlee papers. University College, Oxford).
　　One historian has written recently: 'It is possible to discern a distinct growth in the [Labour] Party's self-confidence, and especially that of its leadership, from the onset of the war ... In September ... Labour's foremost ideological enemy, Fascism, became the nation's enemy as well'. (T. D. Burridge, *British Labour and Hitler's War*, London: Andre Deutsch, 1976. pp. 21–2) But at local level there was much bewilderment, not lessened by the peculiar equivocation of the electoral truce. Was Chamberlain still an opponent, or had he become a potential hero and saviour? The difficulty of answering this question to the satisfaction of the Movement, yet the impossibility of avoiding it, was one factor which pushed Labour leaders towards the May 1940 showdown.
18 LPACR, 1940. Conscription would account for a large part of the decline. Yet after 1940 conscription became far more complete, while membership rose steadily after 1942 and sensationally from 1944–5.Evacuation may also have been a factor.
19 Unpublished diary, 19 September 1939.
20 LPACR, 1940, pp. 188ff.
21 9 September 1939.
22 Scotland was the main base for opposition to Labour's War policy. Seven of the twenty signatories sat for Scottish seats; the Scottish Socialist Party, heir to the ILP tradition, opposed the war on pacifist grounds.
23 Letter to R. C. Trevelyan, 21 October 1939 (Trevelyan papers).
24 N. Thompson, *The Anti-Appeasers* (Oxford, Oxford University Press, 1971), p. 223.
25 N. Nicolson ed., *Harold Nicolson Diaries and Letters 1939–45*.
26 E. F. Williams, *A Prime Minister Remembers* (London, Heinemann, 1961), p. 28.
27 H. Macmillan, *Blast of War 1939–45* (London, Macmillan, 1967), p. 66.

28 Macmillan, op. cit., pp. 71f.

29 Dalton, *FY* p. 305. See also B. Donoughue and G. W. Jones, *Herbert Morrison* (London, Weidenfeld & Nicolson, 1973), p. 272.

30 Sir E. Spears, op. cit., p. 128.

31 Rhodes James, R. (ed) *Channon*, p. 302.

32 ibid., p. 303. Nicolson (1939–45) op.cit., p. 76.

33 Amery, op.cit., p. 370.

34 Nicolson (1939–45), op. cit., p. 77.

35 Dalton, *FY*, p. 308.

36 Amery, op. cit., p. 371. Dalton *FY*, p. 307, 309n. Earl of Birkenhead, *The Life of Lord Halifax* (London, Hamish Hamilton, 1965), p. 453. Cripps, an independent, also favoured Halifax. (Lloyd George papers; *Daily Mail*, 6 May 1940. Cited in Paul Addison, op. cit., p. 101.)

37 E. F. Williams, op. cit., pp. 32f.

38 NEC minutes.

39 Churchill, op. cit., p. 597. According to Halifax, Chamberlain had stated his intention to resign, and the Foreign Secretary had told Chamberlain that he would not succeed him, on 9 May (Halifax, op. cit., p. 219; and see The Earl of Birkenhead, op. cit., p. 454). Addison accepts this chronology (op. cit., p. 100).

40 Cited in I. MacLeod, *Neville Chamberlain* (London, Muller, 1961), p. 291.

41 Dalton, *FY*, p. 312.

42 NEC minutes.

43 Dalton, *FY*, p. 313.

44 Cabinet Conclusions.

45 Williams, op. cit., p. 35. Dalton, *FY* p. 31, Amery, op. cit., p. 374; I. Macleod, op. cit., p. 292.

46 NEC minutes.

47 LPACR, 1940, p. 128.

48 ibid., p. 124.

49 ibid., p. 132.

50 Shinwell turned down a junior post at the Ministry of Food. *Conflict Without Malice*, p. 146.

51 Dalton, *FY*, p. 320.

NOTES FOR CONCLUSION

1 D. Coates, *The Labour Party and the Struggle for Socialism*, (Cambridge, Cambridge University Press, 1975), pp. 19, 134, 39. Coates argues that the Labour Party is inherently incapable of achieving socialism, or even significant social reform, and therefore should be abandoned. His book is the most sophisticated of recent marxist analyses of Labour Party history.

2 Not everybody agrees. R. McKibbin has recently argued ('The Economic Policy of the Second Labour Government 1929–31', *Past and Present*, 1975, No. 68, pp. 95–123) that 'the ability of the state before the Second World War to do more than marginally influence the economy was limit-

ed' (p. 121), and that 'a successful reflation in Britain would probably have required . . . very wide state supervision of the economy' (p. 122). McKibbin's case appears to be that a Keynesian solution was impossible, not because it was inherently wrong, but because too many powerful people would not have accepted the measures necessary to carry it through. Now this is a very hard point to establish. In one sense, anything that did not happen could not have happened because things were as they were: but this does not get us very far, and the limits of historical discussion become extremely narrow unless we are allowed to imagine that some things might have been slightly different. What can be said is that Keynesian-style policies were probably much more available to a British government in the 1930s than to an American one. The national and state authorities which had constitutional power to obstruct the Federal government in the United States had no equivalent here. Our executive was consequently much stronger. Central government had intervened, planned and organised with remarkable thoroughness during the First World War; and, immediately after the period discussed in this book, the British system adapted itself even more rapidly and completely to the direct control of every aspect of economic life. As McKibbin points out, 'Socially there were a number of restraints to treating depression as war.' (p. 104) But to this it may be replied: for the first eight months after September 1939 there appeared to be many restraints to treating war as war. A change of leadership, and by no means an inevitable one, brought about a situation in which restraints were overcome. The same might have happened in the 1930s.

3 See McKibbin's excellent analysis in *The Evolution of the Labour Party 1910–24* (Oxford, Oxford University Press, 1974). Stressing the trade union influence on Labour's organisational development, McKibbin argues that 'the Labour Party was not based upon broadly articulated principles, but rather upon a highly developed class consciousness and intense class loyalties'. (p. 243).

4 R. H. Tawney, 'The Choice Before the Labour Party', *Political Quarterly*, July–September 1932, Vol. 3, No. 3, p. 330. McKibbin (*Evolution of the Labour Party* p. 97) suggests that in 1918 there was scarcely even a wish. 'The socialist objective was . . . implanted into the constitution partly as a sop to the professional bourgeoisie: that this was so helps to explain why the trade unions accepted it as easily as they did.'

5 Quoted in *Parliamentary Socialism,* p. 230.

6 Quoted in R. T. McKenzie, *British Political Parties* (London, Heinemann, 1955), p. 470.

7 Tawney, op. cit., p. 329.

8 ibid., p. 332.

9 ibid.

10 R. Postgate, *The Life of George Lansbury* (London, Longmans, 1951), p. 285. (July 1932).

11 J. M. Keynes, 'The Dilemma of Modern Socialism', *Political Quarterly*, April–June 1932, Vol. 3, No. 2, p. 155.
12 J. M. Keynes, *The General Theory of Employment, Interest and Money* quoted in D. Jay, *The Socialist Case* (London, Faber & Faber, 1937), p. 373.
13 D. Jay, op. cit., p. 275.
14 Lord Duncan-Sandys. (Author's interview).

Bibliography

I have included in this bibliography written sources cited in the text and notes. I have not listed material which has been useful as background, but which I have felt it unnecessary to refer to directly.

PRIVATE PAPERS

Lord Attlee papers (University College, Oxford).

G. D. H. Cole papers (Nuffield College, Oxford).

Hugh Dalton papers (includes unpublished Dalton diary; British Library of Economics and Political Science).

Lord Garnsworthy papers (small collection of papers, mainly correspondence, relating to the Constituency Parties Movement, loaned by the late Lord Garnsworthy to the author).

George Lansbury papers (British Library of Economics and Political Science).

Passfield papers (includes Beatrice Webb's unpublished diary; British Library of Economics and Political Science).

Trevelyan papers (Newcastle University).

OFFICIAL, ETC. UNPUBLISHED SOURCES

Cabinet Conclusions (Public Record Office).

Joint Meetings of the TUC General Council, the Labour Party Executive and the Parliamentary Labour Party Executive; Minutes. (Transport House).

Labour Party NEC minutes, reports and papers (Transport House).

National Council of Labour Minutes (Congress House).

Reports of Annual Conferences of the Socialist League 1933–7.

Report of the Annual Aggregate Meeting of the Socialist League, London Area, July 1936.

TUC General Council Minutes (Congress House).

Bibliography

OFFICIAL PUBLISHED SOURCES. ETC.

Labour Party Annual Conference Reports.
TUC Annual Conference Reports.
Hansard: House of Commons Debates.

NEWSPAPERS AND PERIODICALS

Adelphi.
Daily Express.
Daily Herald.
Daily Mail.
Daily Telegraph.
Daily Worker.
Forward.
Labour Candidate.
Labour Monthly.
Labour Organiser.
Left News.
Manchester Guardian.
Morning Post.
New Clarion.
New Leader.
News Chronicle.
New Statesman and Nation.
Nottingham Guardian.
Observer.
Political Quarterly.
Reynolds' News.
Socialist.
Socialist Leaguer.
SSIP News.
The Times.
Tribune.
The Week.
Yorkshire Post.

PUBLISHED BIOGRAPHIES, MEMOIRS AND DIARIES

Amery, L. *My Political Life*, Vol. 3 London: Hutchinson, 1955.
Angell, Sir N. *After All.* London: Hamish Hamilton, 1951.
Attlee, C. *The Granada Historical Records Interview.* London: Panther
    Record, 1967.
Attlee, Earl. *As It Happened.* London: Heinemann, 1954.
Birkenhead, The Earl of. *The Life of Lord Halifax.* London: Hamish
    Hamilton, 1965.
Brockway, F. *Inside The Left.* London: Allen & Unwin, 1942.
Brown, G. *In My Way.* London: Penguin, 1972 (first published 1971).

Bibliography

Bullock, A. *The Life and Times of Ernest Bevin. Vol. I. The Trade Union Leader 1881–1940.* London: Heinemann, 1960.

Churchill, W. S. *The Gathering Storm.* London: Cassell, 1948.

Citrine, Lord. *Men and Work.* London: Hutchinson, 1964.

Cole, M. (ed.) *Beatrice Webb's Diaries 1924–32.* London: Longmans, Green & Co., 1936.

Cole, M. *Growing Up Into Revolution.* London: Longmans, Green & Co., 1949.

The Life of G. D. H. Cole. London: Macmillan, 1971.

Cooke, C. A. *The Life of Richard Stafford Cripps.* London: Hodder & Stoughton, 1957.

Dalton, H. *Call Back Yesterday. Memoirs 1887–1931.* London: Frederick Muller, 1953.

The Fateful Years. Memoirs 1931–1945. London: Frederick Muller, 1957.

De'Ath, W. (ed). *Barbara Castle. A Portrait from Life.* London: Clifton Books, 1970.

Donoughue, B. and Jones, G. W. *Herbert Morrison – Portrait of A Politician.* London: Weidenfeld and Nicolson, 1973.

Estorick, E. *Stafford Cripps. A Biography.* London: Heinemann, 1949.

Foot, M. *Aneurin Bevan. A Biography. Vol. I. 1897–1945.* London: MacGibbon & Kee, 1962.

Gilbert, M. (ed.) *Plough My Own Furrow: The Story of Lord Allen Told Through his Writings and Correspondence.* London: Longmans, 1960.

Gollancz, V. *More For Timothy.* London: Gollancz, 1953.

Graham, T. N. *Willie Graham. The Life of The Rt. Hon. W. Graham.* London: Hutchinson, 1948.

Halifax, The Earl of. *The Fulness of Days.* London: Collins, 1957.

Hamilton, M A. *Remembering My Good Friends.* London: Cape, 1944.

Harrod, R. *The Life of John Maynard Keynes.* London: MacMillan, 1952

Jenkins, R. *Mr. Attlee. An Interim Biography.* London: Heinemann, 1948.

Johnston, J. *A Hundred Commoners.* London: Herbert Joseph, 1931.

Jones, T. *Diary With Letters 1931–50.* Oxford: Oxford University Press, 1954.

MacLeod, I. *Neville Chamberlain.* London: Muller, 1961.

MacMillan, H. *Blast of War 1939–45.* London: Macmillan, 1967.

Winds of Change 1914–39. London: Macmillan, 1966.

MacNeill Weir, L. *The Tragedy of Ramsay MacDonald.* London: Secker & Warburg, 1938.

Manning, L. *A Life for Education.* London: Gollancz, 1970.

Martin, K. *Editor: A Second Volume of Autobiography 1921–45.* London: Hutchinson, 1968.

Harold Laski 1893–1950. A Biographical Memoir. London: Gollancz, 1953.

Morrison, Lord. *An Autobiography.* London: Odhams Press, 1960.

Mosley, Sir O. *My Life.* London: Nelson, 1968.

Bibliography

Murphy, J. T. *New Horizons*. London: John Lane, 1940.
Nicolson, N. (ed.) *Harold Nicolson Diaries and Letters 1930–39*. First published 1966. Edition cited: London: Collins, Fontana Books, 1969.
Harold Nicolson Diaries and Letters 1939–45. First published 1967. Edition cited: London: Collins, Fontana Books, 1970.
Pethick-Lawrence, F. W. *Fate Has Been Kind*. London: Hutchinson, 1943.
Postgate, R. *The Life of George Lansbury*. London: Longmans, 1951.
Pritt, D. N, *From Right to Left*. London: Lawrence & Wishart, 1965.
Rhodes James, R. (ed.) *Chips: The Diaries of Sir Henry Channon*. First published 1967. Edition cited: London: Penguin, 1970.
Sampson, A. *Macmillan. A Study in Ambiguity*. London: Penguin, 1967.
Shinwell, E. *Conflict Without Malice*. London: Odhams, 1955.
Skidelsky, R. *Oswald Mosley*. London: Macmillan, 1975.
Snell, Lord. *Men, Movements and Myself*. London: J. M. Dent, 1936.
Spear, Sir E. *Assignment to Catastrophe. Vol. I. Prelude to Dunkirk*. London: Heinemann, 1954.
Strauss, P. *Cripps – Advocate and Rebel*. London: Gollancz, 1943.
Thomas, H. *John Strachey*. London: Eyre Methuen, 1973.
Williams, E. F. *Ernest Bevin*. London: Hutchinson, 1952.
Nothing So Strange. London: Cassell, 1970.
A Prime Minister Remembers. London: Heinemann, 1961.
Willis, T. *Whatever Happened to Tom Mix?* London: Eyre & Spottiswoode, 1970.

OTHER WORKS

Addison, P. *The Road to 1945. British Politics and the Second World War*. London: Jonathan Cape, 1975.
Attlee, C. *The Labour Party in Perspective*. London: Gollancz, 1939.
Bassett, R. *Nineteen Thirty-One. Political Crisis*. London: Macmillan, 1958.
Brailsford, H. N. et al. *The Living Wage*. London: The ILP Publication Dept., 1926.
Burridge. T. D. *British Labour and Hitler's War*. London: Andre Deutsch, 1976.
Butler, D. and Freeman, J. *British Political Facts. 1900–1967*. 2nd edn. London: Macmillan, 1968.
Citrine, W. *I Search For Truth in Russia*. London: Routledge, 1936.
Cline, C. A. *Recruits to Labour – The British Labour Party 1914–31*. New York: Syracuse University Press, 1963.
Coates, D. *The Labour Party and the Struggle for Socialism*. Cambridge: Cambridge University Press, 1975.
Cole, G. D. H. *British Trade and Industry*. London: Macmillan, 1932.
A History of the Labour Party from 1914. London: Routledge & Kegan Paul, 1948.
The Socialist Control of Industry. London: The Socialist League, 1934.

248

Bibliography

Cowling, M. *The Impact of Hitler. British Politics and British Policy 1933– 1940.* Cambridge: Cambridge University Press, 1975.

Craig, F. W. S. *British Parliamentary Election Statistics 1918–68.* Glasgow: Political Reference Publications, 1968.

Dalton, H. 'The Popular Front', *Political Quarterly*, October–December 1936, Vol. 7, No. 4.

Practical Socialism for Britain. London: Routledge, 1935.

Dowse, R. E. *Left in the Centre. The Independent Labour Party 1893–1940.* London: Longmans, 1966.

Graves, R. and Hodge, A. *The Long Weekend.* London: Four Square, 1961. (First published 1940).

Greenwood, A. *Love on the Dole.* London: Jonathan Cape, 1933.

Harrison, M. *Trade Unions and the Labour Party since 1945.* London: Allen & Unwin, 1960.

Hynes, S. *The Auden Generation. Literature and Politics in England in the 1930s.* London: The Bodley Head, 1976.

Jay, D. *The Socialist Case.* London: Faber & Faber, 1937.

Jenkins, R. *Pursuit of Progress.* London: Heinemann, 1953.

Jennings, W. I. 'Parliament in Wartime I', *Political Quarterly*, April–June 1940.

Jones, G. P. and Pool, A. G. *A Hundred Years of Economic Development in Great Britain.* London: Duckworth, 1940.

Jupp, J. 'The Left in Britain 1931–41.' Unpublished thesis, London, M.Sc. Econ. 1956.

Keynes, J. M. *The General Theory of Employment, Interest and Money.* London: Macmillan, 1936.

Keynes, J. M. 'The Dilemma of Modern Socialism', *Political Quarterly*: April–June 1932, Vol. 3, No. 2 (and in ed. W. A. Robson, below).

Lewis, J. *The Left Book Club – An Historical Record.* London: Gollancz, 1970.

McKenzie, R. T. *British Political Parties.* London: Heinemann, 1955.

McKibbin, R. 'The Economic Policy of the Second Labour Government 1929–31'. *Past and Present*, 1975, No. 68.

The Evolution of the Labour Party 1910–24. Oxford: Oxford University Press, 1974.

McLean, I. 'Oxford and Bridgwater' in (ed.) Cook, C. and Ramsden, J. *By-Elections in British Politics.* London: Macmillan, 1973.

Macmillan, H. *The Middle Way.* London: Macmillan, 1938.

Marwick, A. 'Middle Opinion in the Thirties: Planning, Progress and Political "Agreement"', *English Historical Review*, 1964.

Mellor, W. *The Claim of the Unemployed.* London: The Socialist League, 1933.

Miliband, R. *Parliamentary Socialism.* London: Merlin Press, 1961.

Morrison, H. *Socialisation of Transport.* London: Constable, 1933.

Mowat, C. L. *Britain Between the Wars 1918–1940.* London: Methuen, 1955.

Bibliography

Murphy, J. T. *Fascism: The Socialist Answer*. London: The Socialist League, 1935.

Naylor, J. F. *Labour's International Policy – The Labour Party in the 1930s*. London: Weidenfeld & Nicolson, 1969.

The Next Five Years – An Essay in Political Agreement. London: Macmillan, 1935.

Orwell, G. *Homage to Catalonia*. London: Secker & Warburg, 1938.

The Road to Wigan Pier. London: Gollancz, 1937.

Orwell, S. and Angus, I. (eds.) *The Collected Essays, Journalism and Letters of George Orwell*, Vol. 1. London: Secker & Warburg, 1968.

Passfield, Lord. 'What Happened in 1931: A Record'. *Political Quarterly*, Vol. 3. No. 1. January–March 1932.

Pelling, H. *The British Communist Party. An Historical Profile*. London: A. & C. Black, 1958.

A Short History of the Labour Party. London: Macmillan, 1961.

Pimlott, B. 'The Socialist League. Intellectuals and the Labour Left in the 1930s', *Journal of Contemporary History*, Vol. 6, No. 3, 1971.

Pollard, S. (ed.) *The Gold Standard and Employment Policies Between the Wars*. London: Methuen, 1970.

Robson, W. A. (ed.) *Political Quarterly in the 1930s*. London: Penguin, 1971.

Samuels, S. 'The Left Book Club', *Journal of Contemporary History*, 1966, Vol. 1.

Skidelsky, R. *Politicians and the Slump – The Labour Government 1929–31*. London: Macmillan, 1967.

Strachey, J. *The Coming Struggle For Power*. London: Gollancz, 1932.

Revolution by Reason. London: Leonard Parsons, 1925.

The Strangled Cry. London: Bodley Head, 1966'.

Tawney, R. H. 'The Choice Before the Labour Party,' *Political Quarterly*, July – September 1932, Vol. 3, No. 3, (and in ed. W. A. Robson, above).

Taylor, A. J. P. *English History 1914–45*. Oxford: Clarendon Press, 1965.

The Troublemakers. London: Panther Books, 1969. (First Published 1957.)

Thomas, H. *The Spanish Civil War*. London: Eyre & Spottiswoode, 1961.

Thompson, N. *The Anti-Appeasers – Conservative Opposition to Appeasement in the 1930s*. Oxford: Oxford University Press, 1971.

The Times House of Commons. London: The Times Office, 1931, 1935.

Tracey, H. (ed). *The British Labour Party*, vol 3. London: The Caxton Publishing Co., 1948.

Trevelyan, Sir C. *Mass Resistance to War*. London: The Socialist League, 1934.

Wilson, T. *The Downfall of the Liberal Party 1914–35*. London: Collins, 1966.

Wood, N. *Communism and British Intellectuals*. London: Gollancz, 1959.

Index

Index

Index

Williams, Tom, 189, 193, 209, 214
Williams, T. E., 207
Williamson, T., 206
Willis, Ted (Lord), 99, 178, 181, 225, 240
Wilmot, John, 134, 135, 173, 207, 232
Wilson, Harold, 71
Wilson, T., 233
Wise, E. F., 14, 89, 200, 216, 218; and
    Socialist League 42–52 passim; econo-
    mic ideas of 60–3
Wood, N., 215
Woolf, Leonard, 175, 216

workers' control, 49, 62, 66–7, 201
Workers' Educational Association (WEA),
    44
Wynne Davies, F., 47

XYZ Club, 36, 37, 201

Yorkshire Post, 153, 214, 237
Young, Allan, 59, 62, 63, 149, 233
Young, Lieut-Comm. Edgar, 176, 177, 181

Zinoviev, Grigori, 88

259